# The
# German Church Struggle
# and the Holocaust

## Scholars' Conference Committee

William Rea Keast, *President of Wayne State University, Honorary Chairman*
Franklin H. Littell, *Professor of Religion, Temple University, Conference Chairman*
Margaret Sterne, *Professor of History, Wayne State University*
William Allen, *Associate Professor of History, Wayne State University*
Max Kapustin, *Director of B'nai B'rith Hillel Foundation; Professor of Near Eastern Languages and Literatures, Wayne State University*
James R. Lyons, *Secretary to the Cisler Library Foundation*
Hubert G. Locke, *Leo M. Franklin Professor-1970 and Director of Religious Affairs, Wayne State University, Conference Secretary*
Kathleen Disser, *Administrative Assistant to Conference Secretary*

## Conference Consultant Committee

Stewart Herman, *President, Chicago Lutheran Theological Seminary*
Gordon C. Zahn, *Professor of Sociology, University of Massachusetts*
Frank Wright, Jr., *Director, Freedom Institute, Iowa Wesleyan College*
C. Arild Olsen, *Vice President, National Conference of Christian and Jews*
John S. Conway, *Professor of History, University of British Columbia*
Arthur C. Cochrane, *Professor of Theology, University of Dubuque*

# The German Church Struggle and the Holocaust

edited by

## Franklin H. Littell

TEMPLE UNIVERSITY

## Hubert G. Locke

UNIVERSITY OF NEBRASKA

WAYNE STATE UNIVERSITY PRESS. DETROIT. *1974*

---

**Library of Congress Cataloging in Publication Data**

*International Scholars' Conference, 1st, Wayne State University, 1970.*
 *The German church struggle and the Holocaust.*

 *Sponsored by the Walker and Gertrude Cisler Library of the Grosberg Religious Center.*
 *Includes bibliographical references.*
 *1. Church and state in Germany—1933-1945—Congresses. 2. Holocaust, Jewish (1939-1945)—Congresses. I. Littell, Franklin Hamlin, ed. II. Locke, Hubert G., ed. III. Walker and Gertrude Cisler Library. IV. Title.*
*BR856.I57 1970  261.7'0943  72-9352*
*ISBN 0-8143-1492-9*

---

# Contents

Contents

## III. Theological Implications

## IV. Personal Reflections

# Preface

The Wayne State University Project on the History of the Church Struggle and the Holocaust was planned in late 1968 and early 1969 through the initiative of members of the staff of the Grosberg Religious Center: Hubert G. Locke, James S. Lyons, Rabbi Max Kapustin. Franklin H. Littell, who had written a number of books and articles in the field and was then President of Iowa Wesleyan College, was invited to serve as chairman and consultant. The sponsorship was assumed by the Walker and Gertrude Cisler Library of the Grosberg Religious Center, and the first International Scholars' Conference was held in 1970.

This is the Conference volume. The papers presented have been somewhat rearranged—thematically, not chronologically—for the readers' use, and no attempt has been made to present the substance of the lively discussions which followed plenary and sectional presentations.

The Conference had three important dimensions apart from the value of the subject matter of the papers: 1) it was international, with participation from Germany, Israel, Canada, and the United States at the sessions; 2) it was interdisciplinary, with a wide variety of academic disciplines represented; and 3) most important, perhaps, it tied together the German Church Struggle with the Holocaust, thus bringing into interaction specialists who had been writing primarily within the context of Christian and Jewish scholarship, respectively.

Special thanks are here expressed by the editors to Susan Wind of Temple University, who made the ribbon copy, and Marguerite Wallace, who saw the work through the press.

# I
# Introduction and Historical Background

# 1
# Church Struggle and the Holocaust

Franklin H. Littell

In a real sense this International Scholars' Conference expresses the first major American initiative in an area to which European scholars, especially Germans, have directed diligent effort for some time. The Commission for the History of the German Church Struggle in the National Socialist Era (Kommission zur Geschichte des Kirchenkampfes im national-sozialistischen Zeitalter) of the protestant church (EKD) has for well over a decade planned and fostered research of high level, publishing an impressive series of monographs in cooperation with Vandenhoeck and Ruprecht.[1] Among other German efforts at preserving and interpreting the documentation, the work of the *Bundeszentrale für Heimatdienst* (Bonn) and the *Institut für Zeitgeschichte* (Munich) should also be mentioned. There was for three years an American Committee, founded at the 1959 Scholars' Conference called by the EKD commission at Tutzing, with a mimeographed newsletter containing scholarly papers and bibliographical and research notes.[2] In the meantime, the volume of books and articles produced by private scholars—usually working without subvention of any kind—has continued to mount. Wilhelm Niemöller, collector of the greatest independent archive on the Church Struggle (*Kirchenkampf*) and himself a diligent writer, deserves special note. The historiography of the Church Struggle has gone through several stages in the last quarter century,[3] and this conference can be said to meet in the fullness of time. We are all grateful to Wayne State University for bringing together representatives of so many different centers and disciplines, and for proposing to help bring order to a field of study which threatens to expand beyond the possibility that any one of us can by personal initiative alone even keep contact with the growing number working in it. Moreover, without a synoptical effort on someone's part, the volume of specialized research by isolates can miss the main point of the tragedy: the self-destructive bent of alienated and dehumanized man in the twentieth century.

The recent work on the Church Struggle is not only of greater volume but also makes use of critically important materials outside the church's own documentation, such as the captured Nazi party files or the microfilmed documents of the security police. The recent publication of John Conway's *The Nazi Persecution of the Churches* and of Eberhard Bethge's biography of Dietrich Bonhoeffer seem to me to indicate how much further along we are now, in both breadth and depth, in understanding the various ways and contexts in which the Church Struggle has meaning for us.

One of the participants in the 1959 Tutzing Conference was the late Alfred Wiener of London. The Wiener Library was then on its way to becoming a major center and resource for the documentation of the Nazi "final solution to the problem of the Jews" (*Endlösung*)—a dimension of the problematic of religion in the Third Reich of which most Christian scholars were still only dimly aware. In recent years we have had the development of the great official center memorializing the Holocaust: Yad Vashem in Jerusalem. Yad Vashem is a memorial, a file of six million murdered persons, and a team of research scholars who—among other things—put out a scholarly quarterly on the Holocaust.[4] The present lack of coordinated effort, or even of awareness of connection, between the two foci of this conference is signalized by the fact that—although the first million who perished in the concentration camps were non-Jews, and their records are available at Yad Vashem—no group of Christian scholars, not even a university sponsored group from the German Federal Republic, has made any use of the materials.

The Jews have been writing their chronicles and histories—for Jews. Some Christian scholars have been writing about the Church Struggle—for Christians. The deeper meaning of the Holocaust and the Church Struggle has scarcely penetrated the American scene at all. Jewish leaders assure me that the American Jewish community has not yet come to terms with the Holocaust—for reasons which are certainly easy enough even for an outgrouper to understand. Less understandable, however—and especially in view of the rising power of the Radical Right in America—is the failure of the American churches to be influenced by the lessons of the German Church Struggle. Even the theological schools give it only a passing glance— chiefly, I think, because it does not fit the kind of self-understanding that American Christendom has of itself. Thirty years ago, as the Confessing Church (*Bekennende Kirche*) was going to its synod at Bad Oeynhausen or the German Jews were facing the dreadful portent of the attack on the synagogues (*Kristallnacht*), there were only two leading churchmen in America who repeatedly and clearly—and with interpretations which still stand the test of time— warned of the true import of the war being waged against the Jews *and* the Christians by the Nazis: Reinhold Niebuhr and George Shuster. Today, so far as the churches are concerned, it is only among the students and younger theologians that the questions constantly arise which the Church Struggle and the Holocaust put to traditional religious institutions, even to the traditional religious language.

It is therefore with great gratitude and anticipation that I welcome the undertaking of Wayne State University to develop a major documentation and research center on the Church Struggle, and a North American center on the Holocaust. I am sure that I express the sentiments of this whole company of scholars in uttering this salutation. The Wayne Project signalizes, among other things, how the energetic concern for Religion as an intellectual discipline is moving out of the church ghettos into the state universities. It also gives promise that the most important events of recent generations of religious history may at last get the general attention they deserve. It is not too much to say that the vigorous intellectual and practical work of the Dutch churches, both Catholic and Protestant, and of a substantial sector of the churches in Germany, is a result in good part of their mastery of the lessons of the Church Struggle and the Holocaust. And the confusion on the American religious scene, in spite of fleeting reference to ecumenism and church renewal and interfaith dialogue from time to time, seems to document that we are still working very largely with the concepts and assumptions of nineteenth-century culture-religion, of the happy time before the flood waters covered the earth.

Most encouraging is the extent to which various aspects of the "problem" have caught the attention and inspired the hard work of scholars outside the theological field: historians, political scientists, sociologists, social psychologists, psychologists, experts in education and in jurisprudence. Since a totalitarian system by definition seeks to conquer all aspects of life from architecture to zoology, such a broad sweep of academic concern is appropriate.[5] It also signifies another very important theoretical consideration: that the major theological problems may often be illuminated not by professionals—who dig like moles ever deeper into the old and proven veins of sustenance—but by so-called laymen working in so-called secular disciplines and idioms. The mounting of this major project, and the response of such an array of scholars with no specific stake in organized religion or official theology, may help to move theology in America out of the monologue which still commands its daily work.

## The Theological Meaning of National Socialism

In theological terms, Nazism was the true—if illegitimate—offspring of a false relationship between the Christian church and the ethnic bloc or nation. And it has its analogues today in places as distant from each other as Alabama and South Africa, Belfast and Beirut. When ethnic history is infused with spirituality, and a political program is mounted on disciplined cadres to return a people to a mythical monism of the past, a frontal challenge to the True Church—on pilgrimage and supranational—is thrown down. The situation is confused, however, because most of the baptized will accommodate in church committees or apostatize, e.g., in White Citizens' Councils, rather than give the head of the Church the undivided loyalty they once promised him.

It was the glory of the Confessing Church to have perceived that a frontal confrontation was involved and not the mere issue of everyday politics in a disaster area. The fact that some saw the sweeping dimensions of the struggle sooner than others, and that even the Confessing Church did not immediately understand the meaning of hatred of the Jews as a hatred of the Jew, Jesus of Nazareth, does not detract one iota from the debt the whole church owes the men of Barmen and what they did. Karl Barth put it directly:

National Socialism, according to its own revelation of what it is—a self-revelation to which it has devoted all the time and chance till now allowed—is as well

*14*

without any doubt something quite different from a political experiment. It is, namely, a *religious institution of salvation.*

It is impossible to understand National Socialism unless we see it in fact as a *new Islam.*[6]

And the men who presented the Memorandum of May 1936 to the Führer of the Third Reich rightly identified Nazism's offense to the True Church:

When blood, race, nationality, and honour are regarded as eternal values the first commandment obliges the Christian to refuse this evaluation. When the Aryan is glorified, the Word of God teaches that all men are sinful. If the Christian is faced by the Anti-Semitism of the Nazi *Weltanschauung* to hate the Jews, he is, on the contrary, bidden by the Christian Commandment to love his neighbour.[7]

Dietrich Bonhoeffer, martyred as the war was ending, drew one concrete conclusion—but a conclusion on which there is still little guidance in Christian theological literature: "If we claim to be Christians there is no room for expediency. Hitler is the Anti-Christ. Therefore we must go on with our work and eliminate him whether he is successful or not."[8]

The problem of discerning and defining the Christian obligation and style to resist illegitimate authority, not to mention illegitimate action by legitimate authority, remains one of the most excruciating agonies of Christians today. The word *Antichrist* is the clue: for the Antichrist is not the honest and open adversary but the one who was once numbered within and has now gone over to the opposition. The misery of the Church Struggle is not first to battle with an open opposition: it is to face the apostasy of the baptized, the convulsion of Christendom.

Before the Church Struggle with Nazism, the Christian corpus gave very little guidance on the matter of resistance.[9] Representative government, in which each citizen shares the responsibility (and proportionately the guilt) for policies implemented by heads of state, is too new a thing in human history for any large body of interpretation to have emerged. But the experiences of the Third Reich remind us that not only absolute monarchs who rule by divine right must be warned and confronted on occasion but also, perhaps especially, those governments which claim to have substantial—if sometimes "silent"—majorities acquiescing in their actions. In a police state, without free access or egress, the moral burden of national wrongdoing on the whole people is certainly no greater than in a society which still has some room for organizing public opinion and pressure.

In even the strictest Marxist areas, however, the lessons of the Church Struggle are bearing fruit. The influence of Bonhoeffer is marked. Western leaders have sometimes criticized Christians in East Germany because they did not denounce Marxism too as a "new Islam" and declare unqualified resistance. In this struggle, however, the first concern has been for the integrity and authenticity of the church—not to defend an ideological Christendom. What is at stake for Christians is not Christendom versus a Marxist state-church, but the freedom of a True Church to serve the human person. To this end, the state must be secularized, not re-Christianized—i.e., rendered modest, problem-solving, and, theologically speaking, "creaturely." In this respect the existence problem of Christians in a Marxist state is not strikingly different from their problem in a society retrogressively committed to "Christendom"—or, for that matter, different from that of Christians living under Muslim sacral governments in the Arab League.

## Secularization versus Spirituality

It is quite wrong to assume that the Church Struggle was a battle to defend Christian Germany against the false teaching of neo-barbarians, just as wrong as it is to assume that the tragedy of this age is the arrival of a second great age of persecution. The tragedy is the wholesale apostasy of the baptized—their eagerness, in the name of "saving the world from atheistic Communism" and "reestablishing law and order" (and let us not forget that Hitler came to popular support and power on these two slogans!), to countenance the most brutal and antichristian of political measures to reconstitute a lost age of religious monism. *Apostasy* not *persecution* is the key word. And precisely for this reason the question which comes to us out of the Church Struggle concerns the nature of the Church as well as the measure of human liberty and the future of the human person.

If we go forward into liberty, we must accept pluralism and voluntarism and dialogue as the essential qualities of religious maturity. Consonant to that is acceptance of the secularization process in significant sectors of society: government, social welfare, public education, higher education, the family.[10] Believing Jews and Christians must learn to distinguish "religion-in-general" (*positives Chris-tentum*, to use the Nazi phrase) and a formless "spirituality" (*Geist-igkeit*), and here any critical mind can distinguish believers-in-general from a faith commitment authenticated by life in history—earthy, concrete. As Hans Buchheim put it:

The claim of the National Socialists, that for a long time there has not been so much "believing" as in the year 1933 or the time of the war, is not false; yet it was in every respect an emptied faith, a faith false in content, intention, and style.[11]

For the Christian, at least, the anchor by which a vague "faith" or "love of humanity" or "spirituality" can be prevented from floating into the maelstrom of demonic ethnic religion (Teutonic, Arab, Anglo-Saxon, African, or pan-Slav!) is precisely his identification with the Israel of God. For him the final version is not some folk community based on racial identity, but a vision proclaimed by Jewish prophets: the Kingdom of God, in which the peoples and tribes of the farthest corners of the earth shall gather about the Hill of the Lord and hear His voice and do His will.

The Gentiles, however, can apostatize: they can take on the protective coloration of their pre-baptismal identity and disappear back into the tribe and prehistory. And when they do, they leave exposed the Jew, the one who—whether he is personally a believer or not—is a sign to the God of Abraham, Isaac, and Jacob. In a way mysterious and awesome, the Jews who perished in Hitler's Europe perished for a truth which the Christians—except for those who stayed Christian and were also hated and persecuted—betrayed: that the Author and Judge of history was made manifest to us out of the Jews. The tragic truth, a truth which the Christian culture-religionists have not begun to grasp even yet, is the truth that most of the martyrs for Christ in the twentieth century were Jews.

The moral claims of religion-in-general died at Auschwitz and Theresienstadt. The pretensions of the Christian intellectuals to a love for humanity—quite divorced from love, even compassion, toward specific persons and groups—foundered on the mechanical precision of the Nazi extermination of European Jewry. The German liberal intellectual, overcome by a kind of spiritual vertigo as he contemplated the vast stretch of humanity, settled for national we-feeling, for ethnic (Teutonic) identity which automatically excluded the Jews. And as Koppel Pinson showed in a study thirty-five years ago,[12] the prevailing combination of Protestant Liberalism and Pietism prepared him for that submission to a false particularity: German folk community. The true particularity, which at the end points to a true humanism, is the truth stated by Pope Pius XI, "We are spiritual Semites," and by Krister Stendahl, "Christians are a special kind of Jews." In a mysterious way, the very particularity of the Jews is the specific against a genocidal folk-identity which is based on regression into an ethnicity infused with piety. In this stage of history, the particularity of the Jews is a testimony to universalism; it is the scandal on which all Gentile racism breaks its teeth. The frenetic effort to reconstitute artificially a religious monolith after the gods have died—whether that monolith be the "German faith" or "Christian America" or Islam—invariably leads from hatred of the Jews to overt forms of attack.

For those who will join me in repudiation of religion-in-general and spirituality without content or integrity, but who are not prepared to use the Christian theological formulation, let me state it thus: we are so situated in our various national and racial contexts that we cannot in fact love humanity without loving concrete, earthy, historic persons and groups. Under pressure, we shall either retrogress to a first love of the Gentile tribe or nation, or we shall love that Israel whose prophets and seers point us toward a day of universal justice and righteousness, mercy and peace. Hatred of the Jews is often the first seismographic reading of the covert emergence of a false particularism, and we must learn to recognize it as such.

Precisely for this reason we bring together Church Struggle and Holocaust at this international conference. For Christians—and not just for the Jewish people—the Holocaust is the most important event in recent church history. For working theologians, it has called into question the whole fabric of Christendom, indeed the very language of traditional religion, just as among youth and students it has rendered the churches incredible. For scholars of other disciplines and vernaculars, political Antisemitism is a code to identify the totalitarian ideologies and systems which are the curse of the twentieth century—whether our eyes are turned toward "the Jews of silence" of Soviet Russia, the Jews of statehood whom Nasser, in a public address on May 26, 1967, promised to exterminate, or the Jews, our American fellow citizens, who are the special target of the Radical Right.

Reference was made to the false spirituality which was so strong in the Third Reich, and against which the men of Barmen and the Confessing Church made their particular stand. In practical terms, the interchangeability of this base ore of devotion was recognized by Hitler himself. He told Rauschning on one occasion: "There is more that binds us to Bolshevism than separates us from it. . . . I have always made allowance for this circumstance and have given orders that former Communists be admitted to the Party at once."[13] For a "true believer" of totalitarian type, one closed system is as good as another!

## The Treason of the Intellectuals

In theological terms, it is this interchangeability which gives special pathos to the irresponsibility of the German intellectuals. For while the common folk were left to the credulity and quick switch of the "true believer," the liberal academics had been very largely rendered incapable of *any* unqualified loyalties—especially to institutional religion! Yet in the end they proved to be as unable to stand against the claims of the folk community as the most unlettered farmer or laborer. Looking on from the balcony, the men of the universities and professions were quite able to perceive the naive and faulty character of unquestioned obedience to any party or group. But when the day of reckoning came, they were without moorings to withstand the overpowering demands of the ideological one-party state. As Albert Einstein noted in a famous statement, resistance came not from the universities but primarily from simple Christian laymen and their pastors. The people of the congregations who remained faithful, and the pastors who held true to the covenant, were living at a level of trust which men who lived from the Fall, from *Techne*, could neither understand nor identify with. According to Christian Theology, human science/invention/artifice entered man's history with man's fall and alienation from God and the created order. The mechanics served Hitler well, being outside the worlds of innocence and trust.

A spirituality which has no relation to a known tradition, a religious moment which involves no loyalties to a known alternative, is what contemporary political Gnosticism offers us. But Gnosticism—the closed system of secret knowledge—of the twentieth century carries political force not noted in the Gnostic heresies which tormented the early Church.[14] "Faith" which is divorced from Judaism or Christianity, the "faith in faith" of which Will Herberg wrote in his classic review of American religion, *Protestant/Catholic/Jew* (1955), in our day sooner or later finds a political channel.

Let our view of the future, then—and it is precisely the hope of things to come which gives history its meaning and shape—be governed by a clear vision. As Jürgen Moltmann has written in his *Theology of Hope,* in criticism of the vague perspectives which mar contemporary neo-liberalism, the transposed eschatology of the crystal *moment,* the *Nun* of existentialism, is far different from the *promise* given Israel.

It is one thing to ask: where and when does an epiphany of the divine, eternal, immutable and primordial take place in the realm of the human, temporal and transient? And it is another thing to ask: when and where does the God of the promise reveal his faithfulness and in it himself and his presence?[15]

We are thrust back upon the essential Jewishness of our holy history in spite of all awareness of the dangers of a linear view of history, pointed out by contextual ethicists and illuminated by linguistic analysis. The truth is that either we shall as an American people look for an epiphany in the American religion, which George Wallace has a better chance to declare than Harvey Cox or Peter Berger or Martin Marty, or we shall confess—however haltingly—the vision of Isaiah for the time to come. The irony of our recent decades as men of education is severe: those who have found the particularity of "Jewish folklore and fable" too confining, too earthy, too finite have ended in the pitiful vulgarisms of Teutonic or Anglo-Saxon or other Gentile ethnicity infused by a vague piety.

Gandhi was once asked to state his greatest grief, and he answered, "the hardness of heart of the educated." It may be that Søren Kierkegaard's iconoclastic word can fix the point: "the greater a man's equipment of knowledge and culture, the more difficult it is for him to become a Christian";[16] anyway, for the purposes of this discussion, the harder it is for him to accept historical involvement, commitment. Romain Rolland telegraphed an international congress of philosophers just before the opening of World War I: "Think as men of action. Act as men of thought." This has not been the record: in the face of one totalitarian threat after another, the men of the universities have copped out. Kierkegaard's presentation of "the Professor" certainly remains the most perceptive exposure of that permanent tentativeness, that spectator's stance, wherein the confusion of the scientific objectivity of accurate reporting with the moral objectivity of the irresponsible has reduced technical progress to frivolity and self-destruction. You may recall "the Professor": the professor, if he could have seen the Crucifixion, would have asked if it were possible to have it repeated so that he could be sure to have an accurate report of all the details! My hope is that at this conference, and in the Wayne Project, we shall not hesitate to draw some of the necessary, if painful, conclusions compelled by study of the Church Struggle and the Holocaust—even when those conclusions come close to home, even when the lessons cast long shadows across the present state of religion and politics in the United States!

Bonhoeffer, of course, knew the academic world well. And he knew the terrible prejudice against involvement in conflict, especially "political" conflict. Many of the opponents of the political coordination (*Gleichschaltung*) of the universities, and of the academic coordinators (*Dozentführer*) installed by the party took the conservative ground: the university, as a reservation for objective scholarship and research, must be kept free of turmoil and conflict. (We hear the same elitist arguments now, from those who in faculty meeting criticize the involvement of their faculty colleagues in anti-Vietnam protests and stop by the office afterwards to pick up their checks for defense research!) The conservatives of the German universities scorned the vulgarization of the Nazi effort, which dishonored the classical standards that had made German universities and scholarship the center of the scientific world. What a difficult decision it was for Bonhoeffer, who knew and loved this Academe—and could have survived the war as a member of a theological faculty in America (while carrying on scholarly work, of course!)—to decide to go back home. Morally, it meant to reaffirm involvement in that most ambiguous of civil acts: tyrannicide. Professionally, it meant to abandon forever any chance of enjoying the academic preserve of "objectivity," of non-complicity. The decision to oppose Nazism was long since made: the decision to cut off the world of Liberal scholarship, and those who defend its aloofness with such passion, was the last and hardest step.

In discussing the lessons of Church Struggle and Holocaust for the man of the university we are speaking not only of university trained mechanics—technicians with university degrees who were as empty of humane education as the bookkeeper at Dachau or the plumber at Bergen-Belsen, and just as ready to follow orders. We are referring to university men of humanistic training. Wherein was the treason of the intellectuals?

If we turn to a specific element, to the professors and writers of German Liberal Protestantism, perhaps we shall learn something about the peculiar perils of our vocation, and also gain a clue as to why Liberal Protestantism in America today is so endemically—if usually covertly—Antisemitic. For the truth is, and this is the tragedy of the intellectuals in many places during the century, that the academics have proven ineffectual in the face of totalitarian thrusts for power and shatteringly confused in the face of the most inhumane of all modern irrationalities: hatred of the Jews.

Looking back on the Church Struggle, in which he played such an important fraternal part, Josef L. Hromadka once wrote:

The liberal theology in Germany and in her orbit utterly failed. It was willing to compromise on the essential points of divine law and of "the law of nature"; to dispose of the Old Testament and to accept the law of the Nordic race instead; and to replace the "Jewish" law of the Old Testament by the autonomous law of each race and nation respectively. It had made all the necessary preparation for the "Germanization of Christianity" and for a racial Church.[17]

Nor is the problem yet resolved in German Protestantism, in spite of the testimony of the Confessing Church. As Samuel Sandmel pointed out in a critical essay on Rudolf Bultmann's treatment of Judaism, the danger point remains exposed. In contrast to the early Church, where—except for Marcion—Jesus and His message were understood to be a continuation of Judaism, Bultmann presses Judaism into the cramped mold of a distorted view of the Law: he describes "a Judaism that never existed so that he can set a special view of Jesus over against it."[18] The parallel to Arnold Toynbee's rejection of the Jews as a "Semitic fossil" is striking.[19] Both reveal the covert Antisemitism of liberal culture-religion. And the references explain why they and their colleagues and followers instinctively respond in opposition to the current manifestations of religious and cultural renaissance in world Jewry.

The problem of liberal Antisemitism is today far more dangerous in America, however, for we have here the last major sector of

Christendom which still lives relatively undisturbed in the balmy days of nineteenth-century culture-religion. The lessons to be learned from the Church Struggle and the Holocaust have hardly penetrated our Protestant seminaries, our liberal Protestant press, our church literature, the thinking and writing of even our ablest older theologians.

Let me illustrate. There was constituted a few months ago, under the auspices of the National Council of Churches and the National Conference of Catholic Bishops, a Working Party of twenty eminent theologians to deal with the theme: "Israel: the People, the Land, the State." In an effort to get behind everyday politics and humanitarian concerns, attention was first fixed upon these theological issues:

1. The Promised Land and Our Responsibilities
2. Our Responsibility for the Holocaust
   a. The Significance of Hatred of the Jews in the History of Christianity,
   b. The Significance of Hatred of the Jews in Islam,
   c. The Uniqueness of the Holocaust;
3. Our Christian Responsibility for Reconciliation.[20]

Letters were sent to heads of seminaries and graduate departments of religion on the chance that somewhere biblical and church historical studies might be going forward which would widen and deepen the discussion. Shortly thereafter a letter arrived from the dean of a seminary which considers itself the bulwark of American Liberal Protestantism. The relevant sentences are as follows:

After reading the topics I must say that I am dismayed and wish to register my strongest protest. If the Christian Church is really concerned for reconciliation in the world, not least in the Middle East, I can think of many more fruitful approaches than this kind of question begging and special pleading effort. The topics are so loaded as to be hardly more than one more propaganda effort to put American Christian support behind present Israeli policies. If peace and reconciliation in the Middle East is one of our fundamental concerns why set up programs that tie in the word like "responsibility" to what is a patently Zionist line of thought. The Christian response to anti-Semitism is surely not Semitism.[21]

Probably the last sentence is the most revealing. I have appended my reply to this paper, for such as may care to take the time to read it. For the purpose of this argument the salient points are these:

1. "objectivity" has led to a rejection of overt involvement in this earthy conflict and the debate which attends it;

2. humanity has become the enemy of any avowed concrete attachments;

3. a general religious and ethical framework has led to rejection of any specific holy history, especially any that has to do with the Jews. In consequence, when push comes to shove, the covert cultural Antisemitism erupts into implied charges that behind the theological study of a group of troubled theologians must lie a sinister Zionist influence.

American Liberal Protestantism is sick, and the theological form of its sickness can be summarized by saying that it stands solidly on ground but lately vacated by the "German Christians" (*Deutsche Christen*) who collaborated with Nazism.

The inevitable result of such initial academic aloofness and doctrinal uncertainty in the German universities and churches was the fatal weakening of the two centers which might have been the chief barriers to the Nazi system. More than that, they predictably produced a generation that came to power amiably inclined toward spirituality and religion-in-general but ill-informed as to the particular claims of the Christian faith and hostile to the particularism of Judaism.

Although there were in fact great differences of opinion among the Nazi leaders concerning the church, the result of religious emphasis was that an increasing number of members left the churches and registered themselves as "believers" (*gottgläubig*) without affiliation. The leaders who were not hostile appear to have been poorly informed about Christian doctrine. Many displayed that emancipation toward historic community and confession of faith which Article 24 of the Nazi party platform encouraged: "The party as such represents the point of view of a positive Christianity without binding itself to any particular confession. It fights the spirit of Jewish materialism. . . ." Goering's statement during the Nuremberg trial seems to have been typical: "I myself am not what you might call a churchgoer, but I have gone now and then, and have always considered I belonged to the Church and have always had those functions over which the Church presides—marriage, christening, burial, *et cetera*—carried out in my house by the Church."[22] This is about as clear a statement based on culture-religion as one is likely to find: it implies the privatization of religion and leaves no doubt as to basic loyalty should conflict arise between state and church.

The most complete formulation of a Christianity that accommodated doctrinally was made by "German Christians," and the best written statement of that position would seem to be Cajus Fabricius's *Positive Christianity in the Third Reich* (1937). Basing his rejection of any objective Semitic basis or unassimilatable dogmatic formulas upon the nineteenth-century liberal tradition of experiential and non-dogmatic religion, Fabricius set out to define the new religion of Germany "in accordance with the basic principles of National Socialism." He was sure that Christianity and National Socialism had the same basic principles because they both had "grown and become as one with the spirit of the German nation throughout the history of centuries." "The living religion of the *Volk* cannot be confined within a narrow scheme. . . ."[23] Such a "narrow scheme" would be some particular historical or doctrinal definition which threatened the mystical base of the Aryan folk community—an entity which Hitler said would be the Nazis' greatest contribution.

The men of the Christian resistance did not view holy history or doctrine so lightheartedly, although they did not always speak as bluntly as the Lutheran theologian Hermann Sasse: "The Evangelical Church has to start every discussion with the avowal that its doctrine is a permanent affront to the morality and ethical feeling of the German race."[24] Nevertheless, they spoke plainly enough to be accused constantly of meddling in politics, to be charged with "fundamentalism" for asserting doctrines not negotiable, and to be answered by a swarm of pamphlets like that of the neo-Lutheran "Ansbach Counsel" (June 11, 1934), which affirmed a general revelation made manifest in the nation and its divinely appointed führer. One is inevitably reminded of the ecstatic affirmation of non-sectarian religion to be found in *The Blue Book* of Robert Welch, commander of the John Birch Society:

I believe there is a broader and more encompassing faith to which we can all subscribe. . . . And I believe it is an ennobling conception, equally acceptable to the most Fundamentalist Christian or the most rationalist idealist, because its whole purpose is to strengthen and synthesize the ennobling characteristics of each man and the ennobling impulses of his own personal religion.

It is hard for man to realize that the Infinite still remains infinite, untouched in

Its remoteness and unreduced in Its infinity by man's most ambitious approaches or that all of man's increasing knowledge leaves the Unknowable just as completely unknowable as before. But I think that, being allowed now to grasp this truth, we should cease to quarrel and disagree over how close we are to God. For we are using a term which, in a literal context, or objectively, has no meaning.[25]

This is, from a biblical point of view, the language of atheism. From the point of view of fascists, it avoids the reproach of outright atheism by appearing to be tolerant and believing.

The "German Christians" were at least logical enough to press the religion of the ethnic base, infused with spirituality, to its logical conclusion: Antisemitism. In their 1932 Platform they appealed to all Christians "of German type" and affirmed "heroic piety." Repudiating all confessional parties, they cited the experience of German foreign missions which "have for a long time called to the German nation: 'Keep yourself racially pure.'" They then went on to condemn association with Jews, especially intermarriage, and even missions to the Jews—"the entry way for foreign blood into our national body."[26]

## Conclusion

We return to the original question: The relationship of the Church Struggle and the Holocaust. When an effort is made to cut Christianity from its essentially Jewish base, when an artificial effort is made to reestablish the myth of Christendom, when the culture-religion of a Gentile race or nation becomes infused with spirituality and historic destiny, we are face to face with the Adversary. Those who attempt to domesticate the church, to make it in corrupted form a mere creature of the state, are of necessity compelled to do two things of grave theological import. First, they are driven to oppose international contacts, to close off all communication with the Ecumene. The importance of the men of the Church Struggle and the universal Christian fellowship to each other is an extensive theme, treated on another occasion.[27] Martin Bormann's model program for the "final solution to the church problem," subsequently published and ably analyzed in the Vandenhoeck and Ruprecht volume on the Warthegau,[28] gives further evidence of how important Bormann—the ablest and most implacable of Christianity's enemies in the Nazi inner circle—thought the cutting off of contacts between the Christians in Germany and the world Christian fellowship to be. Second, on the "final solution to the Jewish problem," the church—even the hard core of the Confessing Church—did less well; and the elimination of European Jewry is the one plank of Hitler's platform which he could count a major success.

In the final paroxysm of "Christendom," as anxious powers strive to resist the process of secularization and the pattern of pluralism which modernity has thrust upon it, Jews and Christians of the pilgrim church have alike been sacrificed to bad politics and low-grade Gentile religion. The crisis in credibility faced by the churches, which has alienated the youth and students and driven the younger theologians to seek a new form of words, has created a wasteland where only a few flowers of renewal give color and bring hope. One is reminded of a child's poem which survived from the extermination center at Theresienstadt, where fifteen thousand Jewish children were murdered.

> Then,
> A week after the end,
> Everything will be empty here.
> A hungry dove will peck for bread.
> In the middle of the street will stand
> An empty, dirty
> Hearse.[29]

Even in America, behind the facade of statistical and institutional success, are heard the rumblings of the preliminary stages of a Church Struggle which affects even the budgets of the boards and agencies. Pathological study of the German Church Struggle can teach us a great deal about the political and theological realities of the twentieth century. One of these realities is that retrogression to sacral society, to a mythical and therefore false harmony, is accompanied by outbursts against the historical people, the Jews, even before "the struggle of the church against the church for the church"[30] sets in. The Jew, who cannot disappear into prehistory, is a surrogate for the Christian, who can.

I have not sought to depreciate the witness of those academics or patriots who—as men who loved culture or their country or both—have fought Antisemitism. I was profoundly moved to read Yevgeni

Yevtushenko's poem "Babi Yar," to which Elie Wiesel called my attention in his book, *The Jews of Silence.* A Gentile, Yevtushenko has borne political and social opprobrium for a patriotism which is humane—a rare thing in any part of the world these days!

> Let the "Internationale" ring out
> When the last anti-Semite on earth is buried.
> There is no Jewish blood in mine,
> But I am hated by every anti-Semite as a Jew,
> And for this reason,
> I am a true Russian.[31]

I am utterly convinced, however, that Antisemitism can no longer be handled at the level of humanitarianism. The very term *Antisemitism,* which we use because it has become part of the language since the nineteenth-century humanitarian pleas, is inaccurate and misleading—because among other things one of its most violent expressions in recent decades is found among so-called Semites, by Arabs to whom the holy war (*jihad*) against the Jews of Israel is a religious obligation. Islam, in dissolution, is producing many of the same frantic responses as Christendom in decay. Of these the most blasphemous is hatred of the Jews.

For me, the problem is basically theological: it concerns the nature of man, his ultimate loyalty, his final identity, his end-time (*eschaton*). The nature of the historical process—as well as its consummation—is itself at stake. Such affirmations cannot be proved inductively, they are not objects of "the historical method," and I do not expect that they will commend themselves immediately to all scholars here assembled. We can, however, establish in negative terms and critical analyses the indissoluble relationship of the Church Struggle and the Holocaust. As for the question whether Jews and Christians share a common future—which may move a theologian to read and think about the evidence—each of us must use his own vernacular, and if we achieve at least a partial pentecost at this International Scholars' Conference, we shall also begin to understand each other's languages in the university and to do something for interdisciplinary cooperation. As we do that, we shall again begin to speak for man—and not continue to contribute to his fragmentation, alienation, and dehumanization at the hands of political and academic machines. We shall also perceive that the most awful figure of this century is the technically competent barbarian—especially when he claims the sanction of religion for his politics of pride.

*   *   *

February 10, 1970

Dear _____:

I have your letter of February 5th, and—frankly—I am shocked more than I shall be able adequately to convey in writing.

The Study Project was constituted under the National Council of Churches and the National Conference of Catholic Bishops. Its priorities were fixed by vote of a group of theologians of front rank (both Catholic and Protestant), in an effort to get behind matters of everyday politics and humanitarian concern to a genuinely *theological* study of Christian and Jewish holy history. In the *theological* sense, do Jews and Christians share a common future? Are Christians "a special kind of Jews"? Did God's purpose for the Jews end with the appearance of Jesus of Nazareth? Does Christianity have a place in Jewish eschatology? What is the meaning of the Holocaust in *Christian* (and not just Jewish) history? In the breakup of Christendom and Islam, what is the significance of hatred of the Jews (what 19th century humanitarians called "Anti-Semitism")? What is the role of Christians in inter-faith reconciliation?

To call this theological concern "question begging and special pleading" and "a patently Zionist line of thought" is to reveal a covert Anti-Semitism which is shocking—in the most precise sense of the word. Furthermore, it reveals precisely the kind of Anti-Semitism which infected and neutralized German liberal Protestantism. The men of the 2nd edition of the *RGG* helped to prepare the way for Auschwitz and Theresienstadt, and when the Day of Reckoning came in the Third Reich liberals like Seeberg, Hirsch, Harnack flunked their exams. Why?—in good part because they were Marcionite heretics in their repudiation of a special relationship of Christians to the people and scriptures of Israel.

I think by now we should prefer to take our stand with the men of the Confessing Church, who witnessed against (Teutonic) culture-religion, and with Pius XI, who declared the truth that Christians are "spiritual Semites.".

In any case, to view a serious theological study of such matters

29

as part of "the Zionist conspiracy"—thank heavens you didn't use that phrase, although your protest has that overtone!—simply indicates the extent to which American liberal Protestantism occupies the ground but lately vacated by the *Deutsche Christen*. Nor is this a uniquely Protestant phenomenon: Catholic culture-religion is endemically Anti-Semitic too. Read Oesterreicher's excellent and detailed description of the efforts made at Vatican II to prevent declarations rectifying the wrongs against the Jews—including even resistance to elimination of the deicide calumny (Vorgrimler, vol. III.)! Read the Anti-Semitic propaganda, complete with vulgar cartoons, which now issues from the Beirut "Christian" centers!

The truth is that Christendom is sick, sick with so wicked a malaise that the baptized destroyed 6,000,000 Jews in Hitler's Europe, so sick that many "Christian" leaders were prepared to look on from the balcony while Nasser tried to carry out his threat of a Second Holocaust in June, 1967.

My earnest plea is that before you join the Neo-Nazis, Communists, and black ethnics (not to mention the American Radical Right!) in automatically considering the essential affinity of Judaism and Christianity "patently Zionist," you examine your own theological commitments. The Jews are not Cherokees, and the wrong done them by faithless baptized is not the same thing as the white man's injustice to the American Indians. There is a demonic quality to hatred of the Jews which makes it more than human cruelty: it is blasphemy. By the same token, the guilt of Christians and the obligation to repent and right the ancient wrong is far heavier upon us.

I refuse to admit, personally, that the fact that I love my wife commits me to "special pleading"—or that it diminishes to any degree the love which I owe all womankind. I also deny that the love a Christian owes the Jews is a denial of his duty to humanity. Quite the contrary: I deny that anyone can love at all unless he loves concrete, earthy, historical persons and peoples.

Sincerely yours,

Franklin H. Littell
Professor

# 2

# The Present State of Research and Writing on the Church Struggle

## John S. Conway

It is unnecessary for me to relate how much we all owe to our chairman, Franklin H. Littell, for his tireless efforts to draw the attention of the widest circles in churches and universities to the lesson of the German Church Struggle. For a generation now he has emphasized three crucial features of these events. First, he has warned of the need to be armed against the tyrannical acts and totalitarian ambitions of governments. Second, he has called on the church to recognize the full dimensions of its responsibilities in the political arena—a challenge which has surely been taken up at least at the level of the World Council of Churches. And third, he has pointed to the essentially ecumenical character of the Church Struggle, which was not something to be left to the Germans alone but was a challenge which the churches of the world could ignore only at their peril.

My purpose in this paper is to raise some of the issues which I feel are of particular significance in the present state of research and to outline some of the many sources which remain to be used by the future scholar of the momentous events of the Church Struggle. The present time, I believe, is particularly opportune for a new approach, because of the increasing availability of substantial quantities of primary materials which afford the opportunity for new insights and directions in research.

I will first sketch briefly the historiography of the Church Struggle. It has been my good fortune, within the last twelve months, to be present at conferences on the same theme held in Scotland for the British scholars, in Munich for the German Protestant scholars, and now here for the North American fraternity. The differences of approach I think are worthy of comment. In Britain and North

So too, I believe, would be the cross-questioning of both churches about some of the areas which now receive little attention. For example, Hitler's wars were fought by Protestants, too. And why was there no Catholic equivalent of the Confessing Church? When are we to get some more thorough sociological analyses of the memberships of the churches? And would it be possible to expect a dispassionate account of the heroic opposition to Nazi tyranny as exemplified by Jehovah's Witnesses?

Perhaps most of all, the tendency of German church historians to isolate their experiences from the history of the rest of society now needs to be looked at afresh. The Church Struggle is of enormous significance in the broad perspective of church history and in the development of the ecumenical movement. And I should mention at this point the recently published work by Armin Boyens, *Kirchen-kampf und Oikumene 1933-39* [Church struggle and ecumene], which for the first time makes splendid use of the archives in Geneva for a study of the relationships between the German Evangelical church and the growing ecumenical movement in its various prewar branches. But at the same time, the outsider cannot fail to be struck by the similarity of the predicament of both main churches with that of other groups in society. The reactions of the universities, the teachers, the lawyers, even the trade unions or the army, afford striking parallels. The impact of totalitarianism on all of these groups surely affords interesting and significant points of comparison. Or perhaps more pointedly, one would wish to study carefully the pathology of these established pillars of society in face of a challenge that they had indirectly nurtured. This should become, I believe, of increasing concern to scholars. For example, the almost total rejection of the pluralism of the Weimar Republic, the constant denigration of the democratic process, the ready acceptance of the mythologies about the Versailles Treaty, and the exaggerated opinions about Germany's place in the world, even the coolness toward the Jewish question, were all facts which churchmen shared with others in the broad band of the educated "clerisy." Much research needs to be done on the pre-1933 attitudes, and on the inability of all these segments of the community to provide a convincing alternative to the authoritarian regime which so many welcomed with so many illusions. It is to be hoped that the disciplines of political science and sociology would lend significant help here.

Foreigners have of course to be particularly careful in such studies to avoid the danger of seeming to seek to create some specific theory of German demonism which would account for Nazi barbarism and excesses by recourse to a theory of German perversion, such as might be gained from a reading of William Shirer's monumental piece of journalism *The Rise and Fall of the Third Reich.* We should be well aware of the need to study the pathology of the Christian church in other situations, and indeed we hope the German historians will help us here. But equally we should all have a vested interest in not seeking to deny the enormity of the Nazi crimes. Too narrow a concentration of self-justifying historiography from within the ranks of the churches, and their failure to relate their experiences to the total picture of the destruction of Western, that is, Christian, civilization by the Nazis has so far had the unfortunate effect of helping little to clarify the most urgent questions about the impact of Nazism upon the twentieth century.

This is all the more remarkable considering the vast amounts of material which are available for the study of the Nazis' policies and tactics. The records of no other modern government are as easily available to the American scholar as are those of the Nazi regime. You will recall that at the end of the war enormous quantities of German records, both official and unofficial, fell into the hand of the victorious allies. It was believed at the time, and perhaps rightly, that these could shed light upon the problem of why so many millions of citizens of the land of Luther and Bach gave themselves so wholeheartedly to the service of the perverted popular national spirit (*Volksgeist*) of National Socialism, and stood by passively while millions of their fellow human beings were destroyed in the monstrous and unprecedented atrocities of Auschwitz or Belsen.

Space does not permit me here to go into the fate of the huge collections of documents discovered in 1945, scattered throughout the country in barns, mines, farm houses, and isolated castles. Unfortunately for us, a large proportion of these records were captured in Silesia or Pomerania where they fell into the hands of the advancing Russian armies. Much of this material, including the archive of the National Ministry for Church Affairs (*Reichsministerium für Kirchliche Angelegenheiten*), has now been returned to East Germany. Access for American historians is still difficult because of the failure to accord diplomatic recognition to that state. The material that fell into Western hands, however, is now almost entirely available and affords enough in the meantime to keep us going. I pass over the huge quantities of military records, and also of the Foreign Ministry, except to note that these are all available on microfilm from the National Archives in Washington.

Among these documents which are of central importance for an understanding of the place of the churches in the Nazi Regime are the twenty-nine volumes dealing with church policy from the Reich Chancellery. These are selectively filmed along with the Foreign Ministry papers, and are indexed in G. Kent, *A Catalogue of Files and Microfilms from the German Foreign Ministry Archives 1920-45*, 3 vols. (Stanford University Press). The originals are now in the Bundesarchiv at Koblenz. The Reich Chancellery acted as a clearing house for many of the policies relating to the churches. It is possible to trace many interesting details because they concerned one or more of the governmental ministries, often in conflict with Nazi party agencies or offices. This source will undoubtedly be of the utmost value in gaining an overall view of the practices of Nazi totalitarian rule. These documents lead to material in the German Foreign Ministry, such as that used in the recent article by Ernst Helmreich in "The Arrest and Freeing of the South German Bishops in 1934," in *Central European History* (June 1969), where he described the part played in this affair by the Archbishop of Canterbury and Bishop Bell of Chichester. Equally important are the documents concerning relations with the Vatican, which complement those published by the Catholic academy in Bavaria, mentioned above.

The collection of documents which were assembled for use at the Nuremberg trials should be noted, both the main trials of the major war criminals and those held later under specific American auspices. Those given the enumeration NG, or Nazi Government, are of particular interest to us. Unfortunately, no archivists were present when these documents were collected, so that for the earlier trials it often happened that they were literally ripped from their original files without any indication of their source, and without leaving any trace that they had been so taken. Of special interest are the documents used in connection with trial no. 11, the so-called Wilhelmstrasse trial, in which Ernst von Weizsäcker was the principal defendant. One of the charges on which the defendants were arraigned was count no. 5 of the indictment, "Crimes against the Churches." For this purpose, the prosecution lawyers assembled a large number of documents from the files of the state secretary, especially those dealing with his relations with the papal nuncio. These were all assigned various, but not consecutive, NG numbers. During the initial proceedings, this portion of the indictment was dropped, as the defendants' lawyers successfully argued that the Wilhelmstrasse's policies toward the churches were not criminal acts. As a result, these documents were not produced as evidence before the court and consequently are not to be found in any of the printed records of the trial's proceedings. The same is true of many of the items dealing with the churches, which were assembled in the P.S. and other series, of which a few—but only a few—were reproduced in the twenty volumes of documents in the International Military Tribunal Blue series. These documents, and most of the defense document books, are to be found in various places in the United States, but as far as I know there is no satisfactory index, except in the Munich Institute for Contemporary History (Institut für Zeitgeschichte), and even there no attempt is made to relate them to the files from which they were taken.

Another neglected area is the place of church policy within the larger framework of the Nazi occupation of the conquered territories from 1939 onwards, for which sources are also available on microfilm from the National Archives. For Poland, the files of the Chancellery of the Governor General, Frank, and a copy of his office diary throw much light on the persecution of the church in that devastated country. Further documentation is available to supplement the material already incorporated in Gürtler's study of the Evangelical church in the Warthegau,[2] the area which was to become the model Nazi district (*Gau*). For Norway, there is now in the possession of the Bundesarchiv, Koblenz, the memoranda of a Norwegian pastor on the measures taken by the Occupation forces against the Norwegian churches. A detailed study is most urgently needed of the material contained on the microfilms which deal with Russia. There still exists a complete set of daily bulletins prepared by the security police entitled *Ereignismeldungen aus der USSR* [Reports of events in the USSR], where reports on the extermination policies of the German invaders are intermingled with descriptions of the highly complex situation of Russian and Ukrainian church life.

Turning now to another vast collection of great interest to our subject, which is readily available in this country, I will describe the holdings of the Nazi party officials.[3] These were all flown out of the Berlin Document Center during the Berlin blockade, and later microfilmed under the auspices of the National Archives and the American Historical Association. A team of researchers was employed to prepare these documents for microfilming and to compile the *Guides to Captured German Records* which contain brief—often far too brief—summaries of the contents. Because of the enormous confusion in the documents after all those years, and because virtually no registers existed, the microfilming project proceeded simply by filming one file after another, regardless of its original provenance, which in many cases could no longer be ascertained. Each Guide includes only those files contained in the crates in which the documents arrived from Germany. The total filming project involved some ten million documents. There are now fifty-nine Guides in all, of which the majority deal with military records. Of most interest to this audience are the Records of the Personal Staff of the Reichsführer SS, the so-called Himmler papers, described in Guides 32, 33, and 39. Since Himmler had his finger in almost every aspect of German life during the Nazi era, these files offer a tremendous amount of evidence for that period. Then there are the so-called Rosenberg papers in Guide no. 28, which include the fifteen volumes of extensive correspondence between Rosenberg and Bormann. These throw a great deal of light on the sinister but widely divergent policies of these two men toward the church. The miscellaneous records of the Nazi party, contained in Guides 3, 20, 35, have a great deal of interesting, widely scattered material.

It is hardly surprising that scholars have so far made little use of these sources, because there is no systematic index of these records or even of the Guides. In order to discover the documents relating to any one theme, e.g., Church policy, it is still necessary to read the entire contents of the Guides. Only the National Archives possesses a complete set of all the films, though individual universities have certain holdings, such as the Himmler papers mentioned above. I am hoping soon to compile a master list for use by all who are interested in these microfilms.

One added difficulty should be mentioned. When all these documents were returned to Germany, most of them were deposited in the Bundesarchiv, where they are still in process of extensive reorganization. Other records, dealing with local areas, were returned to their province of origin, and are thus scattered throughout Germany.

Another interesting collection on microfilm consists of the material collected in the Berlin Document Center, which was never taken to the United States. There are a thousand microfilms of this material alone. Then there is the material which has only been partially microfilmed in Berlin, particularly the great central card index (*Zentralkartei*) of the Nazi party and all its associated organizations, consisting of approximately eighteen million names. Any searching study of the Nazi era must find this source invaluable.

I have dealt here only with those materials readily available in the United States. Space does not allow me to deal in detail with the very numerous church archives, such as the Niemöller Archive in Bielefeld, about which Dr. Wilhelm Niemöller himself will tell us. Many of the diocesan and provincial archives were damaged during the war, but huge amounts of material still remain to be used. We are now entering a phase of research when we can look with dispassionate concern at the complexities and problems which confronted the churches in the Nazi era. I think we have passed through the period of hagiographical self-justifications, and the reaction which led to sharply "revisionist" accounts, though these afforded genuine insights into the significant and often burning issues of the day. We will surely recognize, as Conzemius pointed out, "that historical investigation proceeds dialectically. Without the thesis and the antithesis, the synthesis is hardly possible. But the Church Struggle is not solely a matter for academic research: from its study we must draw concrete lessons for the life of the Church."

# 3
# The Niemöller Archives

Wilhelm Niemöller

When Vladimir Ilyich Lenin came to power in 1917, his first decree was to ensure the preservation of the archives from the days of the czars. This decree, which greatly shocked Lenin's followers, was strictly carried out. We are living, especially in Germany, through a time of rapid changes. The downfall of the Third Reich, the democratization of our political life, a young generation's dislike of anything called "history," the strong attraction of all futuristic claims—these tend to cast suspicion on the study of "archivalia." After all the repeated periods of romanticism, is the intoxication with "history" to come upon us again? Is "history" not designed to escape from the urgent questions posed by the present and the future? Ought one not to sweep up the whole stack of paper from yesterday and the day before and burn it?

I do not want to get mired in these and similar questions—especially as I believe that each one of us will have formed his own opinion, that we may all share the same opinion. As desired and expected, I am now definitely going to concern myself with German contemporary affairs, as we have seen them in the role of contemporaries: a section of history which may hardly be regarded as having been mastered—for old dreams and problems, old slogans and actions, old ideals and mistakes have a way of keeping their vitality for a remarkably long period. The history of the "Strong Man," the thinking in "Friend-and-Foe Patterns," the fairy tales of the victory of the "Victor," the claim that a little evil can be used to achieve a lot of good—all these are old hat and yet always new. Unfortunately, people can time and again be seduced by changes of dress and vocabulary, and fall victim to the seducing powers.

In dealing with the archives in Germany, I must first express astonishment that, in spite of the most unfavorable conditions, so much exceedingly significant archive material has survived. From 1940 to 1942, I was an aide-de-camp in an artillery brigade. Even then it was accepted as a matter of course that any classified material was to be burned in case of immediate danger. At that time, sufficient gasoline was always available and kept nearby. I was never forced to start a fire, but other agencies made more intensive use of this possibility—especially, of course, the definitely political agencies like those of the Nazi party or the Secret State Police.

Those interested, for example, in jurisdiction in Germany will find the greater part of the files of the Dortmund Special Court in the attic of the building housing the Dortmund District Court. These files are a good source for the study of Third Reich jurisdiction and contain invaluable material about the resistance of Jehovah's Witnesses, as well as showing the methods employed by these political courts.

Equally important, perhaps even more significant, is that about seventy thousand files of the Secret State Police are in the Düsseldorf State Archives. They have hardly been touched and certainly have not been systematically researched. It was here that I found the file on the present Praeses Joachim Beckmann of Düsseldorf, head of the Rhineland church. It is one of the most detailed files, comprising no less than 705 pages. It contains not only the resistance story of the former Düsseldorf pastor but also gives deep and reliable insights into the organization and activities of the Confessing Church in the Rhineland. I have reason to believe that nowhere is a better and, on the whole, more reliable picture of the development of the Confessing Church to be found than here. I have written an essay about it—"Aus der Polizeiakte des Bekenntnispfarrers Joachim Beckmann" [Selections from the police records on the confessing pastor Joachim Beckmann], which was published in the volume *"Zur Geschichte des Kirchenkampfes, Gesammelte Aufsätze"* [On the history of the church struggle, collected works] (Göttingen, 1965).

But I must stop enumerating. I merely want to express my hope that the present conference may provide a stimulus for registering and cataloging the scattered and extremely valuable documents in Germany, including the German Democratic Republic and, if possible, from east of the Oder-Neisse line. Only then will it be possible to determine exactly the location of any given material, and to establish what has yet to be searched out and what can be brought together under various headings.

This is not to say, however, that in the meantime nothing at all has been done. Those coming from outside Germany would want to go to the Federal Archives in Koblenz, the Institute for Contemporary History in Munich, and perhaps the Research Establishment for Military History in Freiburg. They will surely not be disappointed. The abundance of existing material is so great that, despite the great interest shown by the Nuremberg Court and the Allied Nations, years of hard work will not suffice to cover it all, and real progress is not to be expected without planning and a division of labor.

For the history of the Church Struggle, it is particularly regrettable that access has still not been granted to the files of the former Reichs Ministry for Church Affairs which was headed by Reich Minister Hanns Kerrl beginning in September 1935. They are in Potsdam. Information about their contents is meager, but as yet there are apparently no plans for making full use of them. There are facts and connections which could be easily ascertained and interpreted if the opportunity to study these documents existed.

We have to ask quite seriously if it would not be advisable to work our way up from the bottom to the top, although working from the top to the bottom is the accepted way and the one that generally offers a greater chance of success. Let me substantiate this by pointing out that in the period we are dealing with (I am now confining it to the years between 1933 and 1945), we have to deal with a "total state," a dictatorship, a Führer state. The meaning of this has been all too clearly summed up by the lecturer G. K. Schmelzeisen in a little book published in 1938. He says: "The power of office of the Head of the Reich comprises the power of *carrying out* all measures necessary in the sense of leadership, the *legislative* power and the *jurisdictional* power. The Head of the Reich is the supreme administrator, legislator and judge of the Reich. He has absolute power of leadership and this is, with regard to its effectiveness, indivisible." The supreme judge is also the supreme executioner and the supreme commander. It is still an open question whether he wanted to be regarded as a prophet, and claimed to be the supreme priest as well.

Criticism is an important part of scholarship. Criticism of the

Third Reich, its leading figures, and the former panegyrists of these men is relatively easy today. After the event, when success or failure has become apparent, it is easy to judge. Therefore it is a particularly interesting question to ascertain what criticism there was in those days; and here one has to start "at the bottom."

To "start at the bottom" is at the same time to "start on the outside." I shall never forget how a leading figure of the Confessing Church described the persecution process. He saw the grouping of the forces of that time in the shape of a spiral. Its center was Adolf Hitler. Then followed the SS, SA, party, NS, affiliated organizations, fellow travelers, the military, helpful persons in economic, cultural, and scientific life, and finally the centrifugal forces and persons representing the sects, Christians, and Jews. Those farthest out were the first to be shaken off. Some came to the fore by raising their right arms and sending cables declaring their loyalty, and indeed there were many (including sectarians, Christians, and adherents of "other faiths"—but never Jews) who crawled ahead and came into favor. For these it is useless to look for documents; they have all been lost or destroyed by bombing. Nobody likes to preserve what may incriminate or speak against him later.

The history of those on the outside of the spiral has always been unduly neglected. This applies particularly to the history of the persecutions of the Christians.

In 1935, I was in the Cévennes in Le Mas Subeyran visiting the museum of the Camisards. I had, of course, heard about the abolition of the Edict of Nantes in 1685. But I did not know much about the Camisard wars between 1702 and 1705 in the south of France, during which at least five members of my mother's family were condemned to the galleys. The inside story of this time, so important in church history, is little known, and little authentic material is to be found in that museum in the Cévennes.

The situation in England appears to be similar. When James I received the Puritan delegation, beseeching him to favor a scriptural reformation of the church, he told them: "If these are the demands of your party . . . I will hunt these people out of the country or worse: I will make them conform." The measures of the mighty, their threats and crimes, stick in the memory. The arguments that spoke against them, the suffering they caused, what the vanquished nevertheless successfully achieved—of these little mention is made.

The history of the Third Reich ought not to go the same way. One should keep in mind that the same method is always used when those in power seek omnipotence: I will make them conform, "Ich werde sie gleichschalten." After the murder of Röhm, along with his accomplices and many innocent persons, Hitler said explicitly: "In this hour I was responsible for the destiny of the German nation and thus was the supreme judge of the German people."

The question was, of course, whether this German people wanted to have, and keep, this supreme judge. At that time, panic spread among large sections of the people, and many could sense the executioner's axe at the nape of their necks. Martin Niemöller then demanded within the Confessing Church that a service of Penance be held in the churches. But he did not prevail. There was—one regrets to say—not one voice which stated in public that murder was murder.

How can one start research "at the bottom"? Let me point out some possibilities which have so far been little exploited but which should not be neglected if the facts are to come out in their true color and if it is to be realized that the acting characters were human beings of flesh and blood. For surely it is not enough merely to relate that the resisters were once in conflict with the powers that be. The motivation and background of their words, activities, and actions must be presented and evaluated, and, if possible, the motivation and background of their faith and ethics as well.

# I

I shall first deal with the individual personalities who acted in one way or another during the Third Reich: by staying neutral in cowardly fear of endangering their jobs or burdening their families, by playing Hitlerian roles while their hearts spoke a different language, or by struggling for a way in which to live their faiths in a dictatorship and for ways in which they might contribute to prepare the way for liberty and justice.

Obviously there is little material to be found among neutrals and fellow travelers. They are sometimes at pains, even today, to prove that others were no better than themselves. But their effrontery is lame because they are lacking alibis. To them, the words of St. Paul in Romans 2:1 apply, "You have no excuse ... when you judge another; for in passing judgment upon him you condemn yourself."

But we are not concerned with judgment but with the ascertaining of facts, and that will keep us busy for some time to come.

Even today it is a pleasure for a research scholar to find a collection of material which is given to him before a household is dissolved or after the death of a contemporary. Although often the only discovery is a hitherto unknown pamphlet or a list of names, for intercession from the period 1934 to 1945 (identifying prisoners, persons banished or prohibited from public speaking) and stemming from hitherto unknown sources, the find is always useful.

Only recently I obtained the criminal files of the then pastor Hans Karl Hack who was sentenced to eight months in prison for "malicious attacks on state and party," and for contravening the "pulpit paragraph." I also acquired the files of senior pastor Dr. Wilhelm Jannasch who was sentenced to two months in prison because of a sermon on the fiftieth birthday of Martin Niemöller, then in a concentration camp, and his intercession for him. The sentence was preceded by a long trial. Thus one can get insights into the jurisdiction of that time, into the often strangely organized consciences of the witnesses for the prosecution, into the dedication of counsel for the defense and of some judges, and finally into the witness of the Confessing Church on which it is rather difficult to come to a valid assessment.

Hans Karl Hack and Wilhelm Jannasch were not the only ones who had to stand trial for their energetic expressions of solidarity with Martin Niemöller. There were others who were demoted as soldiers for the same reason or who were discriminated against in other ways.

This brings me to the invitation to give some information about the material which was accumulated by my brother but which has not yet been extensively studied. Those interested in the development, nature, and activities of the Confessing Church will not arrive at satisfactory results without these materials. It is a striking, indeed remarkable fact that this material has accumulated without planning or any thought of later use in the interests of church history. What is there?

To begin with there are his diaries covering the years 1920 to 1970 and listing all official functions, all conferences, and all encounters with the exact times and names of the persons involved. The years between 1937 and 1944 are, of course, missing—representing the period of detention. But even this gap is balanced by what is probably complete correspondence and records of every visit to the prisoner in those eight years. These records, in clear handwriting, remained in cell no. 1 on Niemöller's leaving Dachau. He found them unharmed on his first visit there after the end of the war.

Then there is the entire correspondence covering everything concerning Martin Niemöller's official functions. He was chairman of the Pastors' Emergency League, a member of the Council of the Evangelical Church of the Old Prussian Union—the biggest "united" church in Germany, and a member of the Council which was the legitimate governing body of the German Evangelical church (the DEK). This correspondence is largely complete and untouched, returned by the Secret State Police after long confiscation. The only part missing is the correspondence with the Minister of Justice (Dr. Franz Gürtner) and with the Secret State Police itself, and this will hardly be compensated by any possible find among official papers.

The original manuscripts of all sermons and other church functions round off the picture. The texts are reliable, as their author habitually kept to his scripts. There is also what is called a "War Diary" listing all occurrences, telephone calls, and visits in the hectic days between the Sports Palace scandal in November 1933 and the meeting with Hitler on January 25, 1934. Then there are his notes taken at all Confessing Church synods, at meetings of the Councils of Brethren and of the trusted representatives. In short, there will hardly be any personality of the Confessing Church who could leave a documentary collection which can even approach such significance for politics and church history.

I do not have time to go into detailed descriptions. I do want to say that the entire collection, amounting to seventy big files, has been returned to its owner after assiduous study in Bielefeld. It will in all likelihood soon be transferred to the headquarters of the Hessen-Nassau provincial church (*Landeskirche*) in Darmstadt. An indispensable and practically inexhaustible source!

## II

I have mentioned the possibility of "starting at the bottom." The Bielefeld Archive of the Church Struggle, which I really started as a private collection in 1933, has belonged to my church, the Evangelical Church of Westphalia, since my retirement as pastor. I collected everything I could lay my hands on, together with what was given to me and what appeared important or necessary for my innumerable speeches and sermons in the Confessing Church and in my small church posts.

Confiscations began in my house in June 1934. Quite harmless items were among those confiscated. But they included forty-one hundred copies of the Barmen Theological Declaration, which the Secret State Police (in a passing seizure of correct theological insight) regarded as dangerous to *their* state. Later, the numerous house searches and interrogations were always carried out for the purpose of getting hold of certain definite publications, leaving the rest untouched. There was not much we gave up. The tactics were always the same: we either delivered up a dozen copies while thousands were saved by others, or we refused to talk and asked the Secret State Police, usually rather uneducated persons, to look and help themselves. Still, there was a lot of trouble.

Never did they guess how much they were missing. This was possible only because in the Confessing Church we had a very good system of distribution in which not only theologians but students, housewives, printers, and civil servants cooperated. It was like a Hydra: where one head was cut off, a new one grew. And this happened not just nine times, as with the Hydra. It is no exaggeration to say that millions of pamphlets and leaflets were printed or mimeographed in that period.

There is sufficient evidence in the Bielefeld Archive that such things were not only pursued by the Secret State Police but also went to the Special Courts for judgment. There is, for example, a whole criminal file against pastors Heinrich Held, Paul Humburg, and Johannes Schlingensiepen (a total of twenty-three pastors and laymen were accused) from 1937. The court concerned itself with no less than thirty-nine pamphlets or leaflets distributed by the Confessing Church at the time. These publications were classified in a special list. Twenty-five bear the note "punishable," and the rest "not punishable." In each case it is hot stuff, and it is interesting to note that the intercession lists are always designated as punishable—the lists which pastors of the Confessing Church read to their congregations every Sunday, stating who was in a concentration camp, who in prison, who was in prison on remand, who had been banished from his congregation or province, who was banned from public speaking, and so on. Measures against members of the Confessing Church were manifold and numerous, and I remember how I once read over a hundred and seventy names from the intercession list to my imprisoned brother's congregation in 1937. May I say in passing that I estimate the number of pastors who went to prison for shorter or longer periods to be more than three thousand.

The underground literature is by no means always recognizable as such at first sight. "Undesirable" items might be published under a title from the field of chemistry or physics. Martin Niemöller's last twenty-eight sermons were laboriously mimeographed in a basement. Their title was, in Greek letters, *Kyrios Jesous Christos*—Jesus Christ is the Lord. Some titles were misinterpreted by the State Police. When early in 1936 Otto Dibelius's pamphlet was printed by the firm of "Martin Niemöller" and of course without the printer's name, its title was "Die Staatskirche ist da" [The state church is at hand]. In their hurry and excitement the Secret Police understood it as "Die Staatskrise ist da" [The state crisis has come] and busily searched for the pamphlet which endangered the existence of the Third Reich.

Now I believe I am right in saying that the Bielefeld Archive of the Church Struggle contains very nearly all the underground literature—at least the Protestant underground literature—the "undesirable," the forbidden literature that never came to the attention of the State Police. This collection can probably be enlarged only by continued research in still undiscovered and unexploited State Police files. Even then the results would not be overwhelming.

Further research would involve working through the existing material, establishing authorship, printers, dates and areas of distribution, and (if possible) editing the lot. This task, however, should be tackled soon, because the last of the authors and those with personal knowledge of what happened are dying out, and without their help satisfactory results are hardly possible. It may be that our friends in the United States are interested in this work and prepared to further it. A certain detective talent, however, is needed to get results.

After the establishment of the Reich Ministry for Church Affairs (or, to be more exact, after Reich Minister Kerrl's fifth decree "for implementing the Law for Safeguarding the German Evangelical Church" of December 2, 1935), all circulars and information bulletins of the Councils of Brethren on all levels of the Confessing

Church were considered impermissible publications. Up to then, the Councils of Brethren in Brandenburg, the Rhineland, and Westphalia (to mention only a few) had issued fifty to seventy thousand copies in fairly regular sequence. At this point, something else had to be found to take their place. Instead of the periodical publications now prohibited, "personal letters" by individual personalities were issued, partly in print, partly in primitive mimeographs. At the same time, items were copied by hand, the State Police were busy searching for certain typewriters and happy when they could confiscate them; however, this did not dampen the zeal of their owners. It would be a great service to research if these items were collected.

### III

Strangely enough, even the newspapers and periodicals of this time can be regarded as sources for the history of the Church Struggle. Of course, everything was made to conform to government purpose—the longer things went on, the more so. But one living under a dictatorship learns to read between the lines if he is not deficient in intelligence. What was permitted circulation in those days is expensive to buy today, but on the whole it is readily accessible.

Unfortunately, the Bielefeld Archive does not contain the official party paper *Völkischer Beobachter.* I was offered it for between four and five thousand Marks, but could not purchase it for lack of funds. There is, however, a complete set of issues of a Bielefeld daily paper. This is a good substitute because in a well-lubricated dictatorship two new papers will be as alike as two eggs. But it is important to have not only the political section but the economic, cultural, and advertisement sections as well. Astonishing things will then come to light. Among the death announcements one may come across the names of people who died in concentration camps, or by euthanasia in so-called sanitoriums. One finds that, starting at a certain date, death announcements of soldiers killed in action could no longer contain a Bible verse and that what persons should desire to express was that their husbands, brothers, or sons had died "for the Führer." There is regular information about where the party held its national Socialist services (*Feierstunde*) to replace undesired church services. Instead of the daily Bible lessons of the Moravian Brethren (*Herrnhuter*), one can read Words for the Day, the Week, the Month from the mouth of the Führer. If one compares the respective orders from Joseph Goebbel's Ministry of Propaganda with such observations, then the steering mechanism becomes apparent—even in church matters.

In 1968 Karl-August Brokfeld, studying to be a teacher, wrote an examination paper entitled, "The Church Struggle in the Bielefeld Press, 1933/1934," a good paper. It is a pity that such papers must be completed rapidly and that it is not possible to have them printed. They could show research workers how to get on with their work, and could suggest that the history of the Third Reich is not complete, even though it seems that documentary proof has been established on how often on a certain day Adolf Hitler screamed, wept, or bit the carpet.

## IV

It is not always easy for the newcomer to find his bearings in the course of the Church Struggle. There are sometimes quite similar situations in state politics or the party and in the Confessing Church, which after all was not a homogeneous quantity, but was often weakened by confessional differences or by divergent attitudes toward the "governing authorities." One can only be ashamed when, in retrospect, it becomes all too obvious what chances to be effective were missed through internal struggles.

Those who would like to go into the subject at one point or another would do well to use a set of twenty-five files into which I put any duplicates I happened to get. This gives a fairly complete and clear survey, making up to some extent for the regrettable fact that Joachim Gauger was unable to continue his fine "Chronicle of the Church Struggle" in 1935.

Starting with this collection it will then be easy to turn to more specialized aspects of the study—like the question of the oath, missions, armed forces, "German Christians," the Pastors' Emergency League, the Councils of Brethren, sermon literature, the question of training, and jurisdiction. I do not want to claim to have come near perfection in any of these. For that, my strength was too weak, my purse too light, my congregation too large. I never had more than a part-time typist available. But I had many friends who kept me supplied and entrusted me with confidential material.

## V

I would like to introduce you to yet another part of the collection. It contains 109 well-filled files containing nothing but *curricula vitae* and related minutiae. Some personalities take up a lot of space: Karl Barth, for example, fills four volumes. But anyone who turns up at some time or some place in the history of the Church Struggle has been registered, and from this preparatory work it would be possible (as some would wish) to prepare a reliable "Who's Who of the Church Struggle."

When the name of Koch turns up, for example, there are many possibilities. First there is the *Praeses* of the Confessing synods, *Praeses* D. Karl Koch. Then there is Pastor Günther Koch from Dortmund, who in conjunction with myself and others as early as June 1933 used to harry the state authorities in Berlin. There is his brother, Pastor Werner Koch, one of Bonhoeffer's pupils, who together with a friend saw to it that the famous memorandum of May 1936, addressed to Hitler, was copied and published in the foreign press—a deed which cost him no less than one and a half years in a concentration camp. There is the *Reichsleiter* Erich Koch, *Oberpräsident* of East Prussia. There is *Oberkonsistorialrat* Dr. Walter Koch, and permanent representative of the Evangelical *Oberkirchenrat*, Dr. Friedrich Werner Koch, in Berlin. There is attorney-at-law Dr. Hans Koch who defended Martin Niemöller at the Special Court in February 1938 and who was killed in connection with the assassination attempt of July 20, 1944.

Who will find his way there? Even so-called experts commit the most astonishing mix-ups. Those who want to safeguard themselves and their readers could do worse than look into the Bielefeld Archive. More could be said about it but I will refrain. I conclude with a stark figure: the archive contains eight hundred and eight files, not to mention an enormous amount of all kinds of literature.

*       *       *

There is a widespread notion among us in Europe that Americans are mad about figures. That statistics can be significant and justified will hardly be doubted today, although their scientific use dates back a relatively short time.

But in regard to the Third Reich and the Church Struggle, it is extremely difficult to provide figures. The Confessing Church always had only those collaborators who did their work without pay and for the sake of the cause. The theologians among them also had to perform their normal pastoral duties. They had no staff, no offices with card indexes, no rooms with shelves. It was a shoestring job that can hardly be imagined today, and although all were ready to make personal sacrifices, traveling expenses and clerical expenditures were very hard to come by. My own congregation was particularly generous although it consisted only of humble people; even today I am not a little proud of having receipts for donations received, bearing such signatures as Friedrich Müller-Dahlem, Wilhelm Niesel, and Martin Niemöller. With the Pastors' Emergency League it can, as an exception, be said that income and expenditures ran up to 2.2 million Marks. But this figure is not reliable because, in addition, congregations helped in numberless cases where help was needed. Such items could not be processed through the books of the central office—especially since there was a policy of having as little money as possible pass through the central office, for the danger of confiscation always threatened.

Those who have always collected will go on collecting to the end. Among the highly important files which have again accumulated during my so-called retirement, there are two which are of particular value to me. One bears the inscription "Statistics," the other, "Materials on the Church Struggle." I have always hoped to make them known and to shape something from them, but now I doubt whether the evening of my life will permit me to do so.

It must be admitted that many things important for reaching the goal were left undone. But keeping in mind that 1,858 pastors were killed in action during the last war, among them a high percentage of the young Confessing Church curates, it may be imagined how incomplete later statements about the persecution are bound to be. And there is the additional fact that provincial churches completely disappeared—and with them, their church administrations from which information could have been expected: Silesia, East Prussia, Grenzmark, Danzig, and parts of Brandenburg. Finally, there is the vast redistribution of population after the war—another adverse factor; the East-West movement plays an important part here, and in the West there are pastors and laymen who were living in the Baltic provinces or the Riesengebirge during the Third Reich.

In 1934, 18,184 pastors were in office. Of these, exactly 20.8 percent were in long-term, active cooperation with the Pastor's Emergency League. They expressly declared that the Aryan paragraph was a violation of confessional status. They promised to fight against this violation with all means. They committed themselves to succor one another in absolute solidarity. Nearly all against whom the state or "German Christian" authorities took measures belonged to this League. But it also counted many retired pastors and many curates among its members, so that the final figure amounted to 4,952 members.

In my personal lists I have collected the following:

Twenty-one names of persons who were, I would say, killed for the sake of the gospel. Direct participants in the action of July 20, 1944 are not included, so that this figure is problematical.

One hundred twenty-five names of persons who spent shorter or longer periods of detention in concentration camps. Duration varied from several weeks to seven years.

Four members of the Confessing Church who were banished and assigned permanent places of enforced residence which they were not permitted to leave for years.

Forty members who were permanently prohibited from public speaking in the Reich. Asmussen and Bonhoeffer, Dibelius and Iwand, Kloppenburg and Friedrich Müller of Dahlem were among them.

Ninety-four pastors and laymen (the latter in the minority) who are known to have been prohibited from public speaking in certain districts or for certain periods of time.

Two hundred twenty-four Confessing Church members are listed as having been banished. This usually referred to their province of residence, more rarely to the district or town of residence.

A list of arrests, more or less complete, arranged according to provincial churches, inclusive of churches from Baden to Württemberg is fairly complete.

It is especially about the prohibition of public speaking and the arrests that the problems of statistics become apparent. Should one collate the numbers of arrests made, or only the names of persons arrested? The figures would differ widely since some persons were repeatedly prohibited from speaking in public, others arrested repeatedly. One man I have in mind is Wilhelm Niesel, who was arrested for the ninth time in May 1941, when traveling to Breslau.

The information given here is reliable but incomplete. May those who can and wish to carry on the job do so!

Caution is advisable about the interpretation of sources. Many things are not easily discernible to later generations because it is difficult to understand what life was like in a dictatorship. There are all kinds of shadings between feigned agreement and unrelenting opposition. Usually, the mental world of outsiders is inadequate when it comes to making judgments. Many upright persons have nobly kept their silence, and one is often astonished at what some contemporaries—who were never heard about because of their silence—suffered, represented, and dared.

After the war, when I was first asked about my life during the time of the Third Reich, I was an American prisoner of war in Austria—billeted under the open sky, living on 452 calories per day. Again and again, our failure was pointed out to me, often rather overwhelmingly, and then I was assured that nothing like Hitler could ever have risen nor been tolerated in the United States. I smiled patiently because I was, and am, of the opinion that "Hitler" waits and lurks everywhere in some form or shape. Sometimes, however, I did not smile but got angry; and then it was a welcome relief that a minister of the Church of Christ gave me my first pack of Camel cigarettes, which subdued the worst of my hunger.

That we (and I am now talking of the Confessing Church) were in need of criticism, we had told ourselves long ago. That is why we made our Confession of Guilt at Stuttgart in October 1945, in which we declared before God and man that we had not confessed courageously enough, not believed cheerfully enough, not loved zealously enough. But nearly a quarter of a century has passed since then. Still we believe that the knowledge of the Confessing Church should continue to be spread, although always in the context of the assurance which at Stuttgart formed the concluding word.

About "The Usefulness and Disadvantages of History for Life" Friedrich Nietzsche has written for his time (in flaming words, as ever) pessimistically, destructively, nihilistically. It is strange that he should be the secret king of minds such as Hitler's and Mussolini's, and strange that countless persons should have become the witnesses and protagonists of a world view in which "the dearest" was to be destroyed, and through which man (surely a term of praise) was to become the superman (*Herrenmensch*).

Can one learn from history and reflect on it? This question, repeated to the point of nausea, is no genuine question. If history had a linear development, if man were really an unequivocal and essentially comprehensible being, then something could be done. Changes in the world and the changeability of man make "learning from history" an illusion, and prognostication of the future questionable.

The Confessing Church in the Third Reich—and with this I want to conclude—hitched itself to the one Man, the only one deserving to be called ultimately "human." It called Him the "one Word of God" and tried with limited strength to serve Him—who with His great power subjects to Himself all powers and forces, men and principalities. It is therefore of paramount importance to state what this weak Confessing Church said, proclaimed, and preached. A little of this was also noticed by its opponent, National Socialism, namely, that the point of decision was precisely here. One of my friends concluded a sermon of his in 1934 or 1935 by saying: "O Lord, Thou alone art our hope, apart from Thee, I know none!" He was arrested, put on trial, and later released. The enemies that listened to him had noticed that the Third Reich was put in a difficult position wherever the "one Word of God" made its appearance. For this reason I am happy to conclude with the words said years ago by our present national president Dr. Gustav Heinemann, a man who, as you know, belonged completely to the Confessing Church: "Its lords"—that is, the lords of this world—"Its lords go; our Lord cometh!"

# 4

# Revisionism and Counterrevisionism in the Historiography of the Church Struggle

Beate Ruhm von Oppen

My title is a terrible mouthful. Let me explain how I intend to deal with it. I shall not confine myself to the Church Struggle in the narrower, purely institutional sense. Nor would you want me to do so. What interests us all are the wider implications of that part of church history, that crisis of Christianity and Christendom.

As for "revisionism and counterrevisionism" in writing and thinking about that era of church history, the allusion to what is going on in the general field of contemporary history is deliberate. The last few years have witnessed some striking reinterpretations of the history of the age of Hitler.

There was A. J. P. Taylor, with his *Origins of the Second World War*.[1] He rejected the version that had been more or less accepted since the Nuremberg trials. But what is currently known as *revisionism* is the interpretation provided by the New Left, for example, Alperovitz, with his *Atomic Diplomacy: Hiroshima and Potsdam* in 1965,[2] and quite a lot in that vein since. The tenor of all this is the reasonableness of the Russians and the obduracy and uncooperativeness of the United States, amounting at times to collusion with the Germans. The historian Arno Mayer digs deeper and goes back further, at least to the Russian revolution and the Treaty of Versailles as an early exercise in containment or counterrevolution.[3]

But what concerns us more is his contention that in the context of the international civil war that began in 1917, World War II and the extermination camps were "the diabolic wages of revolution and counterrevolution. . . ."[4] This is more radical, even, than Peter Weiss in his Auschwitz oratorio *The Investigation*,[5] which mentions the complicity of German industry in the employment of slave labor. It goes a good deal further than Hochhuth who, after a tremendously long build-up, finally lets his pope appear and shows him preoccupied with investments and capitalist calculations:

> . . . von brennender
> Sorge um Unsere Fabriken erfüllt. . . .[6]

You may remember that clever wisecrack. For the benefit of those without German among us I should perhaps add that "Mit brennender Sorge," the famous first words of the anti-Nazi encyclical of Pius XI, are here put into the mouth of his heartless successor to express his "burning concern" for the coffers of the church. The rapacity of Rome is an old theme, dating back to Luther and beyond. The complicity of German firms in the slave labor system is a newer one and undeniable. But to say that that system and the camps that supplied some of the labor were the consequence of the Western capitalists' view of Hitler's Germany as a bulwark against Bolshevism is something else again.

It would be too much of a digression to say more about revisionism in general contemporary history and its possible points of contact with our subject. But the above examples provide another illustration: the difficulty of isolating "historiography." Once political scientists and historians like Lewy[7] and Friedlaender[8] take Hochhuth seriously enough to start their works with favorable references to his play and its historical appendices and message, and then are in their turn accepted as scholarly and cogent, it is not only the public mind that has been invaded by melodrama but the academic mind too.[9] That invasion, its causes and consequences, form part of the story of revisionism and counterrevisionism. And one might be quite prepared to let the academic mind go to pot, if the universities were not the new churches where people look for salvation—provided, of course, they are "relevant."

Ever since Hitler came to power I have been interested in the relevance of religion to Nazism and the resistance to it. It made me go to Dahlem, as a schoolgirl, to hear Martin Niemöller. But *now* when I say that I am working on this subject, the usual question is for figures: what statistics are there? I do not think that relevance can be quantified, though one may be able to draw certain conclusions from church attendance, penalties inflicted on clergy and parishioners, the denominational breakdown of the membership of the SS, and the like.

But, for instance, was the church "relevant" to the man who, among those who tried to kill Hitler, came closest to succeeding? On the eve of his attempt to kill Hitler and bring down the Nazi system—the evening of July 19, 1944, a very tense and busy day— Claus Stauffenberg went briefly inside a church. You will find no mention of this in Guenter Lewy's book *The Catholic Church and Nazi Germany*, not even in the slender chapter on "The Problem of Resistance."[10] Perhaps the incident does not affect his argument— which at most, though not at all, times he limits to the conduct and recorded utterances of bishops and other representatives of the institution. It does appear in a book published long before Lewy wrote.[11] And Peter Hoffmann in his recent book on the resistance[12] even goes into the question of *what* church it was. He has made exhaustive and inconclusive inquiries. So we do not know if it was a Catholic or a Protestant one. I quite like the ecumenical aspect of that uncertainty. Stauffenberg was a Catholic and the son of a Protestant mother—who was never converted to her husband's faith.[13]

But Lewy also goes into questions of theology and motivation. Therefore it is even odder that he does not mention that Stauffenberg had tried earlier to recruit a fellow Catholic for the conspiracy by pointing to the Catholic views on natural law and tyrannicide which, whatever the Protestant view might be, made it the duty of a faithful Catholic to act counter to an oath of loyalty that had been rendered void by mass murder and a ruinous military policy. Both Major Leonrod, the brother officer to whom Stauffenberg had talked in this vein, and his confessor, whom Leonrod had subsequently consulted on the sinfulness of knowing about assassination plans, were later hanged.[14] Lewy mentions just enough of the Leonrod story to make one wonder about the priest and about Cardinal Faulhaber for later praising him "as a fighter against Nazi tyranny." Everything is possible, and I would not put it past the Faulhaber of 1946. But in fact, when one goes to Lewy's source, one finds Mother Mary Alice Gallin has reported something slightly different: a Lenten Pastoral in which Faulhaber "praised the heroism of those who fought against the Hitler tyranny and used as illustration . . . a letter . . . in which a priest from Munich wrote to him: 'What a beautiful day—the exaltation of the Cross! I am condemned to death for being the confessor of a man who participated in the *attentat.*' "[15]

Whatever the possible intricacies of that communication, it strikes me as both mean and misleading to bring out mainly the negative points of that story. Mother Gallin used it quite properly in a discussion of the apparent or real inconsistencies in the attitudes of the church to rebellion. It is, indeed, close enough to the posthumous misappropriation of a *martyr*—or victim—by the establishment to give one an inkling of the rage that anyone not totally uncritical of the establishment might come to feel if this line were followed consistently, with never a twinge of self-examination or whisper of regret.

Then there is, of course, not a word in Lewy about the hanging judge's comment on this Catholic priest for having (as a matter of course) considered a possible assassination of Hitler under the heading of *tyrannicide*.[16] Yet that was precisely what Stauffenberg meant when he spoke to Leonrod about the duty of a Catholic, and the greater freedom of conscience a Catholic might have compared with a Protestant.

What keeps Lewy's resistance chapter so slim? What makes his indictment of the church for collaboration so fat? He sticks to the recorded public utterances of the hierarchs and takes them at their face value. Where such statements *deviate* from the diplomacy that was widely practiced under the dictatorship, they may be used selectively to exclude intimations of opposition. And silence is taken as assent—though we know quite well that it was not always so taken at the time.[17]

But it is not in order to reduce the file on collaboration and increase that on resistance that I urge a less selective view of the Church Struggle. It is in order to take account of the fact that the churches as institutions were and are in a fearful crisis. Unless we regard them as dispensable or even in need of liquidation in the general interest, we must try to see what good they did—as well as what harm—when the challenge to Christianity and to humanity was at its most deadly. And if that is our purpose, it will not do to persist in simple compilations of damning quotations.[18] Even the juxtaposition of staunch laymen and laywomen and the timid clergy, and even that of the devoted pastoral and lower clergy and the diplomatic higher clergy can be overdone. (With this distinction I refer more to the Catholic constellation.) It is, after all, conceivable that if there had been no Concordat, yes, even with its secret annex on the clergy and the armed services, Goebbels would have had no cause to complain about the danger to the National Socialist cause represented by army chaplains at the front. These chaplains were clearly far more important than the Nazi propagandist army bishop Rarkowski whose significance is, I think, exaggerated by Gordon Zahn and Guenter Lewy.[19] I must confess that in all my work on captured German records Rarkowski never impinged on me, whereas the troublesome army chaplains, both Protestant and Catholic, constantly did.[20] Goebbels considered them even more dangerous than he did Bishop Galen of Münster whom, nevertheless, he wanted eliminated as soon as this was feasible, that is, after the war. Quite clearly there were checks and balances of a kind, of a practical and psychological kind, even in the totalitarian system of the Third Reich. They did not balance enough, they did not check *nearly* enough—but they were real all the same. They even saved lives sometimes. It is one of the merits of Peterson's book on *The Limits of Hitler's Power*[21] that he almost *stumbled* on the religious factor among the limits and writes about it without, however, giving it much further thought. He simply takes it as one of the givens of a complex situation, like character traits or the differences between small and big towns.

Eberhard Bethge[22] has given a breathtaking description of the self-deceptions and errors of the Confessing Church. Twice, I think, he referred to the "room to breathe" that Confessors once enjoyed for a time.

The fallacy of the revisionists lies in ignoring that, in order to resist the murderers, people must be able to breathe. Theoretical constructs cannot resist. To postulate a population of perfect resisters does not restore to life a single man, woman, or child. To sneer at those who *did* resist because they do not conform to the current counsels of perfectionism insults not only them but also the casualties they were trying, by their lights, to save. I am not so sure their lights were dimmer than ours. Hindsight is not perspicacity. Neither is there merit in not having been led into certain temptations by the grace of geography or chronology; nor, of course, is there any merit or demerit or moral immunity in genealogy or the accidents of birth. That, surely, is one thing we *must* have learned.

Thus I would say that neither the retrospective expectation of the impossible nor the narrow institutional approach gets us anywhere with our subject—though, of course, questions of the role of institutions are very important, including, naturally, the question of the self-defense of institutions and the cost and benefits, both to their members and non-members. I incline to the view that the self-defense of the church, the *real* church (and I know that the word *real* begs a question), both Protestant and Catholic, had benefits that reached well beyond its own membership. Of course there were moments when the defense of the institution was in conflict with the defense of the faith and of humanity. But to make those moments into a comprehensive indictment of these institutions strikes me as wrong, irresponsible, and unhistorical.

Penitence is one thing—and we have had quite a lot of that here, though we have had other things too, and sometimes one was not quite sure about who was beating whose breast. But I think whole-sale condemnation—even self-condemnation—does not help. There are, I admit, moments when one can understand the revisionist wave that swept over all earlier accounts of the heroism and martyrdom of the Church Struggle. But when a History Scholar in Oxford refers to the churches as "tools of fascism,"[23] revisionism has gone far enough.

The prewar historians of the Church Struggle may have suffered from the weaknesses John Conway has described.[24] Yet they were closer to the truth, I think, than the latter-day perfectionists. It strikes me as significant that George Shuster, who with Reinhold Niebuhr seems to have been one of the first in this country to recognize and denounce the evil of Nazism,[25] was also the first to write a book about the church conflict. The title he gave it, *Like a Mighty Army: Hitler versus Established Religion*, may have been over-optimistic, yet the book, published in 1935,[26] gave an impressive picture of the clash. Then, in 1936, there was John Brown Mason's *Hitler's First Foes: A Study in Religion and Politics.*[27] When, thirty years later, I asked an assistant at the New York Public Library for it, he said somewhat sardonically, "I didn't know he had so many enemies." By then, of course, Hochhuth held the stage and revisionism was in full swing. Mason, incidentally, was a Protestant, writing about the conflict between the Catholic church and the Nazi regime. Micklem was another. He published his book in 1939, under the auspices of the Royal Institute of International Affairs. It is a classic.[28] Lewy uses it exactly *once*, in his chapter on "The Church and Hitler's Foreign Policy," merely for the translation of an announcement read from the pulpits in the diocese of Berlin after the Munich Agreement: "God has heard the prayer of all Christendom for peace," and so on. He uses Micklem's translation in his own argument of church support for Hitler,[29] but does not quote Micklem's comment which follows *immediately* after: "This did not please the Nazis. It ascribed glory to God rather than to Adolf Hitler."[30] And so it goes, I am afraid, in much of Lewy's book. There is a lot one can do with selective quoting and taking things out of their context; and he has done it; and thus what John Conway has called a "brilliant polemic"[31] is built up. Conway was more severe with Friedlaender's book on Pius XII.[32] My guess is that one reason was because by the time he read it, he had seen more of the documents on relations between Berlin and the Vatican; and he knew what Friedlaender must have seen and had suppressed, ignored, or distorted. I had had more experience with the *domestic* documents and developments and therefore found Friedlaender mild in comparison with Lewy. Also, a misinterpretation of this one dead pope worries me less than false simplifications of the complex doings and sufferings of many people.

Perhaps a personal note will help to explain why I feel this so strongly and also feel that—whatever the revival of German Protestantism and its theology in the Nazi era, in response to its almost deadly challenge—Catholics should not be forgotten in all this.

During and after the war I was doing political intelligence work on Germany for the British Foreign Office. We heard and saw more than most, certainly more than the news media, and received more reliable information than the press and radio (television hardly existed in those days). Doing that kind of work gave one a clearer view of the hell of Hitler's Europe than anyone outside had, and clearer, too, than most people *inside* had. It is, I suppose, an experience that leaves its mark.

After the Normandy landings, captured documents began to arrive—including concentration camp records. They conveyed a picture of hell and the virtual inescapability of hell. Then the records of the Reich Chancellery arrived, the records of the administrative, governmental center of it all (though, of course, there was the party chancellery too, and the SS and concentration camp universe had more to do with that). But here was the correspondence of Lammers, the head of the Reich Chancellery. It contained, *inter alia*, the euthanasia or "mercy killing" material. Here were the protests of Bishops Galen and Wurm—one Catholic, one Protestant—of the Protestant pastor Braune and of the Catholic priest Bernhard Lichtenberg. They were like an enclave of heaven in the middle of hell. And of these four it was Lichtenberg who died in captivity. But then he had also publicly pleaded and prayed for the Jews. All these men were brave, Braune perhaps the bravest. But Lichtenberg was imprisoned, maltreated, humiliated, and then died in transit to a concentration camp.[33] It is that kind of thing that stays with one: the palpable, visible proof of courage and fidelity.

These men had kept faith with imbeciles and epileptics and had tried to intervene at the heart—the unfeeling bureaucratic heart—of the political machinery, to get one kind of killing stopped. They eventually succeeded, probably because the factor that had prompted their action—the grief and horror of the next of kin—remained a factor.[34] There were people all over Germany whose institutionalized brothers, sons, aunts died sudden deaths by medical means, and some who might have seen their relatives quite recently and were told that their relatives had died of acute appendicitis, but they knew there had been no appendix since it had been removed years ago. It was these lying death certificates, which one knew bore no relation to the actual cause of death, that may first have conveyed to ordinary, unpolitical people that the country was, in part at least, being run by murderers. It was always individual families who were hit: it was the one person they loved or were somehow attached to who had been made to die; it might happen quite near where they lived, or in an institution farther away; the victims were usually taken somewhere else to be killed; some of the transports became known in the institutions affected—even children heard about them; and here and there smoke from cremation would attract attention. But it was not these—usually avoidable—failures of stagecraft that caused unrest among the people. It was the fact that the families of the victims were leading normal lives among other families leading normal lives, in a state whose laws did not provide for the killing of the incurable—let alone light cases of epilepsy—and whose legal system, despite all political distortion, was still functioning. That the whole program of medical murder was based on a secret order by Hitler, some may have known or heard of by way of rumor. Most had not. The whole thing was surrounded by mystery, secrecy, brutality, administrative anonymity, misleading language, and even by organizations with phoney names.[35] This happened all over the country, and it caused individual grief and collective unrest. The members of the clergy who were approached by the bereaved or those about to be bereaved or who, like Braune, were connected with institutions that housed and cared for the patients the system was now exterminating, these men—Braune, Lichtenberg, Wurm, Galen—could and did use the argument of inexpediency against the policy of extermination. Popular unrest is not a thing a government wants, least of all during a war that demands increasing sacrifices from the people. They also used the argument of illegality. And they invoked the law of God and the dictates of humanity. But it was almost certainly the consideration of the inexpediency of the operation that eventually got it stopped or almost stopped.

Quite an arsenal of arguments—though God and humanity did not cut much ice with Nazis. Expediency did. But even here, what surprised me, coming on this correspondence when I did, was that anyone protested at all—not that there had not been more protest. And this protest was "through channels," the channels that were left in what survived of the old system, the *ancien régime*. Galen also preached in public, referred to the matter in sermons; and at once the radicals, or progressives, of the new regime took counsel on how he could be silenced. They decided it was inadvisable to touch or to kill him during the war. He was too popular in Westphalia—indeed all over the Reich, wherever people pricked up their ears for a voice of dissent. Lichtenberg, on the other hand, was hardly known beyond Berlin and even there his name meant something only to the Catholic minority and a few lively minds outside. Incidentally, his arrest and eventual death were due not to police initiative or the denunciation of one of his parishioners, but to a couple of sharp-eared and vigilant women students from the Rhineland who were sightseeing in his church during a service.[36] It is such human factors, social factors, atmospheric factors one has to be aware of in dealing with those years.

It may have been partly a result of this early conditioning by much of the documentation on the churches that I felt that even Böckenförde was not quite just to the German bishops in his very critical article on German Catholicism in the crucial year of 1933.

This article appeared in the Catholic monthly *Hochland* in early 1961[37] and was, I suppose, the real beginning of the revision of the earlier favorable picture. There was a reply by Hans Buchheim[38] and then a rejoinder by Böckenförde.[39] I felt that Böckenförde was isolating some episcopal statements from their contexts—or at any rate not giving *enough* context for certainty about the significance of the quotation.[40] Shortly before, there was Morsey with his long chapter on the end of the Center party in *Das Ende der Parteien*.[41]

So the nineteen sixties were largely occupied by critical literature, some of it hypercritical, but they also saw the beginning of the documentary series put out by the Vatican and the Catholic Academy in Bavaria and the steady progress of the publications of the corresponding commission on the Protestant side, the AGK or *Arbeiten zur Geschichte des Kirchenkampfes.*

In 1967 came Bethge's *Bonhoeffer,*[42] but to call it that is misleading—to my mind the best single book on the development of events and the feel of the time and, of course, on the figure and role of Bonhoeffer. It is the most vivid, the most telling picture of the era of the Church Struggle likely to be found anywhere.

John Conway's book *The Nazi Persecution of the Churches*[43] appeared soon after, and its very title signaled a change. The book is not about persecution alone: it is also about adaptation and resistance. But it gets back, at last, to the point that the Nazis, whether we call them "totalitarian" or not, once in power had initiative and church policies of their own. They were not friendly.

Readers of German had already been reminded of that in 1965 in Friedrich Zipfel's book, *Kirchenkampf in Deutschland 1933-1945: Religionsverfolgung und Selbstbehauptung der Kirchen in der nationalsozialistischen Zeit* [Church struggle in Germany 1933-1945; Persecution of religion and the self-defense of the churches in the Nazi era].[44] That word *Selbstbehauptung* (self-defense)—which is not simply self-defense—is, I think, a key term in our context.

The evidence of the relationship of the Nazis and the churches is so vast and manifold that the argument about resistance and collaboration can go on forever and lead nowhere—certainly to no understanding—unless certain values and priorities are made explicit. One may have to agree to disagree about values; but at least one then knows what the disagreement is about. By all this I do not mean to say that my own values and priorities are crystal clear to me. But very often in the polemics of the last decade I have had the distinct impression that the basic quarrel was not really so much about facts as about their interpretation, though there are, admittedly, many important facts that we need to know more about. One category concerns the very difficult questions of who knew what when; also, what was knowable at any given stage. Here hindsight is a great hindrance, unless one is aware of its dangers.

These questions are complicated by the hardest question and the most painful answer of all: the question who cared and how much. Caring and knowing are connected—and so are courage and knowledge. In the pressures of the time certain kinds of knowledge were dangerous. There were, undoubtedly, such things as cognitive courage and cognitive cowardice, factors of courage or the lack of it that affected cognition itself. Also much "knowing" was a matter of interpretation. Louis de Jong has shown that the Jews in Holland simply would not or could not believe what was going on in the East.[45] They must have been like the many Germans who knew of deportation but did not know of extermination. In the case of Jews—who were themselves, as we now know, liable to extermination—one cannot say they did not know because they did not care. But since in the case of non-Jews there is always the suspicion that they did not care, or did not care enough, much more contemporary knowledge of the mass killing is now assumed than is probably justified.

The extreme example of wanting to know and taking steps to find out is Kurt Gerstein. It involved complicity. Any knowledge meant a kind of complicity, meant either tacit toleration of the intolerable or attempts to counteract it which invariably involved lies, deception, some harm to others, perhaps even murder. Gerstein himself became part of the system that supplied the gas with which millions of Jews were killed. If his own account is to be accepted—and I do, on the whole accept it, apart from some minor details—he diverted some of the supplies. But his signature is on the receipts for large quantities. He signed for them in order to divert them. A proportion he was unable to divert or destroy. He had joined the SS in order to find out about its murders.[46] This extreme example shows that the courage to see, the courage to know, was far from a simple matter.[47]

The present phase of recrimination indicts knowledge as well as ignorance—knowledge somewhat more than ignorance, however. There is a widespread desire to incriminate. Where so many suffered and died, the desire to find culprits who caused their suffering and death is natural. But such desire is hard to satisfy with the truth. Part of the truth undoubtedly is that there was *less* knowledge of what we now know to have happened at the time it was happening.

But the other and more painful part of the truth is that most men (and most women and children) cared less than they should have cared. They did not love their neighbor as themselves, particularly not the neighbor who had been classified as not-a-neighbor or the millions of Jews outside Germany in occupied Europe—especially in Eastern Europe where they were so numerous and so segregated.

The Jewish experience of forsakenness—the sin of Christendom—is now being visited on Christianity. "Christian" Antisemitism was a deadly reality. But the mainspring and machinery of the twentieth-century mass murder of Jews was not Christian, it was post-Christian or neopagan. Christians did not prevent the murders, but they did not instigate them. And it is surely significant that the Nazi agencies whose task it was to watch opposition to the regime interpreted Christian, particularly Catholic, objections to Nazi neopaganism as objections to Nazi racial policies. Nazis and anti-Nazis were agreed on the synonymity of neopaganism and racism.

And that, to me, is the chief lesson to be learned from that epoch. It does not mean that one ignores the Antisemitism or cowardice or greed or cruelty of Gentiles called "Christians." But it means that there is a difference between Christianity and Gentility, between Christianity and Judaism, on the one hand, and paganism, on the other; and the difference may be one between life and death, earthly, physical life and death—as well as the other kind.

This conference may help us toward the dialectical synthesis mentioned by John Conway, which Victor Conzemius foretold or hoped for when he wrote in 1968.[48] Even earlier Conzemius suggested some such conference as this but could do nothing to bring it about. Incidentally, it might be a good idea to get his outstanding survey of the literature on the Christian churches and Nazi totalitarianism translated.[49] Meanwhile there is my own somewhat shorter and less systematic article, "Nazis and Christians" in *World Politics* (April 1969).[50] I mention it here because church historians may not expect an article on our subject in that political quarterly. Our subject has all along suffered from interdisciplinary as well as inter-denominational segregation. That is why this conference is such a wonderful opportunity to desegregate, to integrate, to bring together what belongs together.

Conzemius, I think, sees the essential as well as the existential connection between the two components of the subject of the address with which Dr. Littell opened this conference.[51]

To sustain the tension between them without short circuits seems to me the only way to illumination or enlightenment on the darkest secret and the best publicized crime of Christendom. The publicity has been retrospective and blinding. The illumination must come from elsewhere.

The Church Struggle was the struggle of the church to be true to its Lord. And I take that to be a vital concern not only to its members but to all mankind. I am not a member, but I am passionately convinced of its importance. What gave me that conviction was precisely the experience of Hitler's millennium and the Christian response to it.

# 5

# Publications on the Holocaust

## Henry Friedlander

The murder of millions of Jews is central to any discussion of Hitler's Germany, because for the Nazis the war against the Jews became the only objective to be pursued with single-minded determination and without any deviation. At times they might compromise with the churches, with the West, even with the Bolsheviks, but never with the Jews. The Nazis persecuted their political and ideological opponents—Marxists, liberals, or churchmen—for what they believed, said, or did; only Jews suffered for just existing. Against the Jews they applied administrative measures without regard for the age, sex, nationality, or politics of their victims; while governed by self-interest and reason, they employed against their actual opponents pseudo-judicial procedures which, however perverted, still granted to the accused a remnant of protection. Even in the camps, political opponents—including members of the resistance—had a chance to survive degradation and torture. Only Jews—and gypsies—were gassed as a matter of policy.[1]

Unfortunately, the papers and discussions have not yet faced fully the interdependence between the Church Struggle and the Holocaust. While Eberhard Bethge (chap. 10) and Beate Ruhm von Oppen (chap. 4) recognized the need to analyze the dilemma of the churches in the Nazi era by showing how they reacted to the fate of the Jews, Ferdinand F. Friedensburg (chap. 13) and the discussion that followed provided for us an example of the failure to understand the central importance of Antisemitism.

As most of the conference members[2] are theologians engaged in the practical work of teaching those not familiar with the Holocaust and are not historians undertaking to do research in it, I shall only attempt to present an analytical survey of the already available literature, concentrating on easily obtainable sources for my study of the Jewish Catastrophe.

## I. The Textbook Treatment

That Germans killed Jews during World War II is widely known but, considering the importance of the Jewish fate in the Nazi scheme, the details of how the murderers killed and how the victims perished are, surprisingly, almost unknown.

In 1961 a study of American high school textbooks showed that their treatment of Nazism was brief, bland, superficial, and misleading. It found that racism and Antisemitism received only perfunctory coverage and that the Holocaust, if mentioned at all, was discussed in a few lines which usually transformed millions shot or gassed into thousands mistreated or killed, and organized mass murder into an excess of traditional Jew-hatred.[3]

There is no reason to believe that these textbooks have improved during the last decade. Moreover, even at the universities, coverage of the Holocaust in history textbooks used today is not substantially better than in those used at the high schools ten years ago. Thus, a survey of Western civilization widely used by college freshmen takes one hundred thirty-one lines to discuss the persecution of Jansenists and Huguenots in its chapter on Louis XIV, but only eight to discuss the persecution of Jews in its chapter on World War II. It mentions Dunkirk and Stalingrad but not Auschwitz and Treblinka. Discussing "conquered and intimidated peoples" it alludes to "mass extermination in the appalling concentration camps," but does not even mention Jews.[4]

Textbooks used in advanced university history courses are not much better. Time does not permit me to give a complete analysis. But perhaps by citing a few random examples I can illustrate their deficiency, and thus the failure of the articulate classes to face the Holocaust, showing how authors who should know better talk about the Jewish Catastrophe only in passing, if they mention it at all.

Thus, R. R. Palmer's survey of modern Europe, often considered the best of its kind, does mention the murder of six million Jews. It even gives the names of some of the extermination centers (but surprisingly they do not appear in an otherwise excellent index).

However, these short, though incisive, comments are submerged in other information and spread across a number of different pages. Nowhere do we find a detailed discussion of the Holocaust, which does not even get its own paragraph. The students, who learn nothing specific, will not remember anything.[5]

Although Palmer's coverage of the Holocaust is unsatisfactory, it is still far superior to that of other authors, who exhibit an ingenious ability to avoid the subject. Thus, Gordon Craig, an expert in German history, does not mention Jews at all. In his text, they only appear in his chapter on Germany as "non-Aryans" fired from the civil service. In his chapter on the war he lists its casualties without mentioning Jews. In his discussion of German behavior in the East he analyzes the mistreatment of civilians with the same omission. Only while talking about the recapture of Kiev does he mention—as an afterthought between parentheses—that the Germans had killed all Jews in that city. Apart from this, the students will not find anything on the Holocaust, not even the names of the extermination camps— except in a puzzling reference where Craig compares the brutality practiced in the camps run by Vichy France in North Africa for "foreigners who had volunteered for service in the Foreign Legion" to conditions in Auschwitz and Dachau.[6]

Craig's book is a rather crass example, but unfortunately it is not unique. Even textbooks concentrating on the twentieth century exhibit a similar blind spot; when they do touch on the Holocaust they are seldom more detailed than Palmer's survey. For example, Stuart Hughes's widely used text openly speaks of the Holocaust, but fails to treat it in detail as a separate subject. True, unlike Craig, Hughes does not submerge the fate of the Jews in that of all other peoples caught by the war. In his coverage of the Nazi regime he sets aside adequate space to describe the attack upon Germany's Jews before the war. He shows how the racist ideology led to the Nuremberg Laws, to the 1938 pogrom, to economic spoliation, and to the flight of the Jews. He correctly points out that "anti-Semitism and the concentration camp together created a demonic atmosphere of torture and frenzy which made Hitlerism unique in modern history," and shows that during the war most German Jews would die "in the holocaust of six million of their coreligionists that ranks as the greatest crime of modern times." It is therefore surprising that after this admirably forthright discussion Hughes only gives eight lines to the Holocaust in his chapter on the war. Students will not find any details about the "greatest crime."[7]

This hesitancy to discuss the Holocaust is not confined to traditional textbooks. We find the same story in the new type of history books—more essay than text—available at reasonable prices in paperback editions. They are well written, beautifully illustrated, and designed for the general public as well as for the college student. For our purposes two of these books on the twentieth century by specialists in German history are instructive.

Felix Gilbert's study in *The Norton History of Modern Europe* avoids mentioning the Holocaust. After the usual passing references to Hitler's Antisemitism and the anti-Jewish legislation of the 1930s, he discusses oppression and resistance in Europe under German rule. But in the two pages he gives to this subject, only eight lines cover the Jewish fate. Without even mentioning names or places he comments that "The number of those who were killed—about six million—is almost beyond imagination."[8] Obviously, with this kind of treatment the deed and the victims will remain an unimaginable abstraction for the reader.

A. J. P. Taylor's study in the British History of European Civilization Library is quite different. Although some historians have ranked him among the revisionists and accused him—unjustifiably, I believe—of downgrading Hitler's crimes, Taylor's treatment of the Holocaust stands out among the bland discussions we find in all other textbooks. True, he also does not provide the details needed for a thorough discussion in the classroom, but this is understandable in a provocative essay; still, though his book is substantially shorter than Gilbert's, he spends more space on the Jewish fate.

More important, Taylor treats the Jewish Catastrophe as an integral part of the Nazi era. With unusual candor he talks about Nazi barbarism without hiding the acquiescence of the churches and of the democracies which, even worse, closed their doors against the victims. Without mincing words, he tells how Jews were segregated, massacred, and finally killed in "gas-chambers of a most scientific type." Unlike all other textbook authors, Taylor sees the Holocaust as "an intrinsic part of the New Order," rejecting the interpretation that views it as "the aberration of a few Nazis or even solely of Hitler himself." Even more unusual, Taylor, concluding that "every civilization has its characteristic monuments. . . . The monument of German civilization was the death camp of Auschwitz," places alongside his text two photographs from the extermination centers.[9]

Some might disagree with Taylor's pedagogical methods. But after reading his essay teachers and students will not bypass the Holocaust. They might even study it further, something that is unlikely after reading the bland and evasive accounts in the other texts.[10]

It becomes clear how unique is Taylor's essay and how pervasive is bland evasion when we look at the college textbooks in German history. Here, if anywhere, the student should be able to learn about the Holocaust; unfortunately he does not. Thus, Marshall Dill's history of Germany in the University of Michigan series adequately covers the plight of the German Jews before the denouement, but, like all other texts, does not seriously treat the Holocaust during the war. In less than one paragraph Dill mentions the destruction of European Jewry. And, once again, an author finds himself unable to discuss the details of these "almost incredible" events.[11]

Coverage is not substantially better in the late Hajo Holborn's far more detailed work. In the last volume of his three-volume history Holborn adequately treats the anti-Jewish repression before 1939, but passes over, in one paragraph, the roundups and the killings during the war. More detailed than Dill, he does mention the specialists (*Einsatzgruppen*) and the extermination camps; he even talks about the Wannsee Conference called by Heydrich, but, hesitant to be more specific, uses the passive voice to tell us that there "agreement was reached on the final program"; he leaves the impression that Wansee was purely an SS affair, thus preventing his readers from discovering that many ministries—including Foreign Affairs, Justice, and Interior—sent representatives to and received memoranda about a conference assembled to coordinate mass murder.[12]

One exception to the usual treatment proves that authors of textbooks could give to the Holocaust as much space as they reserve for other, sometimes less important, topics. Thus, students will find the most thorough discussion in the late Koppel Pinson's scholarly history. In five paragraphs Pinson, a former editor of *Jewish Social Studies*, discusses the brutality, size, and geography of the Jewish Catastrophe; he outlines the development and organization of what the perpetrators called "the final solution," showing also how civil service and industry collaborated. Yet even here the treatment of the Holocaust, though adequate and better than anywhere else, remains skeletal, the minimum acceptable.[13]

The failure to reveal details about the Holocaust is not due to ignorance or ill-will; the authors we have discussed are knowledgeable and humane scholars. How then can we explain their reticence? The answer, it seems to me, is that scholars have been unwilling to recognize and to acknowledge the fact of genocide. Thus, even Stuart Hughes, who, as we have seen, clearly categorizes the murder of the Jews as an unprecedented crime, understandably prefers to see this crime as a macabre excess. He therefore argues, after discussing it, that "these demonic features, however, were not central to Fascism. The tendency of historians to focus attention on such horrifying aspects of the system has frequently obscured the less spectacular side of its relationship to the society and the economy which it dominated."[14]

But Hughes is wrong—and not only by failing to see that SS, camps, genocide were an essential part of the Nazi system—when he contends that most historians have concentrated on the criminality of the regime. To the contrary, a false delicacy seems to prevent most scholars from facing the history of the Holocaust. They seem to feel that it would be offensive to discuss details; here Taylor is a refreshing exception.

The anti-Nazi historian Golo Mann, scion of a famous family, exemplifies this false delicacy. His study of modern Germany, now available in English translation, shows us clearly why historians have been unable to confront the Holocaust.[15] While Mann gives a separate section of five pages to the story of the German resistance, he discusses the Holocaust in passing, when dealing with other matters, and fails altogether to treat the SS, the police, or the concentration camps.

Mann mentions the Jewish fate in a general section on the "Character and Course of the War."[16] There he briefly alludes to the murder of the Jews in Poland as he covers the Polish campaign, the murder of those in Russia as he covers the Russian war, and that "the Jews in France and in the Netherlands" suffered the same fate as he covers events in Western Europe. He makes the statement that "the worst" of all Nazi crimes were committed in "the gas chambers in the extermination camps in Poland where Europe's Jews, millions of them, were killed."

Surrounding Mann's short references are explanations and comments which, it seems to me, are even more representative of historians—and scholars in general—than the examples I have listed.

Mann does agree that "there can be no doubt about a crime which happened in our time and which will cast a shadow on the image of man and his story for ever." But he argues that "the worst" of all, the extermination by gas, "was then known only to a very small number of criminals." Of course, even if we accept this, it does not apply to Russia where, Mann acknowledges, officers and men of the army knew about the mass shootings. Citing Carl Goerdeler's lament: "What have they done to the proud army of the wars of Liberation and William I?" Mann blames the SS and objects to the idea "that the German Army as a whole behaved more brutally than other armies"; as if to prove this point he later discusses the "nightly mass murders" committed by the Allied air forces over German cities.[17]

Thus the deed remains, but the means and the culprits continue to elude us. All Mann tells us is that "the worst crimes were committed by units of the SS and the SD," adding only the curious proviso: "Let us not describe and list these things. But let us not think either that inhuman cruelty is a specifically German characteristic. The French under Napoleon did similar things in Spain—one need only look at Goya's drawings. If the leaders erect a system out of bestiality there will always be a minority willing to obey. This has been so everywhere at all times."[18]

How then does the historian explain the Holocaust? Again Mann gives us the clearest answer: "Just as the Army looked the other way and did not want to know about these things, the historian also does not like to speak of them. These are deeds and figures which the imagination can not grasp, which the mind refuses to believe, however clearly they can be proved by reason."[19] As to the Jewish victims, Mann asks, "Who can visualize four or six million human beings, men, women, and children, picked up at random, in the devilish gas chambers of Auschwitz and Maidanek?" And thus he concludes: "Darkness hides this vilest crime ever perpetrated by man against man."[20] We can only add that if we leave it to the historians and their textbooks, ignorance and distortion will not only hide but also bury it.[21]

## II. Institutes, Bibliographies, Journals, and Readers

The failure of the general literature to treat the Holocaust cannot be explained by a lack of available materials. If anything, we are overwhelmed by the sources. This is of course a general phenomenon in our century; still, it is amazing how much has survived. The Jews in the ghettos and in the camps, driven by the compulsion to inform posterity, recorded everything. Afterwards, the survivors, determined to reveal all, wrote memoirs. The perpetrators who, unlike their victims, wished to hide their deeds, also left for us a complete account. Their documents remain, a tribute to modern bureaucracy and Teutonic thoroughness. Never in history has a crime been so well documented.

To help the student through this maze, a number of aids are now available.[22] The most valuable and detailed of these is the *Guide* published as part of their Joint Documentary Project by Jerusalem's Yad Vashem and New York's Yivo Institute.[23] Basically a guide to bibliographies and collections rather than to individual works, this volume is of inestimable value. With over thirty-five hundred entries (and with exemplary indices) it provides for the student a perfect introduction to any aspect of the Holocaust.

All important items in the *Guide*, which is divided into four sections, have explanatory notes and many entries are annotated with a reference to review articles, thus transforming a simple guide into an essay on the sources. The first section on "The Historical Perspective" lists comprehensive studies and general interpretations on the Holocaust and, as an appendix, on Nazism totalitarianism, and institutions of the Third Reich (party, army, Foreign Office, SS, camps). In addition, it lists as an "Excursus" studies on *The Protocols of the Elders of Zion* and on Arnold Toynbee's comments about the Jews. And as in all other sections, the *Guide* here lists works in any language, published as well as manuscript, mimeographed reports as well as articles and books, general treatments as well as specialized accounts grouped by regions.

The second section lists reference tools: bibliographies, chronologies, biographies, maps, and dictionaries. The third section deals with techniques of research such as the methodology of using eye-witness accounts. In addition, this section includes a valuable discussion of research institutes, archives, and libraries, listing their addresses, their holdings, and their publications.

Section four covers "Documentation." Here are included items on wartime anti-Jewish legislation, on postwar restitution, and on the reaction of non-Jewish organizations (allied, neutral, Christian, etc.). Other items deal with works on the resistance and still others list periodicals and newspapers, including the contemporaneous underground press. Most important, this section also provides the best available coverage of the history, procedures, records, and publications of the War Crimes Trials.

Anyone wishing to pursue the study of the Holocaust further will soon find that a number of institutes have done much of the preparatory work.[24] The earliest to collect and publish materials were organized by survivors soon after the war. Now defunct, the most active one was set up in Munich by Jewish D.P.'s as the Central Historical Commission attached to the Central Committee of Liberated Jews in the United States Zone of Germany. It collected records, now deposited at Yad Vashem, and published a Yiddish periodical.[25]

Of those institutes still functioning the most important is undoubtedly the Central Jewish Historical Commission of the Central Committee of Polish Jews, established in Lublin in 1944 and after 1947 known as the Jewish Historical Institute in Poland. It has the most important collections on the ghettos and the camps located—as were most—in Poland, including the famous Ringelblum Archives; it has published documents, Yiddish and Polish bulletins, and a Yiddish quarterly.[26]

The Yad Vashem Martyrs' and Heroes' Memorial Authority in Jerusalem probably has the most comprehensive holdings of any institute in the West concerned with the Holocaust. Hosting one of the largest documentary collections—both originals and micro-copies—it also promotes Holocaust teaching and research in Israel; a number of Hebrew works, mostly documents and memoirs, have appeared under its auspices. In English Yad Vashem publishes a bulletin and a yearbook which, though they appear irregularly, are an important source for the student of the Holocaust.[27]

The Wiener Library in London is an equally useful and possibly more impressive institute. Specializing in the history of Nazi Germany and international fascism, it has accumulated an unusually rich collection of books, pamphlets, and reports. Expanding its original interest after the war, it now also covers neo-fascism, racial discrimination, right-wing extremism, and the state of Israel. Always concerned with Jewish matters, it is also a center for the study of Central European Jewry, Antisemitism and, of course, the Holocaust.

The Library's archives contain numerous eyewitness accounts and a unique collection of newspaper clippings. Its three published catalogues cover only a small part of its holdings, but they count among the most comprehensive bibliographies on recent German and Jewish history.[28] In addition the Library publishes a unique quarterly *Bulletin.*[29] In it the student will find short bibliographical and research notes; these cover a wide range of subjects, including Nazi policies, wartime collaboration, resistance activities, and Jewish emigration. Of special interest is the *Bulletin*'s survey of the press in Germany and elsewhere, including the neo-fascist papers. Covering Europe, the Americas, the Arab world, and southern Africa, this survey permits us to follow the trial of war criminals, the resurgence of Antisemitism, the activities of the Radical Right, and lately the growth of the militant Left.

Two other institutes are of special interest for Holocaust studies. One of these is the Parisian Centre de Documentation Juive Contemporaine. An important depository of Holocaust materials, particularly concerning France, it has published numerous monographs, catalogues, documentary collections, as well as its own journal.[30]

The other is the Yivo Institute for Jewish Research, the New York successor to the Yiddish Scientific Institute of Vilna. Particularly concerned with the history and culture of East European Jewry, its archives contain important documentary collections on Jewish history in the Nazi era and its library probably possesses the largest number of Holocaust publications available in this country. The Yivo publishes two journals—one in English and one in Yiddish—which contain articles on the Holocaust, and, together with Yad Vashem, the Holocaust Bibliographical Series.[31]

The work of a number of other institutes touches on the Holocaust. Of these we might mention The Leo Baeck Institute of Jews from Germany and the Institut für Zeitgeschichte. The former, with centers in Jerusalem, London, and New York, publishes a bulletin in German as well as monographs and memoirs, some in German and some in English, dealing with Central European Jewry since the Emancipation. Most important, it publishes a yearbook containing scholarly articles, mostly in English but also in German, and a very useful annual bibliography compiled by the Wiener Library.[32] The Institut für Zeitgeschichte, located in Munich, is one of the major centers for the study of the Third Reich. Its scholarly publications include a journal and specialized monographs.[33]

Finally, almost every European country has at least one institute charged with collecting documents and publishing research on the German occupation during World War II. Of these the most important are in The Netherlands and in France. The Rijksinstituut voor Oorlogsdocumentatie in Amsterdam has been most active in the study of the Holocaust, treating the fate of the Jews as an important and integral part of Dutch history under the occupation. All this has been reflected in its collections and its numerous scholarly publications. The Comité d'Histoire de la Deuxième Guerre Mondiale in Paris is primarily known as publisher of the most important journal dealing with Nazi domination and anti-Nazi resistance in occupied Europe.[34]

However, the overabundance of the sources on the Holocaust has not facilitated but inhibited research and its publication. The institutes have served admirably by collecting and preserving the sources; they have contributed much by publishing bibliographies, documents, diaries, and eyewitness accounts. But, with the notable exception of the Parisian Centre, institutes specializing in the Holocaust have so far failed to provide us with studies that approach the qualitative standards we expect in rigorous scholarship.

This is particularly true for Yad Vashem. Its *Studies*, a periodical dedicated exclusively to an investigation of the Holocaust, bears the mark of overly subjective dilettantism. Employing haphazard methods to investigate poorly conceived topics, its contributors seem to use *Studies* to publish their research notes without the disciplined labor of analysis. In addition, these articles, though published in English, usually read like poor translations of pedantic works in a Central or East European language.

Dawidowicz has argued that the reason Yad Vashem and similar institutes have performed so badly is that they are staffed by Holocaust survivors not trained as professional historians.[35] I have no personal knowledge to substantiate or to refute this contention. True or not, it can only be a partial answer.

Basically, Holocaust research has been monopolized by a group of older men and women who, though usually not survivors, have been involved in Jewish affairs most of their lives. Their vociferous attacks upon new and different viewpoints have probably kept many members of a younger generation from breaking into their preserve. Further, I suspect that professional historians as a group have often discouraged graduate students from undertaking Holocaust research. And, most important, neither "Establishment" has been eager to provide the essential support—foundation grants or university appointments—needed to attract young scholars. One has reserved the field for insiders and the other has considered it lacking in academic prestige.

Dawidowicz has also complained that "no American-born Jewish historian that I know of has undertaken any study of the Holocaust, though in the United States at least 1,500 Jews have doctoral degrees in history."[36] As we have seen, this is understandable. Her conclusion, however, that "native American Jews evade, suppress, deny, escape from the very thought or articulation of the Holocaust" applies primarily to the established leaders and older institutions of American Jewry. It does not apply to the next generation, although the evasion by their elders has not made it easy for the young to confront the Holocaust. Thus, I know of at least one young Jewish historian—American-born and Harvard-trained—engaged in research on an East European ghetto, who has, however, been unable to obtain financial support from any foundation, Jewish or non-Jewish.

Considering all this, it is not surprising that the Holocaust is not taught in the schools. Even in Israel, where the schools do attempt to teach it now, instruction before the Eichmann trial, if undertaken at all, was neither consistent, systematic, nor integrated into the curriculum.[37] In the United States, as we have seen, the history of the Holocaust is almost totally suppressed. No public or private school, college or university teaches it; Stern College in New York and Gratz College in Philadelphia are the notable exceptions. If we are to believe a recent catalogue, even New York's Jewish Theological Seminary does not offer a single course on the Jewish Catastrophe.

As you can imagine, the status of Holocaust history is even more dismal in less prestigious educational institutions. Jewish schools—day, afternoon, and Sunday—have not made room for the Holocaust as a subject. In a number of cities, synagogues and, less frequently, Jewish centers have asked me to give a short course on it to advanced students or older adults. But this was always an *ad hoc* program, a sudden inspiration due to personal contact; although the students reacted with enthusiasm, there was never a follow-up and these courses always remained a one-shot affair. With the best intentions, the isolated educator concerned about offering a course on the Holocaust in the school he directs can do little when, without a budget, he must confront institutional indifference and public apathy.

Most striking is the lack of teaching materials. As Jewish history textbooks are not much better on the Holocaust than those used in the public schools, this has imposed a serious limitation on Jewish schools. For the students there are no textbooks; for the teachers there are no study guides. Teaching materials only recently produced by Jewish institutions to fill this gap are inadequate. Poorly conceived and badly executed, they combine the methods of the Sunday schools stressing heroism and martyrdom with the techniques of the "educationists" employing superficiality and gimmicks; the result is an invitation to mediocrity.

A particularly unfortunate example is Joseph Mersand's *Teachers' Study Guide*, a joint publication of the Anti-Defamation League and the Catholic Archdiocese of New York. Designed to accompany a film lecture on the "Writings of the Nazi Holocaust" by Ernst Pawel, the last in a series on "The Image of the Jew in Literature" produced by these two organizations, it illustrates perfectly the error of applying the usual techniques to the study of the Holocaust. Thus under "Classroom Activities and Discussion Topics" Mersand suggests: "A multi-media study of Anne Frank's Diary." As the diary appeared as book, play, and movie, he argues that "a comparison of the three treatments could make an interesting topic for a class report." Also in a "Model Instructional Unit" appended to this study guide, its author, Milton Silver, includes "required writing" which "should be creative in nature." Among his suggestions here are "Additional Entries in Anne Frank's Diary" and "A Series of Letters

Appealing for Help in a Holocaust Situation." This kind of effort, unfortunately not at all atypical, is not only meaningless but also in poor taste.

Other less objectionable examples are two recently published so-called Holocaust Readers. Appearing under semiofficial auspices, they are expensive, hardcover books designed to fill the gap created by the absence of textbooks on the Holocaust. But with inadequate introductions, confusing bibliographies, and almost no annotations, they are not very useful in the classroom; instead, these books have become prestigious items to grace the bookshelves of every Jewish library.

One of these, the better of the two, is frankly, though with hesitation, described by its authors as an "Anthology." True, their decision also to include rare materials, usually translated by them from Yiddish, is meritorious. But they defeat their purpose by printing selections that are far too short to convey real meaning. The student would do better to select an entire work from among the many now available in English. Also, without bibliographical and historical annotations these selections often seem torn out of context. Usually one can not even distinguish between eyewitness accounts and creative literature.[38]

The other reader, published under the auspices of the Union of American Hebrew Congregations, stresses the literary over the historical and the prestigious over the obscure. Most of its selections are from works of fiction long popular and widely distributed. Truly an anthology, this reader does not really treat the history of the Holocaust. Instead, it introduces a new, suddenly popular subject: Holocaust Literature with a capital L.[39]

Unfortunately this is all that is easily available for high school and college students. However, if the schools must use readers, I would prefer an older compilation published in 1949 to fill an obvious need because at that time almost nothing had yet appeared in English. Including eyewitness accounts, often unpublished, and not literary works, then still unknown, this collection still speaks to us with a compelling immediacy totally lacking in its glossy successors.[40]

Surprisingly, more is available for younger children. Of course I do not believe we should teach Holocaust history in elementary school. There are, however, books these children will find worthwhile. Hopefully without the intervention of study guides and anthologies, these original sources can convey to them something about the Jewish fate in general human terms on a level they can understand. One of these is the captivating and haunting *I Never Saw Another Butterfly*, already mentioned by Littell, in which the poems and drawings of Jewish children incarcerated in Theresienstadt tell the story of captivity.[41] At an early age poems like this one can have more meaning than long explanations:

> I'd like to go away alone
> Where there are other, nicer people,
> Somewhere into the far unknown,
> There, where no one kills another.
>
> Maybe more of us,
> A thousand strong,
> Will reach this goal
> Before too long.

Furthermore, younger children could read Anne Frank's *Diary*, which reflects through the experiences of a young girl the anxieties of Jews hiding under the German occupation. Her words, still imbued with hope and expectation, assume a special poignancy through our knowledge that she later perished at Belsen. Her *Diary* should be read together with the one by Charlotte Salomon, who, somewhat older than Anne, tells a similar story in the form of paintings and accompanying text. Drawn in Southern France before her deportation to Auschwitz, Charlotte's pictures, more morbid than the record left in Amsterdam, complement the widely known *Diary* of Anne Frank.[42]

### III. Histories and Interpretations

The failure of our schools to teach the Holocaust is no longer due to a dearth of scholarly books. Enough works are now available for teachers and students to study the destruction of European Jewry in the Nazi era, and, while much remains to be written, the time has come to introduce legitimate courses treating the Jewish Catastrophe. Such courses should not only deal with the events between 1933 and 1945 but should also investigate the causes and origins of the Holocaust. This would obviously involve a history of Nazism, a study of the Jewish past, and an analysis of Antisemitism.

The first of these should pose no problem. The literature on the origins and history of Nazi Germany is large and well known. The second might prove a little more difficult. As a subject Jewish history is almost nonexistent in our colleges; American schools seldom mention the Jewish minority in the Christian world, just as they do not teach about other minorities, something which educated opinion has only recently discovered but which students from minorities— Jewish, black, or others—have always known. However, books on these subjects are easily obtainable; I do not have to mention them here.

The third, Antisemitism, is of course directly connected to the Holocaust, and should serve as an introduction to it. There is, however, some disagreement about its relevance to the Nazis' attack upon the Jews. While some see the hatred of Jews in our times as unrelated to that of earlier ages, almost as *sui generis*, others see it as only the latest, and most ferocious, expression of an old, traditional hostility.

Without trying to resolve this controversy, it might be sufficient for our purpose to state that possibly both viewpoints are partly correct. True, Antisemitism based on race differs substantially from that based on religion. In the Middle Ages Jews could escape persecution by conversion; under the Nazis even those born as Christians could not avoid death if they were descended from Jews. Medieval Antisemites, and most of their modern successors, killed Jews but did not attempt to extirpate Judaism. The Nazis, however, tried to kill every Jew and thus totally destroy Judaism. As Salo Baron has pointed out, the two cannot be separated:

Judaism cannot exist, for any length of time, without Jews, nor Jews without Judaism. . . . The Jewish religion without the "chosen people" is unthinkable. Neither could it, like the other religions, be transplanted from the Jewish to another people. No matter how many adherents it might gain in the outside world, the physical extinction of the Jewish people would sound the death knell of Judaism.[43]

This made Nazi Antisemitism radical, and thus qualitatively different from the earlier variety.

Still, it would be an error to disregard the older history of

Antisemitism. Even if it did not guide the actions of the Nazis, the slogans and images made popular by traditional Jew-hatred were used. And, most important, religious Antisemitism influenced those populations—regardless of whether they were Germany's allies, subjects, or enemies—without whose cooperation, or at least acquiescence, the Nazis could not have carried out their anti-Jewish program.

Numerous studies of Antisemitism are available. An interesting survey by a Catholic historian, one my students have always found informative, might be the best introduction: Malcolm Hay's *The Foot of Pride* (1950).[44] For greater detail, I would suggest Poliakov's scholarly and provocative four-volume study, of which the first volume, most applicable for our purposes, has already been translated into English.[45]

In comparison, works dealing with Antisemitism in the modern period—the nineteenth and twentieth centuries—are surprisingly rare; thus we still lack a scholarly study of its Russian manifestation, essential because in the homeland of the pogroms Right and Left probably first used it for political ends. On Antisemitism's modern uses Hannah Arendt's chapter on the Dreyfus Affair and Koppel Pinson's collection of essays are probably still the best introduction.[46]

More is available on Antisemitism in the lands inhabited by Germans. Several good studies treat it as part of the rise of the "Germanic ideology" in the nineteenth century.[47] A number cover it as part of the fully developed Nazi ideology in the twentieth century. Of these, one shows how Germany's intellectual community in the Third Reich supported the anti-Jewish program of the Nazis.[48] Another, recently published in Germany, illustrates how a majority of university students in the Weimar Republic—and many of their teachers—had embraced racial Antisemitism.[49] But for the most detailed analysis we must turn to the work of scholars concentrating on German Antisemitism.

Paul Massing's history of Antisemitism before 1914 still provides us with the most thorough discussion of the Stöcker movement and of the band of racial Antisemites that appeared after the failure of the Christian Socials (*Evangelische Social Kongress*). He also discusses the reaction of parties and interest groups; of particular interest is his analysis of the Socialist stand. Although they too were not altogether immune, their resistance to Antisemitism retarded its growth before World War I.[50]

Peter Pulzer's more recent history covers, with less detail, the same material, but adds to it a comprehensive analysis of Antisemitism in German Austria. Considering the influence Schönerer and Lueger had on the development of Nazi racism, Antisemitism in Austria, more virulent than in Germany, is of central importance. Basically, Pulzer's valuable study is the only one we have.[51]

Eva Reichman's sociological investigation is an interesting attempt to explain Nazi Antisemitism. Rejecting the view that the Holocaust proves the failure of assimilation, she argues that in the twentieth century, at least in Germany, hatred of Jews no longer reflected an actual group conflict. Thus, a Subjective Jewish Question, based on older stereotypes more dangerous than actual conflict because they could not be corrected by reality, represented a projection on the Jews of German fears and insecurities.[52]

According to Reichman, the psychology of Germans, not their history, might provide an explanation. Several suggestive studies have attempted to do this. Most have analyzed the language of Nazism. Of these, by far the best is Klemperer's dissection of the *Lingua Tertii Imperii*.[53] Using his professional skills and his personal observations, Klemperer, who survived as a Jew inside Germany, shows how the Nazis subverted the outlook of the entire German people—even of anti-Nazis—by manipulating their language. Revealing the hidden techniques of Nazi mythology, his analysis illuminates an aspect of totalitarianism usually hidden from anyone except perhaps a perceptive novelist like Eugene Zamiatin. Another, more experimental attempt to probe the German psyche is a new work that looks for an answer in the nation's visual arts.[54]

Each of these studies proves how central to the Nazi scheme was the image of "the Jews." Thus, for example, Klemperer shows how for almost all Germans World War II became "the Jewish War," as "the Dwarf," usually for effect surrounded by all members of his family, served as an essential antithesis to the image of "the German," always sans relations, as "the Solitary Hero." Norman Cohn has delved deeply into this question of the Jewish image, and his *Warrant for Genocide* is therefore the best scholarly analysis of the mythology of modern Antisemitism.[55]

Cohn, well known for his work on the millennial movements of the Middle Ages, has studied the creation and dissemination of the forgery known as *The Protocols of the Elders of Zion* to illuminate the history of modern Antisemitism. Arguing that Nazi hatred of the Jews is only a modern variation of an older Christian theme, he sees, like Poliakov, the cause for Antisemitism in an earlier rivalry between Judaism and Christianity; in the popular mind the image of the Jews as communistic-plutocratic conspirators is thus a modification of the older image of them as the conspiratorial representatives of Satan. Cohn shows how in the nineteenth century "right-wing Christians, some Roman Catholic and some Greek Orthodox," secularized medieval demonological Antisemitism and how in the twentieth century the Nazis and their allies adopted it as an essential ingredient of their racialist doctrine.

Novelists writing about the Holocaust have basically seen its causes in a way similar to Cohn's. Thus, Schwarz-Bart depicts the recent Jewish Catastrophe as only the latest, though more destructive and more modern, of a long line of persecutions stretching from the Middle Ages, perhaps even from the Hellenistic and Roman world, to our times.[56] A similar thread runs through Wiesel's work. In his latest novel, set symbolically at Jerusalem's Wailing Wall, the experiences of the Holocaust blend—a link and an explanation—with stories of past and present Jewish travail.[57] And in an earlier one, who can escape the demonological interpretation after reading the tale about the survivor who, hiding from the fate of the Holocaust in an East European village, is beaten by the peasants while performing as Judas Iscariot in the local Passion play.[58]

Controversy, however, has centered on the events of the Holocaust, not on the causes. The literature has increased year by year, but few have been able to construct a synthesis. For example, Tenenbaum, writing on Nazi racialism in general, failed by trying to cover too much.[59] Only three scholars have so far successfully attempted a comprehensive history.

The oldest of these, Poliakov's *Bréviaire de la haine*, published in 1951, is still the best survey. Brief, concise, yet still comprehensive, it quotes extensively from original sources. Although unfortunately unavailable in paperback edition, the English translation, *Harvest of Hate*, is undoubtedly the best introductory text for students approaching the history of the Holocaust.[60] Reitlinger's work, published two years later, covers the same ground in more detail. In reviewing how the Nazis developed their plan of extermination, he also describes—country by country—how they implemented mass murder.[61]

These two comprehensive histories cover only one half of the Holocaust. Poliakov and Reitlinger picked as their subject the deed of genocide—the organized plan to kill all Jews. Obviously, they therefore concentrated on the perpetrators. And in their studies the Jewish victims appear only as objects. Still, read together with any of the documentary collections already published,[62] they provide a fairly complete picture of the Nazi deed.

Yet on this aspect of the Holocaust—the conception and execution of the Nazi plan—we now have Raul Hilberg's definitive history, superseding all previously published studies.[63] In his massive work (769 pages of double-column text and numerous charts) based on an exhaustive study of the documentary evidence, Hilberg describes in minute detail all aspects of this plan, adding a convincing and perceptive analysis. And he writes about this macabre subject in a dry and unemotional tone essential, it seems to me, for any scholar interested in retaining his sanity.

Hilberg for the first time presents a clear picture of the destruction process, which the Nazis euphemistically called "the final solution of the Jewish question." He describes the murder of Europe's Jews and shows also how a modern state can and did accomplish genocide. Describing how one step logically followed another, he argues that such deeds could only succeed if based on a plan. And most important, he proves that the Nazi leaders and their SS minions could not have accomplished their task without support from all segments of German society. As H. R. Trevor-Roper commented in his review of Hilberg's book: "The mere technical process [required] national involvement."[64]

Hilberg's impressive study suggests other topics that deserve further investigation. The most important one is the problem of those who acquiesced in the process of destruction by participating in it or by watching it. Undoubtedly, the Nazis could not have murdered the Jews of Europe without the cooperation of Germany's allies and of Germany's satellites. We know the outline of their behavior—the enthusiasm of the Rumanians, the hesitancy of the Italians, the resistance of the Danes—but we still lack the details. We need monographs on every country in Europe; only a few have so far appeared.[65]

Neutral countries and international organizations in the role of spectators had to perform a crucial role. They could have publicized the crimes and rescued the victims or, by abstaining, facilitated the slaughter. Here we still lack good monographic studies on the neutrals and on the central role of the International Red Cross.[66] On the role of the churches, however, we face a constantly expanding literature as the papers at this conference have shown.[67]

The behavior of Hitler's enemies—the United Nations—also deserves serious attention. The Western democracies did not actively intervene to save the Jews, and Russia, clinging to the provisions of the Nazi-Soviet pact, did not even warn its Jews about the mortal danger they faced from German troops. At the time the Allies excused their inaction by arguing that victory on the battlefield had to take precedence and that only the defeat of Germany could save the Jews. Critics have pointed out, however, that Great Britain and the United States did not treat the Jews as a national group deserving protection; in fact, they impeded rescue operations, refusing to bomb the tracks leading to the gas chambers of Auschwitz or even to open their doors to the victims later to be murdered there. But on all this, as well as on the political maneuvers of world Jewry, we still lack detailed accounts. Only one scholarly study has so far appeared; it treats the role of the United States, of special interest to us here. Illuminating the political machinations of the Roosevelt administration, it presents an appalling chronicle of Allied—and Jewish—failures to rescue the victims.[68]

## IV. L'Universe Concentrationaire

The fate of European Jewry might have been sealed in chancelleries and embassies, but the ghettos and camps erected by the Nazi regime became the actual arena of the Catastrophe. Historians find it relatively easy to unravel and explain the deeds of diplomats and bureaucrats, while the denizens of the camp world remain shadowy figures difficult to comprehend. Yet no history of the Holocaust can be complete without insight into this world best described as *l'universe concentrationaire*.

The executioners are undoubtedly the least difficult to understand. Still, we do not yet possess a truly adequate history of the SS as an institution or a satisfying analysis of the technicians of mass murder as individuals.[69] They have revealed themselves, however, in the documents they left behind and in the testimony they gave at their trials. The memoir of the Auschwitz commanding officer, written in a Polish jail before his execution, is a typical revelation which, available in English translation, is easily accessible to us.[70]

Nevertheless, in some ways we find these men incomprehensible; their banal personalities do not fit their evil deeds. The diary of the SS physician Kramer is a good example. In his entry of September 2, 1942, after his first direct contact with radical evil, he records his stilted and conventional impressions: "Went around three this morning to be present at a special Sonderaktion for the first time. In comparison Dante's Inferno seems almost a comedy. It's not for nothing that Auschwitz is called an annihilation camp!" But only four days later, in his entry of September 6, he reveals the shallow preoccupations typical of those callous technicians while performing their monstrous acts: "Today, an excellent midday meal: tomato soup, half a chicken with potatoes and red cabbage, *petits fours*, and wonderful vanilla ice cream. Around eight o'clock out again for another Sonderaktion, the fourth I have witnessed."[71]

The victims have been much harder to understand. Obviously we can not measure the reactions of those caught in the camp world of the Holocaust against the behavior of men in normal times. And attempts to use the psychoanalytical tools fashioned for the study of extreme situations in analyzing their behavior have, in my opinion, so far failed to provide fully satisfying results.[72] Social scientists tend to view the Holocaust as a single event, but, different from sudden, natural or man-made disasters like Hiroshima, it stretched over six years and covered a continent. In retrospect the Jewish victims might appear to have been an undifferentiated mass, but, unlike their executioners, they were millions of separate individuals. The Jews of Europe formed heterogeneous groupings divided by differences in language, custom, politics, and class; each group, facing the Holocaust at a different time and a different place, behaved in its own way in the polyglot world of the concentration camps.

It is therefore not surprising that controversy has centered on the behavior of the Jewish victims. Their decision to comply with and their failure to resist their own destruction have posed the most divisive questions. Thus Hilberg concluded that "the Jewish victims—caught in the straitjacket of their history—plunged themselves physically and psychologically into catastrophe."[73] But some of his critics, viewing all victims as martyrs, have denounced this interpretation as "defaming the dead and their culture."[74] Others have emphasized the few instances of resistance to prove the fallacy of any analysis stressing compliance.[75]

Discussion has tended to focus on the role of the Jewish leaders as reflected in the work of the Jewish Councils, the so-called *Judenräte*.[76] Unfortunately, the controversy surrounding Hannah Arendt's *Eichmann in Jerusalem* has obscured the essential points by turning the discussion into a debate.[77] Arendt's unfortunate choice of language tended to nullify her usually perceptive and often valid arguments.[78] The responses of her many critics—often shrill and vitriolic—have done little to illuminate this controversial issue.[79]

To evaluate these conflicting interpretations we must therefore turn to the sources. The documents are only of value to the specialists. But survivors have published enough accounts for our purposes. If we read them with care and discrimination, we can hope, in part, to understand the camp world.[80]

For the Jews of Europe, catastrophe began long before they entered the concentration camps of the Third Reich. In occupied Russia the Nazis usually dispensed with camps; there the SS in numerous mass executions performed by specialists (*Einsatzgruppen*) murdered the Jews on the spot. Knowledge about most of them has survived only through the statistical reports compiled by the SS commanders. But survivors and witnesses have left accounts about a few of them, such as the killings at Babi Yar near Kiev.[81] Similar massacres, though less organized, were carried out by local fascists and Antisemites in Poland, Rumania, and the Baltic states.

In West and South Europe the Nazis seized the Jews for deportation to the extermination centers of the East. The trains with their human cargo—often a hundred or more stuffed for days into a cattle car without bread or water—moved eastward across Europe, some from as far away as Greece.[82] Before boarding the trains they usually spent days, weeks, or months in transit camps like Westerbork in Holland or Drancy in France.[83]

Many Jews, however, went almost directly from home to train, because sudden and brutal roundups sometimes preceded the deportations. Thus, on July 16, 1942, the Nazis, with the cooperation of the French police, seized thirteen thousand Jews in Paris, confining them at the Vélodrome d'Hiver, in full view of the city's residents, until their deportation to Auschwitz; very young children, separated from their parents, faced these deportations alone—an act as horrible as any the Germans committed in East Europe.[84] A similar roundup took place in Rome on October 16, 1943. There German troops, with the help of the fascist police, plucked Jews from the streets of the city, some from beneath the windows of the Vatican.[85]

In the East the Nazis transformed old city neighborhoods into ghettos which only superficially appeared to resemble their medieval namesakes. Into these ghettos they crowded the Jews of the cities and villages, adding also deportees from Germany, Austria, and Czechoslovakia. Forced to work for the German war economy without the means of subsistence, thousands died of starvation and disease; the survivors were sent to the death camps. Under constant pressure from the German authorities, these ghettos, dressed up to resemble autonomous Jewish communities, became perverted societies whose only goal was the death of their members. Under these conditions self-government became a farce: the ghettos had a *Judenrat*, but no elected leaders; a Jewish police, but no Jewish schools.

These ghettos differed greatly in size and organization; for most of them, including important ones like Vilna, Kovno, and Riga, we still do not have adequate historical accounts.[86] In fact, only the atypical ghetto in Theresienstadt—designed, in part, as a camp for older and privileged Jews from Germany, Austria, and Bohemia—has been analyzed in a major scholarly account by a former inmate. Adler's work, unfortunately unavailable in English, is a model history not yet duplicated for other ghettos.[87]

The literature is most extensive about the two largest Polish ghettos—Warsaw and Lodz. Of these two the Warsaw ghetto, whose life and death has been described in numerous excellent memoirs,[88] remained a viable Jewish community even under extreme pressure and terrible deprivation. Its Jewish Council, selected by the Germans, had to share authority with an intellectual elite and an underground of political parties. Exhibiting an unusual pluralism, Warsaw's ghetto economy retained a private sector where groups organized self-help and where black marketeers became a political factor. The ghetto had illegal theaters, schools, lectures, and, most important, historians whose work, buried beneath its ruins, has survived the war.[89] It is therefore not surprising that when the Germans began their deportations, but not until most Jews had already been shipped with extreme brutality to Treblinka, a youthful political underground—Zionist and Bundist—seized power and organized revolt, an event almost unique in the annals of the Holocaust.[90]

In contrast, the Lodz ghetto community reacted to the imposed pressures and deprivations by transforming itself into a tightly regimented society, hoping to survive through labor for the German war machine. Without the opposition of an intellectual elite or a political underground, its appointed Elder and his cohorts constructed an authoritarian system that did not provide for economic or cultural diversity. As the last surviving ghetto in the East, not dissolved until the Fall of 1944, Lodz produced no historians, few memoirs, and no revolt; only its documents survive.[91]

Eventually all Jews, except those killed in Russia or starved in the ghettos, entered the concentration camps of the Third Reich. At first designed to hold the enemies of the regime, real or imagined, the number of camps expanded rapidly into a large system of central camps (*Stammlager*) and a vast network of subsidiary camps (*Nebenlager*) to hold prisoners from all conquered lands, especially the Jews. To the three original camps—Dachau, Buchenwald, Sachsenhausen—the Nazis added after 1938 eight new camps—Ravensbrück, Gross-Rosen, Mauthausen, Neuengamme, Flossenbürg, Stutthof, Natzweiler, and Bergen-Belsen. Compulsive regimentation, physical brutality, and sadistic torture characterized the camps and made these Teutonic institutions different from those of other totalitarian states. Holding about a million inmates at any one time, the concentration camps came to represent the essence of the Nazi system.

To understand this system, we must turn to books by former inmates. Eugen Kogon's account, originally composed for the United States army, is still the best introduction. Centered on but not confined to Buchenwald, Kogon's work, treating both SS and inmates, is an analytical description of the camp world's organization, structure, and function.[92] Kogon's clinical report alone, however, does not make it possible to comprehend this surrealistic world. For this we must turn to the accounts of other former inmates. Perhaps two of these can complement Kogon's book: Elie Cohen's medical study, originally a Dutch thesis in psychiatry, and David Rousset's impressionistic memoir, more a literary work than a journalistic report by a French academician.[93]

For the Jews of Europe the camp world included yet another, even more demonic, dimension: the death factories. Although the SS killed in all camps, they concentrated the mass extermination of the Jews in the killing centers of the East. There, in the "scientific" installations of Treblinka, Maydanek, Belzec, Sobibor, and Chelmno, they used gas chambers and crematoria to practice mass murder on the assembly line. Few escaped to tell about it, and those have found it difficult to talk about their experiences. For this reason Steiner's documentary novel is probably the best report we have about these camps.[94]

The SS established its largest killing operation in the Upper Silesian concentration camp Auschwitz. Comprising three camps, it became a giant complex. Camp number one, Auschwitz proper, served as the central camp, and camp number three, the I. G. Farben installation Monowitz, served as the industrial labor camp. Camp number two—Birkenau—served as the killing center. In its gas chambers the SS murdered millions; the flames belching from its crematoria chimneys turned night into day while the stench of burning human flesh pervaded the entire camp.

We now know a great deal about Auschwitz-Birkenau. There have been trials, plays, and a great number of memoirs.[95] The best of these is Primo Levi's eyewitness account. Levi, an Italian Jew, reports about his Auschwitz experiences in the dry tone and comprehensive detail of an observant scientist.[96] Different, but equally illuminating, are the short stories, terrible in their simplicity, about the Auschwitz experiences left to us by the Polish poet Borowski.[97]

In May 1945, the Third Reich collapsed. But against the Jews of Europe Hitler won his war. Still, some Jews survived; for them the gates of the camps opened in the spring of 1945. This is another story. Those who wish to follow it should start by reading Primo Levi's second book, the best available account of the days and months that followed the liberation of Auschwitz.[98]

# II
# Historical
# Political Considerations

# 6

# Problems of Resistance in National Socialist Germany

Peter Hoffmann

## I. Introduction

Even a brief description of the external events of the "resistance" in Germany from 1933 to 1945 would require a series of papers. Any attempt at a full account would fill several weighty tomes. Twenty-five years after the collapse of Hitler's regime in Germany, the literature dealing with the twelve years of his reign numbers tens of thousands of titles, and there are literally thousands of books and articles on the events and problems of resistance to the National Socialist regime. This fact, on the other hand, makes unnecessary the repetition of what may be considered matters of record.[1] A few basic facts can thus be listed without any attempt at development and merely as outstanding indicators of the varied and complicated course of events.

The resistance or opposition, as a struggle against Hitler and National Socialism, and as a group of activities endangering the lives of those who engaged in them, began years before, but certainly not later than the moment Adolf Hitler was appointed Chancellor of the German Reich on January 30, 1933. The men and women who had the insight and the will to resist the regime of the National Socialists spent five years in relatively powerless frustration for reasons such as the largely self-imposed impotence of the Social Democrats, the largely Moscow-imposed passivity of the Communists in 1933—and the destruction of their organization by the Gestapo (*Geheime Staatspolizei*) in 1934—36—and the ambiguous position of most of the army (*Reichswehr*) leadership. Individual Social Democrats risked much; many risked everything in resisting the policies of the new regime, some in public, some in clandestine, underground activities.

But their leadership had not recognized the true nature of the National Socialist regime at its inception, and they had not resorted to any measures which would promise effects—such as a general strike or an armed uprising, for which many Socialists were fully prepared. There are reasons for this, too, which may be seen in the organizational and bureaucratic tradition of the party, and which must be seen in part in the severe unemployment situation that seemed to forbid experiments such as a general strike. It is also easier to judge an event correctly after it has occurred than to judge it while it is taking place; but the fact still remains that the Social Democrats did not act energetically in opposition to Hitler in 1933. Many believed it would be better for the party if they emigrated and waited in Prague, Paris, or London until the freak apparition of the Nazis disappeared of its own accord within a few months.

Similar beliefs were held by many Communists; but added was the Moscow party line that fascism was the agony stage of capitalist society and would actually speed up the process toward socialism, so that from a long-range point of view, the dictatorship of Hitler could be welcomed or at least tolerated for the short time it would last.

The position of the army leadership concerning the new regime was in part a carry-over from General Seeckt's non-political army (*unpolitische Armee*) of the Weimar Republic which had really meant a denial of support to the Republic.[2] This factor had been important in keeping the road to power open for an extremist of the Right such as Hitler. But now, in its reverse manifestation as lack of opposition to an unconstitutional and criminal regime, it had the effect of helping Hitler to win and solidify his power. The position of the army leadership became clear as early as February 3, 1933, when Hitler announced his war plans to a group of high-ranking generals.[3] It was confirmed again and again—for example, during the two-day (June 30 and July 1, 1934) murder spree of the SS against the SA leadership and some other "enemies," including two brigadier generals of the army, and also when General Freiherr von Fritsch was removed as Chief of Army Command in January 1938 on trumped-up charges of homosexuality.[4]

Even the two major churches at first reacted either favorably or passively to Hitler's government. Their leaders, too, like so many others, either did not understand the nature of the new regime, or were too inert, or both. But the churches not only were the first large organizations left intact (as organizations) by the seizure of power (*Machtübernahme*) that began to resist, to a large extent as organizations, the policies of Hitler's regime; they also remained unique in this respect throughout the period from 1933 to 1945, although their resistance remained limited to certain issues and methods.[5]

On the other hand, there were in all groups and classes of the population farsighted individuals who did all they could to oppose the regime and, specifically, to prevent the war for which Hitler was preparing. In this category are prominent names such as Dr. Carl Goerdeler, General Ludwig Beck, Fabian von Schlabrendorff, Ewald von Kleist-Schmenzin, Ernst von Weizsäcker, Hans Oster, Wilhelm Leuschner, Dr. Julius Leber, Max Habermann, Dr. Dietrich Bonhoeffer and Dr. Klaus Bonhoeffer, Dr. Hans John and Dr. Otto John, Dr. Hans von Dohnanyi, Dr. Hans Bernd Gisevius, Admiral Wilhelm Canaris—to mention only a few almost at random. Along with many others, those individuals organized the first serious attempt to overthrow Hitler on the occasion of the Sudeten crisis.[6] They made their plan hinge on the assumption that they could act *only* if the outbreak of war had either occurred or was irreversibly imminent after marching orders had been put into effect. When, because of the attitude of Great Britain, a compromise was reached and Czechoslovakia was amputated by a decision of Great Britain, Germany, France, and Italy (the Czechs were merely informed of this decision), the conspirators believed it would be a mistake to attempt to remove a successful Hitler, who seemed to be not a criminal but a national hero. They had banked on a hard attitude by Great Britain that would force Hitler to give up his annexation plans or actually to start the war he threatened to unleash. Obviously this hope had been unrealistic.

Despite the further successes of Hitler—annexation of the Sudetenland, annexation of Austria, occupation of "Rump Czechoslovakia" (Hitler's terminology)—this unusual group of conspirators from all political persuasions and social classes, once brought together by the threat of a war that the German government had been about to begin wantonly, stayed together and continued in their efforts to overthrow and later to assassinate Hitler, even from 1939 to 1942, the years of his most triumphal successes. Such practical Christians as Dietrich Bonhoeffer and Eugen Gerstenmaier were active in those attempts and plans.[7]

Lack of support from the only power factor in the state that could be expected to provide it, the army, continued to plague the opposition. Despite some ambiguity in the attitude of SS leaders such as Himmler or Wolff from 1943 to 1945, neither the SS or the SA, nor others of the private armies of the regime were ever likely to support a *coup d'état*. But in addition to this, all of the approximately eight to ten attempts on Hitler's life that were made by the conspirators in 1943 and 1944 failed for the most bizarre reasons—reasons and circumstances which must be studied carefully and thoroughly to be understood and believed.[8] This is also true of the most famous of all attempts, the one made on July 20, 1944, which was the third attempt of Colonel Claus Graf von Stauffenberg (no other would-be assassin had made more than one), and for which Stauffenberg and four of his closest co-conspirators paid with their lives on the same evening. This attempt was followed by a barbaric wave of persecution during which hundreds of the best men and women of the nation were executed, and hundreds more were thrown into concentration camps, including wives and children of conspirators and of suspects who were being tried or who had already been executed.[9]

Such remarks can only vaguely indicate the scope of the opposition to Hitler during the twelve years of his regime. As has been stated, the large outlines of the external events are clear and undisputed, and a detailed record of the attempts to overthrow and to assassinate Hitler is available. However, three aspects which are disputed and will continue to be disputed seem to deserve further discussion: the demarcation of the terms *resistance* and *opposition*; the intellectual and ethical substance of the movement; and its continuing importance and implications.

## II. Resistance and Opposition

Historically there were two main tendencies in the attitudes toward resistance and opposition against Hitler from within Germany. In Allied Western countries, the strongest tendency was to discount all opposition to Hitler in Germany—except perhaps the real or imagined opposition of those who had been thrown into concentration camps—and to acknowledge as true opposition besides the above-mentioned type only the opposition of emigrants who wrote, spoke, or fought against their homeland, preferably in Allied uniforms. Examples of this were not infrequent, and the moral sincerity of such individuals must not be challenged without good reasons. Willy Brandt, a Social Democrat of long standing and now Chancellor of the Federal Republic of Germany, served on the Allied side during the war in a Norwegian uniform after he had been active in the Socialist underground in Berlin;[10] and Otto John, who managed to escape to Lisbon and finally to London after July 20, 1944, worked for the intelligence service (MI 5) of the British army during the remainder of the war and for a while thereafter.[11] These two are perhaps the most famous examples but by no means the only ones. In Allied Communist countries the prevailing, and for a long time the only permissible, tendency was to acknowledge as opposition only that of Communist, Communist-led, or Communist-inspired groups. The claim that Communists are the vanguard of all progressive forces in society is an article of faith and has been written into the Soviet constitution.[12]

Another strong tendency was diametrically opposed to the prevailing Allied Western position. Especially in Germany after the surrender of May 1945, under the indictment of the theory of collective guilt, and under the pressures resulting from policies closely associated with the name of United States Secretary of the Treasury Henry Morgenthau,[13] it was almost a matter of course for many Germans to claim opposition and resistance where there had been none, and to inflate the concepts to the point where they lost meaning altogether by including such things as the mere failure (not open refusal) to make a small contribution in money to the state winter relief (*Winterhilfswerk*) or to the Nazi public welfare (*Nationalsozialistische Volkswohlfahrt*) or absenteeism in shop meetings, or successful draft-dodging for selfish reasons.

If one looks in from the outside of these two extremes, one can recognize the nucleus of true resistance and opposition. Some pointedly formulated theses will indicate a few of the limits within which and conditions under which this resistance will become recognizable as the movement that it was. It would take up far too much space, but it would not be difficult to set forth so much information and description that a balanced and true picture would be created; but the provocation to controversy resulting to a large extent from the necessary brevity of the "theses" to be advanced here may serve as a useful stimulant for discussion and investigation.

Opposition to Hitler in Germany was very much in existence despite the wartime and postwar Allied propaganda to the contrary, and the Allied governments knew very well that it existed.[14] It is attested by the hundreds of thousands of German citizens, including hundreds of clergymen, who filled the concentration camps long before the war—and long before Jews, Poles, Russians, Ukranians, Gypsies, Belgians, Jehovah's Witnesses, and countless others found themselves there.[15] It is also attested by the fully documented contacts between its members and representatives of Allied governments before and during the war.[16] The opposition in Germany was indeed widespread, and its adherents were numerous; and it was recruited from all social classes, political groups, and ideological and religious persuasions.

The largest amount of support Hitler ever received in a free popular election (which rules out any election or plebiscite that took place after January 30, 1933, though the Reichstag election of March 5, 1933 was not yet completely controlled by the National Socialists, and other parties were not yet outlawed) was hardly more than a third of the popular vote. Only a few months after unemployment in Germany had reached its peak in February 1932 with 6.13 million, the National Socialists in July 1932 attracted 37.4 percent of the vote. The figure declined by November 1932 to 33.1 percent which represents a loss of two million votes.[17]

As far as can be determined, Hitler did have the support of the majority of Germans (though it was quite silent unless otherwise ordered) from about 1935 to the beginning of the Sudeten crisis of August/September 1938. But in the autumn of 1938 and through 1939 the mood in Germany was very gloomy because of the prospect of war and its further expansion, as reported even by observers whose expected bias would lead them to see things in a different light.[18] According to Albert Speer, whose memoirs are the most honest and sincere to come from the inner circle around Hitler, the mood after the victory over France was still a depressed one.[19] World War I was still remembered. It was clear that England had not been defeated, and it was doubtful if in the long run the United States would stay out of the war.

Yet at no time during Hitler's twelve years of power did a majority of Germans resist or oppose actively or even passively the National Socialist government and its major policies. When there was discontent, as in the face of the threat of a repetition of World War I, and during the World War II years, when Allied bombs were destroying German homes and Hitler sacrificed entire armies unnecessarily, the discontent was rarely vocal. With the exception of some isolated though noteworthy instances, it did not go beyond the complaining stage.

Active resistance on a large scale would have been indeed surprising, both because of basic facts of human nature and society, and because of the prevailing circumstances in which the individual citizen was forced to live. Those circumstances are usually summed up under the heading "totalitarian state." An important psychological factor was that many Germans—in the army, police, administration, and industry—were caused to play active parts in the oppression of foreign nations. All Germans were forced to do this indirectly as members of the nation in whose name other peoples were being suppressed. They were forced to take part in oppression vicariously, be it consciously or unconsciously, whether they consented or not. Resistance to such participation would have put Germans in a psychological and social position similar to that of American soldiers in the occupation army in Germany in 1945 if they disobeyed the orders against "fraternization" with the German population; and it would have put them in a much worse physical position—committal to a concentration camp and almost certain death there. Trial and execution for treason were not at all uncommon for such offenses, as the ominous red posters in Germany frequently made clear.[20] By indirect participation in oppression, however, the feeling of being oppressed was somewhat reduced. It must also be considered that there was, during World War II, a very real threat to the national existence of Germany from the outside that was not made less by the realization that it had been provoked by the German government itself.

On the other hand, the power of the totalitarian state was ubiquitous through its police, the secret political police, and through the countless organizations and informer networks of the SS, SD, SA, NSDAP, NSV, NSKK, HJ. The Gestapo alone numbered at least forty thousand men from 1943 to 1945.[21] These organizations infiltrated all of German society, even groups with years of experience and expertise in underground conspiratorial operations such as the outlawed Communist party (KPD). When the Socialists, Julius Leber and Adolf Reichwein, negotiated with members of the underground KPD Central Committee on June 22, 1944, to see if cooperation for the planned *coup d'état* with clandestine Communist organizations was possible, there was a Gestapo informer present. The two Communist functionaries did not suspect him, but Leber did, and he refused to come to a second meeting after one of the Communists had addressed him by name, which was a violation of the conditions agreed on before the meeting. Reichwein went to the second meeting, July 4, 1944, and was promptly arrested along with the Communists. Leber was arrested on July 5. All participants of the meeting were executed, with the exception of the informer.[22]

Under such conditions, neither organized nor spontaneous mass uprisings had any chance of success—and hardly any chance to occur. This may be difficult to appreciate without personal experience, but the evidence for a similar lack of opportunity in like circumstances, let us say, in Cuba, Russia, China, Korea (North and South), or in Spain, is clear and contemporary enough to illustrate the point.

In addition to the difficulties already mentioned there were serious obstacles to resistance or opposition that were felt by individuals who had the will and the ability to oppose the regime or some of its policies, though naturally at the risk of their lives. All members of the armed forces and similar organizations were required after 1943 to swear personal allegiance to Hitler as Head of State and Supreme Commander of the armed forces.[23] While this was a shield behind which many retreated to evade responsibility or to soothe their consciences, many others had sincere scruples about breaking the oath, although Hitler had broken his own oath a thousand times.[24] For those who understood that the regime could not be removed without the assassination or summary execution of Hitler and other leaders, additional scruples arose regarding the permissibility of murder, even if it meant killing a mass-murderer, and many were opposed to killing humans regardless of terms and circumstances. Usually, however, such arguments were not consistent because they did not include or derive from a position of fundamental pacifism. But subjective honesty and sincerity can rarely be denied with justification. This is illustrated by the fact that scruples against killing in general contributed to the failure of the *coup d'état* on July

20, 1944, when the conspirators did not move so ruthlessly against the functionaries of the regime as they could have. The men who risked and gave their own lives to overthrow the National Socialists must be considered sincere in their scruples against shooting Goebbels, SS leaders, or uncooperative army officers on that fateful day.[25]

The only instrument with which Adolf Hitler's regime could have been overthrown was an army—German or Allied. The German army therefore played a key role in all *coup* planning. But the motives for the attempts on the dictator's life and position were not primarily or predominantly military, nor even political in the narrow and common sense of the term. They were generated for the most part outside the army, and the military conspirators were so far from taking a leading position in the plans that they refused consistently to act even as the executive arm of the opposition unless the civilian groups gave them evidence of complete and feasible preparations for an orderly transition to a civilian post-*coup* government, for the installation of a new cabinet that could take the reins within hours, for the promulgation of a new (temporary) constitution, and for negotiations with the Allies that would with reasonable certainty result in the preservation of German national unity and to a large extent at least in the preservation of German territorial integrity.[26] Certain members of the armed forces were merely willing to provide executive power for a *coup*. General Beck, who had resigned as chief of staff in August 1938, when Hitler would not listen to his protests against the Sudeten policy, was still one of the most respected leaders of the conspiracy in 1944, but less as a general than as a man of integrity and wisdom with statesmanlike qualities. Even in Beck, a military man by origin, the motives of opposition were most of all ethical and philosophical. Even though the army alone could provide the instrument for a *coup*, the impulses and motivations were those of men like Dietrich Bonhoeffer, Hans von Dohnanyi, and Julius Leber.

Obviously, a definition of *resistance* or *opposition* in one or two sentences would be either too broad or too narrow. There were many methods of resistance and opposition, depending on the opportunities available to individuals and groups, depending on how far those willing to resist or to oppose were prepared to go, and depending also on what method seemed to them most appropriate to their motives or to the desired results. As methods and actions often overlapped, groups, origins (social, political, intellectual), and attitudes distinguishable by the terms *resistance* and *opposition* also overlapped in individuals as well as in groups. Active clandestine attempts to undermine and overthrow the regime structure might be coupled with open defiance in the same individual, as in the case of someone who refused to shoot prisoners in Russia and was involved in the *coup* conspiracy at the same time. There were stages, too, through which many progressed from passive resistance to open defiance and to overt or clandestine sabotage, and eventually to active opposition with the aim not merely to obstruct the functioning of the regime in its war efforts, economic operation, political and criminal activities (indoctrination, murder of Jews) but to overthrow and remove it as well. Methods and stages included such manifestations as remaining uninvolved in activities and policies of the regime, covert and "camouflaged" criticism in writing (a novelist or historian might describe and criticize in Napoleon I or Charles XII qualities that he recognized in Hitler) or from the pulpit,[27] sheltering and hiding Jews and other fugitives or enemy agents (which certainly constituted a stage beyond the one of hiding, let us say, a relative who had been classed as a "half-Jew" according to the Nuremberg Laws), slowdown in factory work, and sabotage in the manufacture of submarines or airplanes, espionage for the Allies (a famous example for ideologically motivated espionage is the *Rote Kapelle*),[28] attacking and obstructing a government activity such as the euthanasia program (church leaders were successful by 1941 in their attempts to halt this program),[29] counterpropaganda and agitation, self-sacrificial manifestations and drastic protests such as those of the Scholl group in Munich in 1942 and 1943,[30] and planning and preparing for a *coup d'état* and for the assassination of Hitler.

### III. Intellectual and Ethical Substance

Much early resistance was politically oriented and motivated. This means only that it was *less* fundamentally motivated by ethical and perhaps religious thought than later when many had progressed to different positions—a matter of degree. All political thought is ethical thought even if it tends to follow a prepared ideology or set of ideas once accepted as good by implication without further analysis. The progression to fundamental ethical thought requires a further effort, a more personal decision, almost a secession or declaration of independence of the individual from a society that follows given or imposed patterns of behavior relatively without resistance.

However, many opposed the regime on fundamental grounds from its beginning. Ewald von Kleist-Schmenzin was one of those who never compromised and who was dismayed at the lack of opposition to the new regime when he wrote in 1933: "Soon there will be a proverb—spineless like a German government official, godless like a Protestant clergyman, honorless like a Prussian officer." [31] When Kleist's son, Ewald Heinrich von Kleist, asked his father early in 1944 if he advised him to make an attempt to assassinate Hitler should he have an opportunity, the father told his son that he must try it by all means—knowing that it meant almost certain death for his son. But the attempt could not be carried out. The father's role was discovered, and he was beheaded after July 20, 1944. The son, who was serving at the front, escaped the purge.[32] Fabian von Schlabrendorff, Dietrich Bonhoeffer, Wilhelm Leuschner, Julius Leber, and Nikolaus von Halem are some of those who held the same or similar attitudes.

Others took longer to realize fully the true nature of the regime, to resolve their misgivings and scruples about the legality of clandestine opposition that amounted to high treason under the laws of the regime. All the peaceful and legal means of opposition that might have been effective had been abolished and suppressed, but it was still a considerable step forward to the claim of an unwritten, fundamental "mandate" for opposition in the absence of legal means.[33] A man as intelligent as Albert Speer (who, however, admits he was tempted by the almost unlimited opportunities for working in his chosen field, architecture, and that he "sold his soul to the devil" for them) never quite saw or wanted to see the truth before February 1945.[34] Not much was heard from General Ludwig Beck on the occasion of the shootings of June 30/July 1, 1934. And General Kurt Freiherr von Hammerstein-Equord, acknowledged by a critic such as John W. Wheeler-Bennett as one of the most fearless of Hitler's enemies,[35] did little more than remark upon hearing that Brigadier Kurt von Schleicher had been shot in the "purge": "Now they are starting to murder even gentlemen."[36] In September 1939, Hammerstein was ready to launch an attempt on Hitler's life, but he got no chance to try it.[37]   Arthur Nebe, head of the Reich central Criminal Police Office, and Count Wolf von Helldorf, as well as many civilians who agreed to be put on a list for a post-Hitler government, joined the opposition late, but usually from the same or similar motives as the early members. Many key figures in the armed forces who saw clearly the true situation, who saw the criminality of the regime and knew of the vast murders committed by it, and who knew the military situation of Germany to be hopeless, never quite made up their minds what to do about it. Fieldmarshal von Kluge, involved in high treason but insisting on "doing nothing before Hitler was dead," wavered to the end and finally committed suicide when his involvement was discovered by the Gestapo.[38]   Fieldmarshal von Manstein was always charming and obligingly polite when his participation in a *coup d'état* was solicited. He fully understood what the conspirators were up to, and he even assured them of his cooperation as soon as they could establish a new, "legitimate" government. But beyond that, he preferred to play the role of "only a soldier" (*Nur-Soldat*)—without any sympathy for Hitler, aware of the crimes and of the impending disaster that was likely to bring to an end the national sovereignty and unity of Germany as well as the existence of the German army, yet claiming that his participation in a *coup* might disunite or even break up the army.[39]

Even such fearless men as General Olbricht, who participated actively in the *coup d'état* attempt of July 20, 1944, and since 1938 had been involved in most of the earlier plans, and General Fromm, who sympathized with the opposition but preferred to be on the winning side, hesitated and wavered at crucial moments. Captain Hermann Kaiser—who kept the official diary in the Staff of the Commander of the Home Army, General Fromm—described the average attitude among most of those in the army who were sympathetic to the cause of the opposition (though by no means among all of them) when he wrote in his private diary in February 1943: "The one wants to act as soon as he is given an order, the other wants to give orders as soon as action has been taken."[40]   "The one" was Olbricht, "the other" was Fromm, and "action" meant the assassination of Hitler as the initial step in a *coup d'état*.

Much has been written about alleged pro-Nazi attitudes on the part of Claus Graf von Stauffenberg.[41]   It is true that Stauffenberg did not engage in high treason and in attempts to overthrow and assassinate Hitler in 1933; but in the years following Hitler's rise to power, he grew increasingly critical, and finally decided that his supreme warlord was a criminal and must be killed.[42]

The lack of opportunism in almost all the principal conspirators, including those in the armed forces (among whom were many civilians who only wore the uniform because they had been drafted for the war, or who had practiced "internal emigration" into the relative protection of army or navy service), is clearly demonstrated by their actions, their statements of purpose and motives, and their sacrifices. Dietrich Bonhoeffer returned voluntarily to Germany from America in 1939 because he wanted to be among his people in the coming times of trial.[43]  Adam von Trott zu Solz also returned in 1940 from a trip to the Far East and to the United States, although he could have stayed abroad in honorable exile and washed his hands of whatever happened in Germany. Julie Braun-Vogelstein urged Trott in New York in November 1939 to stay and to "represent another Germany." "I must return," Trott answered without hesitation, "to help to make Germany a place that can be represented."[44]  Schlabrendorff and the elder Kleist, too, could have stayed in England when the war was about to break out, but they believed the only way for Germans to fight Hitler was from within.[45]

The generals had not acted. Those with insight and in positions of responsibility at the top of the military and political structure looked on, "doing their duty," to be sure, while Germany was driven into the greatest disaster of her history. Stauffenberg became convinced that the colonels must act if the generals failed. He told his wife in the summer of 1944 that he believed he "must do something to save the *Reich.*"[46]  A friend, Peter Sauerbruch, son of the famous surgeon, reports these words by Stauffenberg: "I could not look the wives and children of the fallen soldiers in the eyes unless I did all I could to prevent these [further] senseless human sacrifices."[47]  In June 1944, Stauffenberg said: "The issue now is not the Führer, not the fatherland, not my wife and four children, but the entire German people."[48]  A few days before the attempt of July 20, 1944, he said: "Whoever dares to do something must know that he will probably go down in German history as a traitor. But if he failed to do it, he would be a traitor before his own conscience."[49]  Berthold Graf von Stauffenberg, somewhat less optimistic than a would-be assassin had to be, told his wife on July 14: "The most terrible part of it is to know that it cannot succeed, and that one still has to do it for our country and for our children."[50]

General Beck said to Max Habermann, the trade union leader, on the morning of July 20, 1944: "Now the issue is only this: the action against the criminal regime must come from within the German people itself. The consequences, after all that has happened, and after all that has not been done, must be suffered by Germany."[51] In addition to its moral value, the uprising against Hitler would result in some relief for the fate of the German people after the Allied victory, Beck believed. But he did not think that unconditional surrender and the occupation of Germany by Allied forces could still be avoided.[52] Even so, he insisted that the attempt against Hitler be made. It will be difficult to attribute such an attitude to mere class interests, or to a willingness to end the war merely because it was lost.

The full range of the ethical, religious, and patriotic convictions of the conspirators became manifest even more impressively after the failure of the *coup d'état.* An hour or two before his arrest on the evening of July 20, 1944, General Fellgiebel, one of the leading men in the conspiracy, refused to commit suicide (an escape was out of the question), though he was not religious and made it clear that he did not believe in a life after death: "One stands, one does not do that."[53] He was beaten and tortured by the Gestapo, but he did not betray the many lower-ranking officers who had participated in the *coup* at his instigation. Only two whose participation had been too overt to be denied were hanged with him, while many others who were deeply involved survived.[54] Ulrich von Hassell, the former German ambassador in Rome, and after 1938 one of the most active conspirators, wandered through the streets of Berlin after the *coup* had failed, refusing to seek shelter with friends because he did not want to endanger them. He was hanged on September 8, 1944.[55] He had not given away anyone, and neither had Schlabrendorff, Trott zu Solz, and many others who were beaten and systematically tortured.[56] The great number of active conspirators who were never arrested speaks volumes for the fortitude of those who were tortured, tried, and executed after July 20, 1944, and whose families, including small children, were thrown into jails and concentration camps.[57] In the French resistance, by comparison, the general rule was that whoever was captured by the Germans was expected to try to keep silent under torture for twenty-four hours so that others who might be compromised could get away.[58]

Before Roland Freisler's People's Court, where the conspirators were tried in the last months of the war following July 1944, many were silenced by the judge when they tried to explain their motives. Brigadier Helmuth Stieff could only stammer "for Germany." But Peter Graf Yorck von Wartenburg managed to get in a few more words: "The essential connection in all these questions is the State's claim of total authority over the citizen, to the exclusion of the citizen's religious and ethical obligations to God."[59] Hans-Bernd von Haeften told Freisler: "In my opinion, the world-historic role of the Führer is that of a great executor of Evil."[60]

Detailed accounts of the executions of the men and women of the opposition sound like hagiographic lore, but they are true. Their last letters and orally transmitted statements are heartrending documents, but they reflect an immense strength of conviction and fortitude. Many conspirators died slowly and painfully. Many were strangled gradually, and films were made of the executions after the first great trial of August 7 and 8, 1944,[61] with the cameras fully visible to those to be executed. The films were taken back to the Führer's headquarters. In more than one respect, the deaths of the men and women of the opposition are a legacy that deserves to be remembered.

## IV. Importance and Implications

The right to resist and oppose unjust rule has been taken for granted in most times and societies of the West. It was implied in Roman natural law, in feudal law and customs, in Luther's acts of conscience (particularly those against the Emperor), and in the doctrines of Johannes Althusius and John Locke. In 1804, Friedrich Schiller wrote his concept of the inalienable right to resist into *Wilhelm Tell:*

> When men oppressed can not find justice, when
> The burden gets to be unbearable,—
> Then they with confidence and courage reach
> To Heaven and fetch their eternal rights
> From where they hang as indestructible
> And as inalienable as stars themselves.

*111*

Then Nature's old primeval state recurs
Where man to man stands up in opposition,
And as a last resort when nothing else
Is of avail, the sword is given them.[62]

But there was more at issue in the opposition to Hitler. After World War I something of what it meant could be noticed: the attempt to overcome and transcend nationalism after it had triumphed so horribly for four years. Before this new attitude could strike roots in Germany, the country was "occupied" in a real sense—occupied after January 30, 1933, by a gang of criminals disguised as politicians with top hats and uniforms, and as popular leaders with paramilitary organizations far stronger than the regular armed forces, whose leadership nevertheless gave at least tacit approval to the new regime. Yet even to those who recognized this situation, it was not as clear and unambiguous as it was, let us say, in France or in Norway during the German occupation. The oppressors of Germany in Germany were not so obviously foreign and illegitimate as in non-German countries. Traditional patterns of loyalty to the government in power were associated with patriotism; they had to be transcended by the German opposition to Hitler.

When the opposition did make this transition, it often did so with great consistency. Colonel Hans Oster, who ranked immediately under Admiral Canaris in the Military Intelligence, repeatedly warned the Royal Dutch government of German intentions to attack in 1939 and 1940. He regarded an attack on a neutral country as illegal. He viewed Hitler's war as a world civil war, and he acted in what could be called "self-defense of humanity," or "world domestic policy." [63] Helmuth Graf von Moltke, an expert in international law, who served in the legal branch of the High Command of the armed forces (OKW) during World War II, wrote to a British friend, Lionel Curtis, in 1942: "We hope you realize that we are willing to help you win the war and the peace."[64] Dietrich Bonhoeffer told Dr. W. A. Visser't Hooft, Secretary General of the World Council of Churches, in 1941, when it seemed that Hitler's march of triumph could not be halted: "If you really want to know—I am praying for the defeat of my country because I believe that it is the only way to pay for all the suffering that it has caused in the world."[65]

Such attitudes clearly point to the future, to the transition beyond a narrow patriotism. A good part of the German opposition may be viewed as paradigmatic, as a model for a new international-ism and for an interpatriotism that transcends the dividing lines of nations, races, and cultural or economic or technological conditions. In an age of world-wide communications through means of trans-portation and information such as has never before existed, and in an age in which the very existence of mankind is at stake paradoxically partly because of its scientific success and partly because of the resulting multiplication of its numbers—in such an era the German opposition not only worked for the German people, for peace in Europe, and against a criminal regime but it also made a contribution to the humanity-wide opposition against the constant threat of oppression of men by men. It has made a contribution to the demythologization of ideologies (*Weltanschauungen*), to the breaking down of vicious patterns of group behavior. It has contributed to the demotion of politically oriented, group-oriented, violence-generating values, and to a reemphasis of humanistic, religious, and ethical values.

# 7

# Objective and Subjective Inhibitants in the German Resistance to Hitler

William Sheridan Allen

The objective difficulties facing the internal opponents of Hitler's terroristic regime are so generally understood that it may seem otiose to consider subjective factors.[1] The Third Reich has long been described as a totalitarian dictatorship and it certainly was that in intention. But research has shown that the "totalitarian model" is inadequate—and possibly misleading. Hitler's government did not exert the same amount of control at all times or over all its subjects equally. Control progressed in intensity and reached its apex during the war; it was also selective, being the most completely exerted over Jews and the less so over other segments of German society. In fact, pockets of potential opposition were always present. Furthermore, for all its totalitarian intentions the Third Reich still contained elements of "politics" within its operations, and the extent and limits of these must be understood if one is to understand the objective framework in which resistance to Hitler had to function.

The pretensions of the Third Reich are well known: a monopoly of force, of politics, of organization, and of information. As for force, Hitler's development of the SS meant that only the army had enough potential counterforce to hope for success in a direct confrontation. But to employ this counterforce required conspiratorial preparation; overt recruitment and planning could be easily suppressed by Hitler's other instrument of force, the Gestapo. Nor could mass revolutionary action take the place of the army as an initial counterforce since the Gestapo was designed to detect and prevent even rudimentary organizational preparations for popular uprisings. Fundamental opposition, therefore, aiming at the forcible overthrow of the government had to be covert and had to depend upon making use of the German army. This put distinct limits upon resistance, not the least of which was the way in which it compelled a reliance upon basic values by anyone engaging in such resistance. The act of conspiracy alone was punishable by death and the risk of discovery was high. Intermediate or temporizing stances as to whether the regime ought to exist were excluded by the regime itself and everyone in Germany knew it in those years. Circumstances compelled commitment, and this objective factor had significant subjective implications.

With respect to the other monopolies claimed by Hitler's government (information, politics, and organization), the regime was clearly not omnipotent. Nazi censorship and propaganda, for example, could not prevent oral exchanges of information or access to outside sources of information through the radio—if one used these methods cautiously. Goebbels did manage to convince most Germans that he was exerting control over the minds of most other Germans and this was a powerful inhibitant to resistance. It isolated opposition at least as much as the Gestapo surveillance and official terrorism did. Again, internalized values became crucial if one were to act in the face of this.

Through coordination (*Gleichschaltung*) virtually all forms of social organization in Germany were either destroyed or controlled by the Nazis. But there were important exceptions. They included informal centers of primary cohesion: friendships and families, neighborhoods or factories or small villages. United action was possible beyond that instigated by the Führer. But apart from these circumscribed groups there were the churches and they were most important as independent formal organizations because of their size, their geographic extension, their emotional and ideological bonds, their deep organizational roots, and their ability to convey information through the pulpit or pastoral letter. The regime clearly suffered them unwillingly and their independence was qualified. But adherence to the churches was not exceptional; total commitment was not required of their members.

The regime's control over political decision-making seemed so obvious and absolute that scholars have tended to overlook the ways in which political legitimation and accommodation also operated and were essential to the system. Quite apart from its control mechanisms, the political stance of the Third Reich engendered if not support at least ambivalence from precisely those elements which still enjoyed precarious semi-autonomy: the army and the churches. The leaders of these institutions belonged to the rightist side of the German political spectrum. However much they might oppose the Nazi party, it belonged to their ideological pool: nationalism, anti-bolshevism, and authoritarianism. The same political rule which made it difficult for liberals to attack Communists in the interwar era made it hard for conservatives to disavow the Nazis in Germany. "No enemies on the Right" was a formula which could be overcome only with an effort.

A second political factor was the apparent absence of acceptable political alternatives. Many moderates and conservatives supported Hitler's installation of the Third Reich as the only choice other than a Soviet Germany. Throughout the Nazi years this political dilemma continued in force; there were many who grew to abhor Hitlerism but saw it as less evil than Bolshevism or chaos.

A third political consideration was the assumption that National Socialism had overcome Germany's persistent pluralistic disintegration. The inability to develop a political system that could unite all segments of society had been the major problem of both the Wilhelmine and Weimar governments, though both had unceasingly and unsuccessfully sought national fusion. But Nazism claimed to be an integrative movement; it seemed to harness the masses. Thus those who opposed it seemed to be reactionaries, or at least anti-modernizers. The regime's mass basis coupled with its espousal of many traditionalist tenets—no matter how ultimately spurious these might be in reality—were arguments superseding and reinforcing its dictatorial weapons. The point is that the Third Reich legitimized itself politically and that, too, belongs to the objective factors making resistance difficult.

None of this ignores Hitler's terroristic practices and his desire for totalitarian control. But even these aspects had their own built-in limitations. It was precisely Nazi dependence upon terror and Nazi aspirations toward all-inclusiveness which—paradoxically—forced Hitler to avoid direct confrontations over unpopular measures such as the attempted prohibition of Corpus Christi processions in the Rhineland. Overt popular opposition, even in non-fundamental matters, might break the totalitarian myth. If naked force were needed in too many instances, Germans might begin to wonder whether the emperor had any clothes at all. Reckless repression, especially against the Nazi constituency of Center and Right, might also destroy the image of Nazi legitimacy as a government by popular support. Terror had to be spent carefully, upon selected targets, over agreed upon issues, and this forced Hitler to restrain his savagery.

What all this suggests is that objective facets of Nazi Germany drove its opponents into one of two directions (excluding accommodation, fecklessness, and martyrdom). The first was fundamental resistance which seemed to imply conspiracy and a *coup d'état* to overthrow the regime. Things might have been different if a revolutionary situation had developed in the Third Reich. On the model of earlier revolutions, for example, new possibilities could emerge if the confidence of the ruling elite had been shaken ideologically (as the Enlightenment affected the aristocracy of eighteenth-century France) or shattered by an external crisis (as happened to czarist Russia in World War I and to fascist Italy in World War II). Since this did not happen in Nazi Germany, it remains only a theoretical possibility, though it also motivated hundreds of thousands of German Social Democrats opposed to Hitler. In fact, a *coup d'état* was thus doubly problematical since even if successful it would apparently confront not only a still intact elite but one with vast mass backing as well.

The other option was not to overthrow the government but to compel it to modify its policies, perhaps even in fundamental ways. This required popular solidity in opposition. That is, the government would have had to decide that it was riskier to suppress its opponents than to accede to their demands. Obviously, no avowedly fundamental threat could be posed by any such action. Where open revolutionary defiance was shown, for example, by the Munich students of the "White Rose" or earlier by the Social Democrats or the Communists, the regime was willing to be utterly ruthless even against large numbers of Germans. The only possibility was to work within the plebiscitary nature of the regime, using its need for mass backing against it by circumspect political guerilla tactics. Again, the objective situation seemed to force even opponents of Nazism to deal with Hitler on terms set by him.

Thus even a cursory analysis of objective factors in Nazi Germany shows that they meld into the subjective qualities of the resistance. Other subjective inhibitants have been noted, too. For example, the most fundamental resistance was the conspiracy culminating in the assassination attempt against Hitler on July 20, 1944. Historians from Hans Rothfels to Peter Hoffmann have insisted that in the last analysis the motivation of the conspirators was ethical repugnance for the entire Hitlerian system. But a conspiracy of generals and aristocrats in a country where the army has been a traditional bastion of feudalistic autocracy immediately suggests other motives. Could this resistance to Hitler have been based on such upper class values as nationalism and snobbery? The Nazis were vulgar in style, origin, and program, and it is only common sense to wonder whether Germany's upper classes felt repugnance for their rule on this basis alone. If so, the July 20 conspiracy may be interpreted as a *fronde* and its failure explained by the weakness inherent in such an approach.

Nationalism is another motive expected of the generals since Hitler's reckless foreign policy not only turned the world against Germany and therefore threatened her with destruction (this was evident to the farsighted at least by 1938) but, furthermore, the Allies explicitly stated that Hitler and his party were insurmountable obstacles to any understanding with Germany. The army and the conservatives ditched one regime that ran counter to national interests in 1918; were they trying to do the same in 1944? In short, are we dealing with a caste motivated primarily by self-seeking concerns rather than by ethical considerations?

The documentary evidence argues against this supposition. It is true that aristocrats were heavily involved in the July 20 plot; yet closer examination shows that most of them were not Prussian Junkers but noblemen from western and southern Germany. More to the point, they were determined to transcend traditional class and ideological lines. They actively sought to include Socialists and even Communists in their ranks and they also paid heed to the ideas and values of the working-class left. Finally, their debates do not show conservative noblemen on one side and Social Democratic trade unionists on the other. Instead there was a fluid mixture of positions. The common denominators were a fundamental rejection of Nazism as an indecent, lawless system and a desire to create something new which would be immune to the ills that had produced Nazism.

Thus the "caste-*frondeur*" argument is relegated to the shadowy realm of potential subconscious motivation. Nationalism as a selfish motive cannot even be accorded this much. On the one hand, the various appeals to "national heritage" were clearly euphemisms for other values, as might be expected in a country with so variegated a tradition as Germany. On the other hand, there is simply no documentary evidence that the July 20 conspirators sought to eliminate Hitler in order to strengthen Germany's position in international power politics. Their ideas as to the peace terms obtainable by an anti-Nazi German government were exceptionally naive and they did use nationalistic arguments to recruit supporters (especially from the army, where such terminology appeared most "realistic"), but they were consciously ready to sacrifice Germany's material possibilities in return for expunging the national dishonor of Nazism. There is only *one* instance of the idea "win the war first, then cope with Hitler" being attributed to a conspirator (Stauffenberg, in Joachim Kramarz's book of that title) and even that is a dubious quotation.

A variant point (and a subtler subjective element) is that noted by George Romoser.[2] The majority of those involved in the July 20 conspiracy did come out of the conservative movement of the Weimar Republic and it is strikingly evident that their constitutional proposals derived from a deep distrust of the masses. Therefore, Romoser asks, are we not dealing here with a simple extension of the "Conservative Revolution" ideology from the Weimar period? Did not this condemn them to ineptness?

The conservative-authoritarian tradition was doubtless a predisposing element in the thought patterns of the men around Beck and Goerdeler. But it was also a logical response to the way Hitler came into power and the unique mass basis of his regime. Surely the conspirators had far more reason to fear the German masses, having seen what a mass manipulator of Hitler's dimensions could do with them, than they had cause to abhor some abstract demonic Jacobinism supposedly inherent in popular democracy. Thus their constitutional proposals are understood more as an attempt to prevent a recrudescence of Nazism than as the expression of a despairing philosophical outlook. That is why even the Social Democrats in the conspiracy, though reluctantly and with reservations, accepted these constitutional concepts. The immediate practical problem of securing a new regime established by *coup d'état* against a mass based government required some authoritarian measures to isolate and punish the

Nazis, or at least to prevent a counter *coup*, until educational denazification could build a firmer foundation. Objective imperatives superseded subjective inclinations.

In what way, then, *did* subjective factors inhibit the effectiveness of the July 20 plot? Conspiracy to overthrow the Third Reich by force had to be based on fundamentalist motives. In other words, the politics of conspiracy required finding the lowest common denominator for diverse elites, namely, a desire to restore national decency and the rule of law (*Rechtsstaat*). The expressed ethical motivation was also the most hardheaded practical solution to the process of developing a conspiratorial coalition. This does not exclude the possibility of other, baser or higher, motives. But it does indicate that the dialectical relationship between ruling and opposing elites in the Third Reich forced a moral affirmation upon Hitler's fundamental opponents.

Once this became the basis of action it not only limited further the size of the conspiracy (moral insight being a highly selective gift—more so than determination or courage) and thus impaired its chances of success but it also tended to become an end in itself. The temptation was strong to be righteous but ineffective, since moral resistance was the one thing that was always possible in the Third Reich—though usually at the price of one's life. Effective resistance was harder to accomplish.

Perhaps this helps to explain both the recklessness of men like Goerdeler and the apathy of men like Beck, both of whom were willing and ready to pay the highest price to overthrow Hitler, but neither of whom was efficient about it, beyond forging a coalition. It also gives a new sense to Brecht's aphorism about how regrettable it is when heroes are required. The subjective necessity for ethical fundamentalism, forced by objective circumstances, was a major inhibitant to successful resistance in Nazi Germany.

Paradoxically it was the exact opposite—that is, the *lack* of moral fundamentalism—that inhibited the leaders of the other option: mass based opposition to the Third Reich. Here we refer directly to church officials, since they were the only leaders with still intact organizational ties to a popular base. Of course their opposition was no conspiracy to overthrow the government. But is it not also "resistance," and perhaps more significant because successful, to thwart the goals of the regime? The best-known example was the mass protest through the churches which forced Hitler to abandon his euthanasia program, though only after seventy thousand Germans had died in the gas chambers. It was Bishop Galen's publicly calling it "murder" that defeated Hitler in this respect. The Nazis were also kept from removing crucifixes from Bavarian schools, or capturing organizational control of the Evangelical churches, by open mass defiance in support of church leaders. That the Nazis did not modify their intentions, and even continued circumspectly to murder incurables and arrest preachers, simply substantiates the fact that the Nazis were forced to retreat against their will. Here resistance, however limited, was definitely effective.

But it was limited; further resistance was never tried. Were subjective factors the reason? By applying to the churches the same arguments brought out above in discussing the July 20 conspirators, one can assert that church resistance was undertaken principally for motives of self-interest, out of organizational egoism. This, indeed, was also a key to its success as open defiance. It was possible to get mass backing for church based resistance, or opposition ostensibly based on religious doctrine or practice, precisely because the regime accepted that as a motive which was neither a fundamental threat nor openly assailable. There is an interacting cynicism involved here, based on mutual fear and self-defense, in which both the government and its potential opponents agree that self-interest alone is an acceptable motive for opposition. Viewed this way, the Church Struggle would not even have happened if the state had been more politic in its treatment of the churches.

And indeed, both churches gave abundant indication that they desired reconciliation with the Third Reich. They consistently showered gratuitous and unsolicited declarations of loyalty upon Hitler. And Hitler saw the need to be politic, too. After *Gauleiter* Adolf Wagner tried to remove crucifixes from Bavarian schools, Hitler summoned him to Berlin and informed him privately that if he ever tried anything that stupid again, Hitler would not only dismiss him from the office of *Gauleiter*, he would personally shoot Wagner.

Was there equal reason for the church leaders to fear mass hostility toward more extensive opposition moves? The evidence of the Church Struggle suggests the opposite. Congregations generally stood solidly behind their pastors. Among Catholics, overall church attendance increased during the Third Reich. When several Nazi officials called for the execution of Bishop Galen because he had accused the government of murder in the euthanasia conflict, Goebbels decided "that the population of Münster could be regarded as lost during the war, if anything were done against the Bishop ... [plus] the whole of Westphalia." When Niemöller defied the regime, contributions to his church in Berlin-Dahlem rose noticeably. When Rosenberg tried to get Germans to substitute Nazi rituals for baptism, marriage, and funeral ceremonies conducted by the churches, he discovered almost total popular noncompliance. Carefully kept statistics in Thuringia for the first six months of 1943 show that there were 37,280 such ceremonials conducted: 35,853 in churches and 1,427 by the Nazi party. The 1940 census shows that some 95 percent of the German people were affiliated with a church, and the evidence suggests that loyalty usually accompanied membership.

All this implies that much more was possible through church opposition in carefully graduated steps. A following was there if skillful, forthright leadership were present. And this, of course, is precisely why the regime curtailed its ruthlessness in its confrontations with the churches. The most ironic statistic of the Third Reich on this was that more Catholic priests and Protestant ministers died in the German army than were put into concentration camps: from an actuarial point of view it was safer to oppose Hitler than to support him.

The conclusion is inescapable that church-led resistance was primarily limited by subjective factors rather than by objective ones. It was the refusal of church leaders to oppose Nazism from a base of fundamental considerations that prevented them from being more effective. Yet the fundamental tenets of the Christian religion were violated by Hitler. One could possibly reinterpret Christ's prime injunction to "love thy neighbor," but it seems impossible to get around the explicit language of the First and Fifth Commandments in evaluating Nazi Germany. Admittedly ignorance and doubt shrouded many of the crimes of the Third Reich (the use of code words for "the final solution of the Jewish problem" and the location of the extermination camps outside the boundaries of the Reich indicate the regime's desire to mask its murderous policies). But there were also occasions when Hitler espoused murder openly. Nor was this a late development. Even before he came to power

Hitler publicly endorsed the brutal Potempa murders of August 1932. His actions during the purge of the SA on June 30, 1934, were known to all; yet only Martin Niemöller called for an equally visible protest against murder. Not one Catholic bishop protested the murder of the head of "Catholic Action."

The failure of the church leaders to remain faithful to their own doctrines, to oppose the regime in obedience to the principles they taught their congregations, meant in effect that they were supporting it, except on those few occasions when Hitlerian policies ran directly counter to their obvious organizational self-interest. This applies even to a leader like Cardinal Faulhaber, who helped smuggle Jews out of Germany but insisted that he was doing so as an individual, not as a churchman. Privatization made religious leaders "part of the problem," for Hitler's regime was so largely based on the myth of universal popular support that the official acquiescence of the churches was a vital factor sustaining the Third Reich and permitting it to work its wickedness freely.

Just as the focus on moral fundamentalism hampered the July 20 conspirators, so the lack of this impeded the extension of church opposition. Yet the further difference also needs noting: to the churches was given a better opportunity to change the government, at a lesser risk, if they had only combined the tactics of moderation, which they employed so well, with fundamentalist goals.

Resistance *was* possible in the Third Reich, though only with skill and caution. One problem was the temptation to be moral rather than effective. But without the ability to recognize immorality and without the determination to do something about it, effective resistance was not possible either. The particular tragedy of the Third Reich was not that there were insufficient martyrs or even insufficient heroes. It was that the objective circumstances demanded men who combined moral insight with practical determination. Ironically the men of determination were too obsessed with morality to be practical while the guardians of morality determined to be practical even at the expense of morality. In this sense subjective factors were as significant as objective circumstances in inhibiting resistance to Nazi Germany.

# 8

# The German State and Protestant Elites

Frederick O. Bonkovsky

## I. Introduction

For a quarter of a century, commentators have marveled over the Protestant resistance to Hitler. Of all German institutions, only the Protestant church, more specifically the segment known as the Confessing Church, consistently opposed the regime to its end.

Recently there have been three major attempts in the English-speaking world to deal with the relationship of church and state in Nazi Germany. John Conway's *The Nazi Persecution of the Churches: 1933-1945* is a well wrought historical approach.[1] Beate Ruhm von Oppen surveyed the more polemical literature and engaged in the debate herself.[2] Finally, in March 1970, the Institute for the Study of Religion and Societal Conflict at Wayne State University in Detroit brought together scholars in the field for an international conference.

Surveying the literature and the current discussion one comes away with intellectual indigestion. After two decades of research and writing the proper historians are concerned that so much evidence remains unculled. Antirevisionism has followed revisionism and now threatens to divide and multiply. The German Church Struggle can be used to illustrate everything from the scourge of the American Radical Right to the value of church-state separation. But overall, the discussion seems to have advanced comparatively little. Historians tell each other about untapped sources. Theologians debate the nature of the Christian faith, the more sociologically minded concern themselves about its German manifestations.

All this work is very worthwhile, but it is not enough. The

fundamental question, Why was the Confessing Church successful where all others failed? is left unanswered and even unasked. A more analytical approach would be useful. It would aid in ordering the mass of material and thereby increase understanding. This essay argues that the category of elites and their interaction is a revealing way to understand the Nazi-Protestant confrontation. The resistance entailed a conflict between leadership groups (*Führungsschichte*) in German society.

The fundamental hypothesis is that Protestant churchmen best resisted Nazi political coordination because of their strong hold on elite tools and skills. The opposition was founded in the historic power and importance of Protestantism and its leaders. The manner in which churchmen first defended their positions is an intriguing story. Indeed, all significant resistance to the regime was tied to the ability of the Protestant elite to maintain and reconstitute itself in the face of Nazi attempts to destroy it and usurp its prerogatives.

The first step in noting the social mechanism of the resistance is to draw a distinction between mainline Protestants and other German religious groups, whether Roman Catholic or sects. Leaders of the latter rarely reached true elite status in Germany. Catholic resistance was thus a function of German-Vatican (interstate) relations or of individual conscience rather than a result of German social interaction. Sect opposition, often heroic, was nonetheless easily overwhelmed for it was exclusively personalistic in origin. The tradition of radical separation from society explains both the absolutist nature of sect resistance and its tragic defeat.[3]

In all of Nazi Germany it was only the mainline Protestants, drawing on the capital of four centuries, who comprised an elite able and strong enough to resist the new order. The Evangelical religionist combined education, knowledge, special skills, and a firm select position in German culture. His natural allies were other members of the traditional elite, more particularly Junker and army leaders.

Nations, especially in time of stress, are held together as much by common understandings as by technological trappings. Machiavelli and Rousseau were repeating the wisdom of Greece and Rome when they noted the value of religion in maintaining the state. The Nazis recognized the importance of religion. There eventually arose a situation in which the regime proposed a counter faith. Protestant churchmen responded uncertainly and conservatively at first, but finally moved toward all-out resistance. Their symbols, skills, and methods (conviction, cross, communion, and communication channels) proved resilient where those of university or labor union leaders, for example, crumbled under the Nazi onslaught.

## II. The Historic Relationship of German State and Protestant Elites

A usual concomitant of western nation-state development has been some form of state-church conflict usually resulting in separation, *de jure* or *de facto*. In some instances this took the form of anticlerical revolution. Germany's development was extraordinary. England, France, the United States, and even the Soviet Union preceded her in "secularization" or some form of disestablishmentarianism.

In Germany, the effect of Luther's reformation was to drive out one form of clericalism in certain regions but to cause its replacement with deep ties between church and state. *Cuius regio, eius religio* was the official description of church-state cooperation after 1648. Two centuries later, in 1848, a liberal anticlerical revolution resulted in failure.

The two great heroes in the long struggle for German national identity and unity were deeply religious men. Luther and Bismarck perceived themselves to be devout. Both asserted Protestantism to be an integral ingredient in German life and personal self-definition.

Luther, the first modern German national, may be taken as the expression par excellence of Germanic consciousness. Politics and Protestantism were integrally mixed in his career. Attempted church reform soon became political struggle. Luther appealed to German princes for defense against Spanish and Romish opposition. A German monk successfully challenged the Pope and the Emperor. The German language was born in his translation of Scripture. Soon, most of what was to become modern Germany found itself under the spell of the Reformation and was divided, religiously and politically, from old Europe.

Half the Protestant territorial gains were reversed in the Counter-Reformation and the Thirty Years War. By 1648, Germany was devastated and decimated—its unity destroyed—its politics became the plaything of foreign princes. But Germanic consciousness defined itself by at least some of the spirit and specifics of Luther's revolution.

Modern Germany might have arisen in many ways. It came about through the leadership of Prussia. Had Bavaria or Austria been central, the pattern of unity and certainly its religious aspects would have been greatly different. It is a striking fact of Prussian history that its elites, more particularly its imperial family and general staff, were avowed Lutherans and champions of Christianity.

William I, king of Prussia from 1861 and first German kaiser (1871-1888), ruler of Prussia and Germany in their most momentous years, was well known for his piety. Christianity in its Lutheran form was "the bread of his life, the comfort of his pains, and the measuring rod for his actions." His motto was, "Because I know I am powerless in God's hands, I am powerful against all the world."[4] Under such a kaiser, the state church reached great heights of influence and became in fact an official agency of government. The offices of Provincial Bishop (*Landesbischof*) and Preacher to the Court were immensely important.

Lutheran pietism attracted many of Germany's upper classes. The von Moltke family was deeply religious. Bismarck too claimed firm belief in the ethic of the Sermon on the Mount.[5] The Iron Chancellor once wrote: "We ourselves can do nothing; we can only wait until we hear the footsteps of God echoing in the events of time: then we spring forth and grasp the hem of His garment—that is all." Bismarck's daily devotional guide was replete with marginal notes.[6]

In imperial Prussia, political and religious elites moved in the same circle and mutually supported each other. The ties between Protestantism and the Prussian-German state were strikingly revealed in Bismarck's *Kulturkampf* (culture battle) against the Catholic Church and the newly formed Center party (*Zentrum*) in the 1870s. It is instructive that this campaign was early on the agenda of a united Germany.

By the end of the decade the *Kulturkampf* had ended in an uneasy truce. The Center party achieved precisely the position Bismarck had feared, holder of the balance of power in the Reichstag. A residue of anti-Catholicism from the *Kulturkampf* was now joined to pro-imperial and antiparliamentarian sentiments. Protestantism, more particularly Lutheranism, comprised the religion and underlay the ideology of the court of the kaisers. It constituted the ethical basis of imperial Germany. Elites were unified in their attitudes. Every German kaiser and almost the entire Prussian nobility were practicing Lutherans. The officer corps was perennially more than 80 percent Protestant.

On the other side of the coin, the official Protestant church maintained its tradition of cooperation with the state. The anarchy of the peasants' revolts in the 1520s had driven Luther to a stern "law and order" position in which he justified extreme governmental repression on the basis of Romans 13. Luther accepted at face value the Pauline injunction of obedience to civil authorities, who were assumed to be agents of God. It was probably not unimportant that Luther's life and reformation had been preserved by the German princes.

The historic Lutheran pattern was one of cooperation between church and state. Where Lutheranism was the official religion, this presented no great problem for the church. Pastors were part of the lordly ruling class. Princes were assumed to be under God's sovereignty and hence obedient to his servants. Thus religion and the state were intertwined and mutually supportive.

A somewhat different attitude characterized the smaller Reformed Protestant group. According to Calvin, the church is not only the organ of salvation but is also called to Christianize the entire community. Although the Genevan was vague on the problem of resistance to the state, his followers were known for their insistence on freedom of conscience. John Knox, for instance, held that church officials possess the right and duty of leading opposition to a tyrant, even to the point of death. The upper Rhineland and northwest Prussia were influenced by Swiss and French Calvinism, but radical Calvinism was never well established in Germany.

Calvinism emphasized the worldly calling of Christians. The Reformed Germans followed this pattern, tending to be bourgeois and politically liberal.[7] Because Calvinism emphasized the individual conscience, it was the original point of departure for many sectarian movements. When resistance to Hitler formed within Protestantism, the bulk of active opposition was grounded in either the Calvinist or pietist wings of the established church, probably because these traditions had placed a strong stress on the individual responsibility of the believer.

During the nineteenth century, the German Protestant churches gradually united. This union took place under the sanction of the territorial princes. Church elections were subject to state approval. The old principle of *cuius regio, eius religio* was recalled in the derivation of the authority of the provincial church (*Landeskirche*) from the secular ruler. The official head of the Prussian church was the king of Prussia, later the kaiser of Germany. In return, the state paid clerical salaries and gave official support to religious activities.

In 1922, the major Protestant denominations came together into the United Evangelical Church of Germany. Composed of twenty-eight provincial churches plus the Prussian synod, this church elected national officers to handle church affairs out of a Berlin bureau. The Evangelical church with about forty million official members accounted for about two-thirds of the German population; the Roman Catholics and a few small Protestant sects claimed most of the other one-third.

Whatever the theory of democratic Weimar, the church remained a favored institution even though it retained its monarchical sympathies. Loyalty to the church was deeply imbedded in German culture. The Weimar government did not attempt to change ecclesiastical structure. Although the constitution called for separation of church and state, the pastors were paid by the state, and government machinery was used to collect taxes for the support of the church. Even the socialists continued the practice of paying a forty-million-yearly "indemnity" dating from the time when the Prussian kingdom had seized church property for needed funds.[8]

The church maintained its preferred position. Protestant leaders identified with and remained part of the old elite. The young Tillich gained fame precisely because he was an exception to the rule. Most clergymen, like most officers, mouthed the theory that World War II had been lost by weakness at home (*Dolchstoss Theorie*) and detested Versailles and the Weimar arrangement it fostered.

Eighty percent of the Protestant pastors belonged to parties of the right. The church officially condemned leftism. Pastors who joined socialist parties were boycotted and those who became Communist were excommunicated.[9] Church spokesmen repeated nationalist and revanchist sentiments. Martin Niemöller, for instance, had refused to turn his submarine over to the British as ordered, saying, "I have neither sought nor concluded this armistice. As far as I am concerned, the people who promised our submarines to England can take them over. I will not do it!"[10]

By and large, pastors remained monarchical and refused support for the Republic.[11] Fearful of the threat from the left they welcomed the Nazis as a strong force which might be able to end economic and social chaos. As Niemöller stated after the Ruhr crisis, "We lacked leaders, we lacked a real goal, and, above all, we lacked the inward and moral urge to national action."[12]

The Nazis promised to provide all of this. Many churchmen were therefore willing to see the rise of a regime which would restore (traditional) virtue and moral strength, recreate imperial Germany, and oppose atheistic Bolshevism. But National Socialism also proposed a German domestic revolution. The resistance grew precisely when the Nazi upheaval challenged the positions and status of the religious elite. At first there was considerable confusion, for Nazism cast itself in the role of champion of pre-republican privilege. But as the Third Reich came to full power, it sought to displace the traditional elites and create its own religious leaders. This was a new form of disestablishmentarianism and anticlericalism. The clever attack was not on the faith per se. It was aimed only at the religious elite. Protestant leaders and the state had previously worked hand in glove. The Nazis drove Protestant leaders into opposition.

### III. The Nazi Revolution: Challenge to the Protestant Religious Elite

Elites exist in and take their strength from their milieu—the society which surrounds them. Elites are constituted in terms of the ideas, values, symbols, and skills which they control. Only as long as their symbols are accepted, their methods held legitimate, and their skills found desirable by society in general do elites maintain their positions.[13] Their "goods" must appeal to the community for favored roles to be continued.

The Nazis challenged and attacked traditional Protestant elites in many ways. The regime posited values, ideology, symbols, and skills counter to those of historic German religious life. In this way, the Nazis directly contested the place of former leaders, religious as well as secular. Ultimately that challenge took physical form.

*"Theology": The Contest over Values, Ideas, and Ideology*

Nazism, even under wartime conditions, never achieved the absolute coherence and unity it is sometimes pictured as possessing. Through the 1920s and 1930s, the movement and then the regime had various spokesmen who often spoke differently on the same issue. Ultimate authority rested in the Führer, of course, which in many areas he failed to exercise. Moreover, the Church Struggle is replete with instances of Hitler's changing his mind (for example, with regard to the imprisonment of Niemöller).

There never developed a clear-cut Nazi pseudo- or counter-Christian doctrine. But the new order challenged the very basis of the Christian commitment. The two most influential Nazi philosophers were Hitler and Alfred Rosenberg. Rosenberg was strongly anti-Christian. Hitler's attitude was at least a-religious, though for political reasons he often gave other indications.

In *Mein Kampf* Hitler insisted that all religions were alike in their dis-value. They would have no future in his new Germany. The Italians, he said, could be both Christians and pagans at the same time. But the German *Volk* took these matters too seriously. Christianity, a slave religion of Jewish origins, would be rejected by true Germans. But as Hitler gained in authority, he was notably less willing to make such statements. Instead, in the late Weimar and early Nazi years, he was cast as the champion of traditional German values.

The burden of the ideological attacks was thus carried by Alfred Rosenberg, author of *The Myth of the Twentieth Century*. In that work and others like the extreme anticlerical *An die Dunkelmänner unserer Zeit* [Concerning the obscurantists of our era], Rosenberg sought to take from Christianity such concepts as "sacrifice" and "blood" and give them secular, Nazi, and anti-Christian meanings. A transformation of the churches based on a new message, one of heroic German racism, was intended. The "tormented saints" would be replaced with German heroes; the Jewish "words of prophecy" and songs to Jehovah, with praise to the Führer.[14] Secretly, lesser Nazis went even further, as programs at a Nazi student organization make clear.[15] National Socialist ideology was thus a perversion of and a challenge to traditional Protestant teaching.

*The Battle for Social Control: Symbols, Skills, and Communications Channels at Issue*

The Nazi movement and party were themselves a kind of secular religion. The Führer's role was that of omniscience incarnated. Specific Protestant counter-churches were also founded and supported. The most important was the German Christian church officially begun in 1930. The new church proposed both a new doctrine (positive Christianity) and a reorganization of church structure. It counted among its founders two sons of the kaiser, August Wilhelm and Eitel Friedrich. No one is sure exactly what role the Nazis played originally, but it is believed that Goebbels had a hand in organizing the church. Clearly, the regime supported the new church as part of its revolution.[16]

In 1932, Joachim Hossenfelder, a former member of the illegal *Freikorps* (rightist paramilitary formations) and a pastor in Berlin, became head of the German Christian movement. Rosenberg was its leading theologian. Nazi racial principles were advocated. Jesus was pictured as an Aryan. God's interest in the Teutonic people became a scriptural principle. Utilizing nineteenth-century romanticism, Rosenberg discarded as Jewish much of the Old Testament and the writings of Matthew, Luke, and Paul. The latter had corrupted Christianity into a servile religion. The doctrines of sin and grace were rejected. Protestantism was charged with dividing the German people and bringing national weakness and military defeat. Only a "positive Christianity" without the guilt of sin was fit for such a great race.[17]

In the early months of 1933, while they planned the take-overs of other institutions, the Nazis made plans to unify, nationalize, and thus to coordinate (principle of *Gleichschaltung*) the Protestant churches. A Reich church would be far stronger than twenty-eight provincial churches. But it was imperative that the Reich church be sympathetic to Nazi ideas and the Reichsbishof be a man suitable to their concerns.

Passing over the controversial Hossenfelder, Hitler chose Ludwig Müller, a rather ordinary military chaplain whose major service had been in East Prussia. Hitler himself explained to Müller what the Nazis sought: a unified church prepared to accept the party's political leadership. Müller announced his readiness to assist and on April 25, 1933, was named Hitler's "Delegate and Plenipotentiary for all questions concerning the Protestant Churches."[18]

Thus the Nazis were creating a new elite, establishing new leaders and a new organization. The next step was a usual one: to confirm the arrangements by plebiscite. Since all Protestants (except the sects) seemed to agree upon the establishment of a Reich church, the specific issue was who would be chosen the first national bishop.

The Nazis and "German Christians" supported Ludwig Müller. The traditional elites, however, sensing their positions were being challenged, drew up their own plans for church structure and nominated as their candidate the head of the Inner Mission, Friedrich von Bodelschwingh. In the election, von Bodelschwingh defeated Müller by a considerable majority.

Bodelschwingh's victory indicated that the traditional symbols, professionalism, and communications channels had not been significantly disturbed by the Nazis. In response, the Nazis followed a pattern which was to become familiar. They declared the first election illegal and set up another for July. They then set about disrupting the old church machinery. The Evangelicals were denied access to news media. Church officers were caused to resign for "reasons of health." After most offices had been filled with Nazi supporters, von Bodelschwingh also quit in despair.

In this way the Nazis achieved by force and violence what they could not accomplish by competition with the traditional elites. The debates between the two groups attracted so much international attention, however, that von Hindenburg expressed his concern in a letter to Hitler.[19]

Müller was appointed to fill out von Bodelschwingh's term and the Nazis announced a "reorganization celebration" for July 2, 1933. All churches were to fly the swastika and all pastors were to offer thanks for the Nazi "revolution" and to ask for divine blessing on the government. Müller was confirmed in a "national synod" in Wittenberg, a place which suggested that a second historic German Protestant church revolution had occurred. A huge procession was held in Berlin. It ended at the Kaiser Wilhelm Memorial Church to symbolize the new assertion of *cuius regio, eius religio.*[20]

By this time most other German institutions (for example, parties, unions) were well on the way to political coordination. The Protestant elites, however, were far from defeated. Hitler found it necessary to intervene in the church dispute directly.[21] On the eve of the church elections, July 22, he made a radio appeal to the nation calling for the election of the "German Christian" candidates and promising that the state would thereupon guarantee the "inner freedom" of the church.[22] The "German Christians" won the election. But since the Nazis had unseated most of the Evangelical leaders and brought to the polls thousands who never attended church services, the significance of the victory is far from clear.

In fact, the Protestant church had not been brought into line. The Nazis continued in the creation of a counter-elite and a counter-organization. In September the Prussian synod reinserted the Aryan paragraph into the statement of church polity, this time going so far as to exclude from church membership anyone of Jewish descent or any person who had married a Jew. Hossenfelder had the Gestapo remove several pastors, including Niemöller, from their parishes in retaliation for their anti-Aryan sermons.[23]

The local pastors, however, remained obstinate. Müller's attempts at church reorganization were so unsuccessful that his entire cabinet resigned and he found himself without support from either the Evangelicals or the "German Christians." To assert his authority, Müller took increasingly stringent action in late 1933 and early 1934.

The Evangelical youth groups were forcibly incorporated into the Hitler Youth. In January Müller announced that disciplinary measures would be taken against any pastor who refused to obey his directives. He further declared that all church services must be identical in form and called for an end to the teachings of forgiveness of sin and a "suffering Christ." He forbade any remarks or attacks against the "German Christians" and announced that Hitler was to be considered the supreme authority of the church.

When even these measures were not sufficiently successful, there followed direct attacks on the resisting churchmen. During January 1934, Niemöller was harassed by the Gestapo. A bomb was thrown into his parsonage and his meetings were broken up by Hitler Youth. After a particularly strong sermon entitled "God Is My Führer," Niemöller was given a second "leave of absence" from his pulpit. But the prestigious Dahlem congregation brought so much pressure to bear that Hitler himself ordered the pastor's return.[24] Other pastors were not so fortunate. By the end of February 1934, some seventy had been put into concentration camps.

Hitler was now personally involved in the effort to break the old elites. In March, during an audience with leaders of the churches of southern Germany, the Führer flew into a rage. Albert Speer notes that this was one of the two such genuine periods of anger which he

observed as Hitler's colleague. The leader shouted that the Evangelical church had collapsed in 1918 and the remains were an "append-
age of the Roman Catholic church," on one hand, or of the Marxists,
on the other. Before he dismissed them, Hitler called the opposing
pastors "traitors to the state."[25]

The fall of 1934 brought a new barrage of attacks as additional
Nazi officials became involved in the Church Struggle. Harassment of
pastors increased. Niemöller's parsonage was bombed and he was
beaten on the street. In the communications war, church phones
were tapped. Frick, Minister of the Interior, forbade the publication
of any news of the Church Struggle. Rosenberg vigorously pursued
his publicity of Nordic myths and substitutes for Christianity.[26]

On August 2, 1934, Field Marshal von Hindenburg, president of
the Reich, died. By the Enabling Act, Hitler now became both
chancellor and Reich president. A week later, a National Protestant
Church Synod was convened. Its large Nazi majority approved the
"coordination" of provincial churches into a Reich church. Moreover, the synod passed an ordinance obliging all pastors to take the
same oath as a civil servant, pledging their loyalty and obedience to
Adolf Hitler, Führer of the German people and state. The protesting
Protestants saw this as a direct challenge to their ordination vows, as
it surely was.

There followed Gestapo harassment of various church leaders and
the dismissal and "protective custody" of Niemöller and other Evangelical leaders as well as Bishops Wurm and Meier who had headed
the resisting provincial churches of Württemberg and Bavaria. The
National Synod approved the ecclesiastical legalities of this Nazi
repression. Thus the new elites made warfare on the old.

## IV. The Protestant Resistance as Traditional Elite Response

To the Nazi attack upon status and the symbols, organization,
and professionalism which undergirded their elite position, the Protestant leaders first responded in a way primarily defensive and
conservative. But in spite of their hesistancy, their overall conservative attitudes, and their fundamental theology of cooperation with
the state, the traditional elites were ultimately forced into open
defiance by the Nazi attack.

In theory, opposition based on religion should have been no

more successful than the opposition of the army, the universities, and certainly the labor unions. Yet "the most active, most effective, and most consistent resistance came from the churches."[27] The explanation is to be found in the fact that the Protestant church leaders were able to maintain considerable control over symbols, ideology, professional identification, and organization and communications channels. Moreover, where control was lost to the Nazis, the traditional elites were at least partially successful in establishing new institutions.

## The Response from Tradition

It should not be surprising that the primary Protestant position was a conservative one. The first goal of the resistance was to preserve its traditional place in German society. Historically, Protestant behavior and theory had been conservative about society and the state. That conservatism was now useful in combating a revolutionary challenge.

Martin Niemöller, the leading figure of the early resistance, aptly symbolizes the conservative stance. Niemöller came to theology after achieving national fame as a World War I hero and recipient of the Iron Cross. He studiously maintained his strong nationalist sentiments even in the seminary. Thus he studied at Münster, rejecting Bonn because it was then in the occupied zone. Upon graduation, Niemöller's fame as naval hero served him well as he was appointed youth and charity work coordinator for the Westphalia Inner Mission. Thereby he gained experience in church politics and wide acquaintance with church officials.

His nationalist and conservative attitudes served Niemöller in good stead. In 1931 he was called to the Dahlem parish in Berlin, probably the most prestigious Protestant church in all of Germany. The congregation was made up of professional men, high-ranking government officials, and military officers. By this time, Niemöller had published his autobiographical *From U-Boat to Pulpit*, which found ready acceptance in his parish. The book was widely read in Germany and in many countries. Hitler recognized Niemöller by name in 1931.[28]

In his first months at Dahlem, Niemöller preached fiery Evangelical sermons, avoiding all mention of political matters.[29] He was friendly with many of Hitler's supporters and on occasion gave the

Nazi salute himself.[30] Niemöller welcomed Hitler's seizure of power in 1933 and approved the Nazi economic plans. Worried about the growing secularization of Germany, Dahlem's pastor seems to have hoped that Hitler could revitalize the churches.[31]

Almost immediately, however, there came the challenge from the "German Christians" to which Niemöller and others responded almost reflexively. A radical "German Christian" spokesman called upon Hitler to be the interpreter of the scriptures and claimed that God had "set his seal on the Third Reich." Arguing that Christ had been an Aryan and that "the maintenance of racial purity [was] a commandment of God and Christian duty," he called on all Christians to join the Nazis in the battle against "internationalism, Marxism, free masonry, and pacifism." To facilitate this, the "German Christians" called for church reorganization.[32]

Perturbed over the threat to church organization and the attack on traditional theology, the church office in Berlin issued a statement in March 1933, contradicting "German Christian" views.[33] Two days later, in response to the March 5 voting returns, the Prussian general superintendent, Otto Dibelius, warned pastors to maintain their traditional allegiances, organizational and theological.[34] On the first Sunday in Lent, Niemöller surprised his congregation by saying that although normally and historically politics had no place in the church, "something is happening which is of importance to our fate and that of our nation: something, moreover, with regard to which we must personally take up a conscientious stand. . . ."[35]

In defense of the privileges, the traditional arrangements, and the ideology which gave them elite status, Niemöller and others objected to the new church organization and doctrine.[36] But as late as May 1934, Niemöller still used the Nazi salute and held to Luther's position of loyalty to the government so long as scriptural theology was not threatened.[37]

The basis for early resistance to Nazi tampering was strictly conservative. When the "German Christians" called for church elections to be limited to Aryans, Niemöller and colleagues called for a return to the "confessions of the Reformation."[38] Karl Barth challenged Reichsbischof Müller's reorganizational ideas by insisting that reform could arise only from an inner conviction of the Word of God.[39] To the Nazi attack on Jews and their families, the resisters replied that converted Jews should not be discriminated against. But they did not, in 1933, protest the increasingly evident general Anti-semitic policy.

As church organization and communications channels came under Nazi control, the older elites established counter channels, still under the rubric of maintenance of the past. Deposed church officials joined together in the Young Reformation Movement. In August 1933, the Pastors' Emergency League (*Pfarrernotbund*) was formed under Niemöller's leadership and by the beginning of 1934 it included about one-third (six thousand) of the German Protestant pastors. Denied the official channels of communication, the League made use of circular letters and declarations which were often read from pulpits.

Thus the resistance was successful in maintaining at least some of its skills and symbols and in creating new means of communication with fellow professionals and hence with society in general. The names of arrested pastors were read at worship services and prayers were said for their release. Collections were taken for their wives and families. Such publicity, domestic and eventually foreign through cooperating churchmen abroad, put considerable pressure on the Nazis and led to prison releases and grants of amnesty.[40]

The high point of the traditional resistance was the Barmen synod convened in May 1934. Here in a fundamentally conservative gesture the traditional elites reasserted control over ideology, symbols, and profession by establishing a counter-organization and communications network to the Nazi controlled Protestant church. The Confessing Church, while new, was seen as a return to true Protestantism.

Vowing to oppose the illegitimate authority of the Reichsbischof and the "German Christians," the protesting pastors formulated their position in traditional terms.

The inviolable foundation of the German Evangelical Church is the Gospel of Jesus Christ, as it is witnessed to by the Holy Scriptures and as it comes to light anew in the Confessions of the Reformation. . . .

We reject the false doctrine that the Church is able or at liberty apart from this ministry to take to itself or to accept special "leaders" (Führer) equipped with power to rule. . . .

We reject the false doctrine that the State can become the single and total order of human life, thus fulfilling also the Church's vocation.[41]

Barmen was concerned with those things which affected the

church directly. It spelled resistance to the Nazi attack on the historic ways of German Protestantism. Similar attitudes were reflected in the sermons of Niemöller and other Confessing Church leaders. But no mention was made of the state per se, except where it infringed on the church directly. In this traditional resistance, there was no concern for political matters as a whole.[42]

At the end of the Barmen synod, some ten thousand persons gathered for a service of worship. They departed while singing Luther's hymn, "A Mighty Fortress Is Our God," which became the sign of traditional resistance throughout the Nazi period. Thus both Nazis and resisters referred to Martin Luther for legitimacy. Who were the Wittenberger's true successors became precisely the question.

*The Broadening Resistance: beyond Tradition—toward Politics*

Thanks to Nazi and "German Christian" indecisiveness, traditional resistance was effective for some two or three years (1933-35). But in January 1935, Reichsbishof Müller's schemes for church control having proved failures, Dr. Wilhelm Stuckart of the Ministry of Education presented a memorandum to Hitler which reviewed the church-state situation and suggested a plan for achieving Nazi goals.[43] Attacks on the churches increased. In July 1935, Hanns Kerrl, formerly Prussian Minister of Justice, was named both national and Prussian Minister for Ecclesiastical Affairs and commissioned to carry out Stuckart's suggestions.

Though there were never any programs from the new ministry, its import was clear. Church matters were placed directly under a state bureaucracy, effectively destroying the former Reichsbischof's control. Previously, the institutional struggle had lain between two ecclesiastical hierarchies. Now a new direction was taken. Kerrl cared little for the niceties of theology or church structure. He simply wanted to coordinate completely all religious matters with the purposes of the state.

Kerrl's first move was placative. In September 1935 he granted amnesty to all pastors who had opposed Müller's administration and returned some provincial ecclesiastical authority. Müller's power was given to various church commissions charged with reinstituting church discipline in place of the arbitrary rule of the Reichsbischof and the "German Christians."

Some traditional leaders hoped for a brighter day. But the Evangelicals found in the very existence of Kerrl's ministry a challenge to church autonomy and their positions. It indicated an open Nazi refusal to abide by the historic rule of church-state cooperation. Niemöller responded with a circular letter calling for continuance of the struggle:

We are in danger of losing God's grace through our own disloyalty. Therefore we must ask our brethren to examine their hearts to see if they are ready for the future struggle.... In recent months we have been waiting for the decisive success of our Church administration and for the official recognition by the State of the Confessing Church. But we have only received one disappointment after another. Many of us are therefore tired and despondent. But we must recognize that it is our faithlessness which has caused us to put our trust in men rather than in God.[44]

Kerrl's response was more efficient and ruthless than Müller's had been. He deprived arrested ministers of their salaries, thus putting their families in difficult circumstances. A blow at Confessing Church attempts to train ministers was struck by the proclamation that state officials would examine all theological candidates. Kerrl also moved to get rid of opposing pastors indirectly by giving a minority of the congregation the right to ask for a new pastor. Karl Barth was dismissed from the Bonn faculty for not signing a loyalty oath to the Nazi government. (The theologian moved to Basel where he conducted seminars for young German theologians and continued his writing against the Nazis.)

By December, the conflict between traditional elites and government was becoming clear. Kerrl demanded an end to the Confessing Church at precisely the moment when the larger Nazi revolution culminated in the totalitarian breakthrough of 1936. Niemöller replied that the group would not disband until the "German Christians" were removed from authority. When Hitler threatened to bring Niemöller before the People's Court, the pastor challenged the Führer's authority over church affairs.[45] Thereupon, the Gestapo seized the funds of the Confessing Church and confined Niemöller to his apartment.

Resistance grew increasingly strident. Anti-Nazi sermons were printed and translated. Classes and church leadership groups discussed the problem of the church and the regime. Admittance was contingent upon the possession of cards signed by the Confessing Church pastors.[46] Niemöller collected large amounts for the resistance and for the aid of arrested pastors and their families. So easy was it to raise money for this cause, that Niemöller once said, "Money lies on the streets."[47] The societal base was holding for the traditional elites. When von Ribbentrop, thinking it would increase his standing with the British, applied to Niemöller for membership in his church for "reasons of state," Niemöller refused.[48] The Dahlem congregation supported its pastor against the Nazi foreign minister.

Conflict between regime and church increased still further when Hitler in 1937 began to draft pastors. Permits for printing religious literature were denied. Young theologians were refused teaching certificates. Confessing Church youth were barred from the universities.[49] Arrests increased so that some five hundred Protestant ministers were incarcerated in that year alone.

The year 1937 was one of pitched battle. The old elites were now in open opposition to the regime. Hitler Youth had to be forcibly restrained from their attempts to disrupt church services. Gestapo orders to cease publication and distribution of newsletters were flouted. When new church elections were planned for July, the Confessing Church termed them a fraud and urged church members to resist the Nazis by not voting.

Sermons became increasingly anti-Nazi. Niemöller preached his last on June 27, 1937, basing it on the account of the persecution of early Christians in Acts 5.[50] On July 1, the World War I hero was arrested and imprisoned. The Nazis planned a secret trial, but that was not to be. The churches announced they would toll the church bells and hold prayer meetings during the proceedings. When the authorities forbade a church meeting in Dahlem, a near riot resulted. The staid congregation took to the streets, astounding the police.[51] From prison, Niemöller proclaimed that the authority of Kerrl and the "German Christians" was illegal.[52]

In October, Niemöller's trial was postponed. But Otto Dibelius, who preached in Dahlem during Niemöller's absence, was arrested and brought to the bar. In court, Dibelius won an astonishing victory over Kerrl and was released. Finally, in February 1938, Niemöller was tried and found guilty only of printing documents against government orders. The pastor was fined two thousand marks and given a seven month sentence which the court found he had already served.[53] Niemöller's case was surely aided by international press coverage and by the large crowds of Germans and foreigners milling around the courthouse.[54] On March 2, 1938, Niemöller emerged from the courthouse to the cheers of the crowd. He was, however, immediately seized by the Gestapo and taken into "protective custody." He spent the war in concentration camps, receiving good treatment.[55]

## V. The Spill-Over into Politics

Of necessity, resistance grew increasingly political and secretive. Bishop Wurm of Württemberg, though threatened and arrested, protected not only the ministers of his synod but also became the champion of other enemies of the state. Protesting the persecution of Jews and euthanasia for the insane, Wurm developed a "natural rights" argument which overturned the Lutheran position of cooperation with authority. The bishop further urged that resistance not be limited to church concerns.[56] Wurm, however, was a small voice among the many pastors and church leaders who turned a deaf ear to the cries of anguish from the ghetto.[57]

If the high point of the ideological clash was in 1936-37, by 1938 the Gestapo and Confessing Church were locked in a struggle to the death. The Nazis' aim was to crush all resistance.[58] The church elites, which had previously been conservative, were now driven into silence or direct opposition. Even in conservative East Prussia, church leaders intervened in and halted Nazi attempts to regiment the peasantry.[59]

"By the middle of the summer of 1938," a Gestapo official noted, "the situation in the churches was characterized by weariness with the struggle, by uncertainty of purpose, and by lack of courage."[60] Yet several of the Confessing Church leaders openly noted the dangers and tragedy of the Austrian *Anschluss* and the possibility of war over Czechoslovakia in 1938. They called for services of prayer for peace in which it was suggested that the policies of Hitler would lead to war and would be God's punishment on his sinful people.[61] The Munich Conference obviated the need for the services, but when the plans fell into Nazi hands, Hitler took them to be final proof of the disloyalty of the Confessing Church.[62]

In 1939, eleven thousand of the eighteen thousand Protestant pastors rejected Nazi attempts to settle the religious conflict. Throughout the war the Confessing Church refused to pray for military victory,[63] and many leftists joined the churches as a symbol of protest.[64] Of the thousands imprisoned, it is estimated some five hundred pastors or Protestant church leaders died in concentration camps. Among those were Ludwig Steil, defender of the Jews, and Karl Stellbrink, critic of the war. Other famous war critics, who survived, were Helmut Thielicke and Hanns Lilje.

Thus the Protestants who remained steadfast in their opposition became political critics and opponents of the regime. More and more, the old elites separated themselves completely from the new. By the war years, the ideologies and symbols controlled by the conflicting groups were contradictory at many points. The old elites who had first tried to accommodate the new within a "conservative-revisionist" theological schema, ultimately found it necessary to reconstitute themselves into a "true religious and Christian" elite.

Seen strategically, a major Nazi error with regard to the church was the positing of new ideology and new symbols. Eventually, this left the traditional field to the Evangelicals. The war having drained off much Nazi energy, the Confessing Church controlled traditional methods, symbols, and skills. Insofar as the resistance was successful, the Confessing Church evidenced elite solidarity, cohesion, and professionalism. It had a ready-made organization, educated and influential leaders, meeting places, and other communications channels. Most importantly, the traditional elites had great popular legitimacy based on extremely significant symbols and widely accepted and deeply felt ideology.

The historic unity of religious and political elites in German society increased the relevance of religious elements once church leaders entered the political sphere. Many political opposition groups were strongly oriented toward religion, as the Nazis themselves realized.[65] Not only were old group and family ties important. The Protestant resisters provided the moral undergirding and conviction which became the political philosophy for active resistance to Hitler. Protestant leaders also played key personal roles.

An important figure was Bishop Otto Dibelius of Prussia. An early opponent of Nazi power, he resisted attempts to force his resignation from church councils. More decisively, his justification for political resistance was important in church and army:

The struggle will never come to an end until the State has realized its limits. . . . The moment the State wishes to be the Church, and have power over the souls of men and over the preaching of the Church, we are, in accordance with Luther's words, bound to offer resistance in God's name; we shall most certainly do so.[66]

Dibelius and Helmut Gollwitzer carried on the critiques of Nazi injustice which Niemöller outlined in his last sermons.[67] Since German political theory was lacking in a theory of "natural rights," the work of the Confessing Church in this regard was particularly valuable.

Christians were the only group which could justify breaking the oath to Hitler and the state. Dibelius's arguments that Christian man must be ultimately responsible to a power higher than the Führer were especially relevant in traditional Prussian officer corps circles.[68] Further, as Protestantism was part of an international movement, many of the contacts with the Allies were made through church leaders. The church was able to lessen the sense of isolation felt by Germans who wished to oppose Hitler.

The Protestant politico-religious opposition was evidenced particularly by three groups in which church leaders played key roles: the Oster cell in the *Abwehr* (counter-intelligence service), the Kreisau circle, and the Beck-Goerdeler group. Membership of all three groups was comprised of precisely the traditional Protestant elites described above: nobility, army, clergy.

The most famous member of the Oster circle was Dietrich Bonhoeffer, whose entire family was also numbered among the resisters. Bonhoeffer, choosing to return to Hitler's Germany from the United States, detailed a sophisticated theory of Christian political resistance.[69] He felt deception was his religious duty; thus he gave the Nazi salute, cheered at Nazi rallies, and avoided giving grounds for arrest. He explained he did not wish to be put aside for a small matter—choosing to save himself for something big.[70] For this reason he was also willing to serve in the armed forces.[71]

Oster himself, son of a pastor and personally very religious, exercised significant control in the counter-intelligence staff through his influence over Admiral Canaris. Oster was able to secure important positions and travel permits for members of the resistance as well as to spare the lives of Jews and even of members of the opposition. Hans von Dohnanyi, Bonhoeffer's brother-in-law, was also a member of the counter-intelligence staff and assisted Oster. Klaus Bonhoeffer, Dietrich's brother, worked for Lufthansa and involved his chief, Otto John, and other businessmen in various plans to resist Hitler. Hans Gisevius, working out of the counter-intelligence, made contact with Allen Dulles in Switzerland and informed him of the resistance movement.

The Oster cell was convinced that if the army was to move against Hitler, there would have to be assurances from the Allies concerning post-Nazi Germany. Dietrich Bonhoeffer was dispatched to Sweden in May 1942 to make contact with the British through Dr. George Bell, bishop of Chichester. At the same time, Hans Schönfeld, a German representative to the World Council of Churches in process of formation (and a later contact of Allen Dulles), went to Sweden to discuss what Gerstenmaier had told him of the work of the Kreisau and Beck circles.[72] This action came to naught when Anthony Eden expressed concern that the pastors were being used by the Nazis. Britain would need evidence of overt resistance, he said, before taking the plotters seriously.[73] Here the matter rested in spite of Bell's entreaties.

When Bonhoeffer was arrested in 1943, the resistance lost both an important leader and contact with England. Bonhoeffer remained influential, however, even from prison as officers and others sought his advice. To one officer who asked about shooting Hitler at a staff meeting, the pastor replied that Hitler must be killed, but the political consequences must also be detailed. He assured the plotter that a Christian was justified in using violence.[74] In April 1945, during the final spasms of Nazism, Bonhoeffer was hanged at Flossenburg Prison in Berlin.

Helmut, Count von Moltke, manager of the family estates in Silesia, created the Kreisau circle with the purpose of planning post-Nazi Germany. Like Bonhoeffer, von Moltke returned from abroad to participate in German national life. Moltke's religion was that intense, mystical Lutheran pietism found among many of the Prussian nobility. At first he opposed all violence, believing the Nazis should be left to run their course to self-destruction. In 1943, however, he agreed that Hitler must be killed but counted it an act of God that he was arrested before the attempt on Hitler's life and thus did not partake in the bloodshed.[75] Two pastors were prominent in the Kreisau circle, Poelchau who was later the chaplain at Tegel prison and carried secret messages for members of the resistance, and Gerstenmaier who became a liaison man for the resistance in general.

Eugen Gerstenmaier was the one member of the Kreisau circle who steadfastly held that force must be used against the regime. Removed from his Berlin church office by the Nazis, Gerstenmaier publicly criticized the regime and argued that no German owed loyalty to a tyrant.[76] He was able to persuade von Stauffenberg to forget his conservative training and officer's oath to join the July 1944 plot.[77] Gerstenmaier also convinced Socialists to cooperate with Goerdeler and worked to bring together older and younger members of the resistance between whom considerable friction existed.[78] Gerstenmaier was the only prominent member of the July 20 plot who escaped execution.[79]

The Beck-Goerdeler group was made up primarily of Protestant officers. Many of these men were nervous from the very beginning about Hitler's leadership and specifically plotted his overthrow at least as early as 1938.[80] Thereafter Beck, a retired general, worked with Goerdeler, former mayor of Leipzig, on the plan that eventually resulted in the July 1944 attempt on the Führer's life. Until von Stauffenberg was drawn into the group, however, the generals lacked the moral conviction to act.[81] Hence the importance of the religious elite, even in the July 1944 plot, was considerable. The Protestant elites provided members for the resistance, but most importantly detailed the theoretical justification and ethical foundation for the political act.

The Protestant opposition was thus of signal importance not only because it opposed the regime and resisted political coordination but because it also provided the foundation and architects for the major political resistance attempts. Repeated and regular Nazi attacks ultimately forced the old elites into open opposition. In this new role, a few churchmen became the ideologists and leaders of the groups bent on toppling Hitler. Equally instructive is the fact that most political resistance figures were from the traditional Protestant-monarchical-military elite.

Social conflict may be understood as revolving about eight "values." The political process is central in determining how these are allocated.[82] In summary one can compare the relative success which the Nazi religionists and their Protestant resisters achieved in the competition over power, wealth, respect, skill, enlightenment, rectitude, well-being, and affection. More specifically, a religious elite through its skill, enlightenment, and power should be able to bestow some form of wealth and well-being, share rectitude with its supporters, and gain for itself respect and affection.

The Nazis possessed a monopoly on national physical power. But they failed in the attempt to translate this into dominant religious strength. Unable to contest traditional enlightenment, the Nazis proposed a new "Gnosis," but their tenure was too short-lived for it to take firm rootage. For a time, the regime could bestow a form of wealth and well-being and could withhold them causing severe deprivations. The troublesome thing was that Christianity proposed radically alternative definitions and referents for these symbols. This fact, plus the war, undercut mundane Nazi promises and left the older elites with some social control.

The church conflict revolved about elite skill, perceived rectitude, and attributed respect and affection. The success of the opposition lay in its ability to maintain itself with regard to these in spite of state harassment. The successful establishment of a counter-organization, the Confessing Church, and the continued communication and professional ties between churchmen are evidence of their skill and of the support they received.

Because the social role of religion is built about rectitude, this was a central pillar of the Protestant resistance. The regime might be powerful, its ecclesiastical arms far more formidable than the Confessing Church, and, had it been given a generation or two, morals might have been reversed. But the Nazis could not so swiftly overturn four centuries of German Protestantism.

At least where religious men were concerned, rectitude remained the province of the traditional elite and, with it, spiritual well-being, transcendent wealth, and non-temporal power. Army officers of conscience thus turned to churchmen for guidance. Marxists sought the fellowship of Christians.

The Protestant elites survived National Socialism and constituted its only domestic opposition because of their historic power and their elite skills. They are remembered for their success. They are honored because they represented one of the few vestiges of moral courage in Nazi Germany.

147

# 9

# Hitler's Challenge to the Churches: A Theological Political Analysis of *Mein Kampf*

Michael D. Ryan

## I. Introductory Remarks

Few ventures in life are more precarious than the interpretation of recent history, especially when eyewitnesses are present to detect undue bias and ignorance of the facts. I hasten to add that a sortie into history is doubly precarious when the interpreter is a theologian, for theologians are notorious for the relative ease with which they turn the turbid facts and events of human life into the eternal verities of Sin and Grace, or, if they happen to be Lutheran as I am, into Law and Gospel.

But let us not have it the easy way. Let us not simply assume that the Christian faith, of which we speak, is the gift of God, is true faith as opposed to all that the world may offer for our believing, hoping, and caring. Let us agree for the sake of dialogue that in history we must acknowledge every witness and every commitment to some particular community's ultimate truth as constituting a faith. If we do not do this, then we cannot speak seriously of a contest of faiths. The churches in our narrative would simply embody the true and the good, and Nazism simply the evil and the false, in which case we might as well hold a worship service praising God for having granted us the possession of truth and then be dismissed.

But this is not to say that we are not interested in truth. It is just that our judgment of the true and the false will be within the limits of history with the result that the true will be humanly true and the false humanly false. In this frame of reference our enemies must always remain men actualizing their own potentialities. They cannot be written off as demons displaying satanic forces. But again this does not preclude the possibility of being shocked at the disclosure of what men can do and be. In Dietrich Bonhoeffer's terms this revulsion before the human can be an experience in the presence of both the tyrannical despisers of men and the *despisers* of the tyrannical despisers of men.

Two further words of caution are in order as we approach the subject of the Church Struggle under Hitler. Our purpose cannot be to rehearse once more the indictment of history against the German people or against the German churches. There is nothing that we can say about it here that has not already been said by Germans themselves. For years after World War II leading German scholars laid bare their guilt in acts of self-recrimination far more penetrating than the accusations of outsiders.

Our ultimate purpose is to answer the question, What can America learn? And it is precisely in this task that we must exercise special care. Let us seek whatever lessons we can for America and, as we discuss, let us draw our historical analogies between Germany and America with as much skill and finesse as we can muster. Some people might argue that no analogies between Nazi Germany and America are possible; that post-World War I Germany as a central state in Europe with strong neighbors and a relatively homogeneous population bears no resemblance to America during the same period, much less to America today. I could not share this view. We must draw historical analogies if only because of two very significant constant factors—anticommunism and racism. Both were, and have been, strong tendencies in Nazi Germany and America. Our task will be to specify the respective contexts for these forces so that the differences as well as the likenesses between the two situations can be appreciated. I do not think that this can be done definitively, given the complexity of the task, but it is one which under the pressure of our present history simply cannot be avoided. Our great opportunity at this conference is that scholars representing both situations are here to cooperate in the venture. What follows now I offer as an attempt of an American to understand the faith of Adolf Hitler and his persecution of the churches.

## II. "Ach, die goldene Stimme!"

When you stop to think about it, it was one of the strangest, certainly among the least expected, alliances in history that stopped the Nazi war machine and rolled into Germany to meet at the Elbe River in April 1945. Who would have been more surprised than Alexis de Tocqueville could he have learned that the two giant nations whose character and destiny he predicted with such amazing accuracy would first be joined in a military alliance before falling into the separate spheres of influence that he foretold? Russian Communism, dedicated to the radical overthrow of capitalism, employed weapons supplied by that very system to defeat Hitler's armies in the East and to conquer Berlin! What an absurd idea! It is a truth stranger than fiction, yet it happened. Why?

Sometime during the winter of 1958 I was settling down in my seat in a motion picture theater in Tübingen, Germany. The film was *Der Arzt von Stalingrad* [The physician of Stalingrad], the story of a German military doctor and his fellow prisoners who surrendered to the Russians at Stalingrad. On the screen scenes of the battle flashed while a narrator described the situation. Twenty-two German divisions had been encircled by the Russians. The Führer had ordered them to hold their ground, to make no effort to break out. One German division after another, sent from outside the iron ring, piled up on the preceding one and collapsed in the effort to rescue the trapped army. From November 25, 1942 to January 31, 1943 the battle raged. Bitterly, the narrator commented on the unquestioning obedience of the officers and men who gave themselves as grist for the Russian mill.

Suddenly, a broad mellow voice could be heard above the din from the screen, starting slowly and rising to high speed harshness— Hitler instructing the German people on the meaning of total war. Behind me someone said in tones dripping with irony and loud enough for most to hear, "Ach, die goldene Stimme!"

There at Stalingrad the tide of battle turned and the Communist armies began their slow and bloody journey to Berlin. Hitler had won the battle with Marxism in the beer halls and the streets of Munich in 1920 only to lose the war with Marxism at Stalingrad. These dates— 1920, 1933, 1943—and the events that they represent constitute the anatomy of the Nazi phenomenon. The underlying unity behind them, and what, I believe, accounts for the strange alliance of capitalism and communism was the power of that golden voice and the world view that it proclaimed as the fighting faith of the German people.

### III. The Fighting Faith of Adolf Hitler

What I am about to say may seem like an attempt to revive that well-worn idea of the "Great Man" view of history, only with a completely negative connotation for the word *great*. The question of the causes of the National Socialist revolution has elicited a multitude of answers both within and without Germany. The conflict of scholarly opinion has been very well documented by John L. Snell in a volume that he edited and entitled, *The Nazi Revolution: Germany's Guilt or Germany's Fate?*[1] Here is a brief sketch of the range of the answers:

The guilt of General Kurt von Schleicher and the military clique around him (Gordon A. Craig, pp. 67-72)

The social impact of militarism (J. J. Schokking, p. 58)

The sick psyche of Germany, 1918-1933 (Zevedei Barbu, pp. 85-89)

The result of a popular movement for mass democracy (Gerhard Ritter, pp. 76-84)

The idea of a synthesis of nationalism and socialism emerging at a time when nationalism was in its most degenerate state (Friedrich Meinecke, pp. 46-50)

The result of the crisis of German capitalism (Franz Neuman, pp. 35-38)

The product of European power politics (Ludwig Dehio, pp. 9-12)

The impact of Hitler's own person (Alan Bullock, pp. 1-8)

Other scholars in separate works have traced the roots of the so-called Nazi mind deep into German history, but with special emphasis on the nineteenth century. Most notable are those by Peter Viereck,[2] George Mosse, and Hans Kohn. Kohn's book, *The Mind of Germany: The Education of a Nation*, is remarkable for its brilliant style, its erudition, and its rather glaring bias. The reader is informed that "the leading German scholars at the turn of the century made little effort to understand western thought"[3] (meaning the turn to the twentieth century). But this statement was plausible only because any serious discussion of the impact of Friedrich Schleiermacher and those thinkers after him who represented both a profound interest in Western thought as well as continuity with Kant and the eighteenth century was omitted. This would have included Albrecht Ritschl and his school in theology, the philosopher Wilhelm Dilthey, and the historical theologians Ernst Troeltsch and Adolf Harnack. The threads of continuity between the National Socialist propaganda and the thought of nineteenth-century Germany rather quickly fray and break when one gets beyond outright Antisemitism and Pan-Germanism. While all of the interpretations of the causes and the historical roots of Nazism have some basis in the total context of the political, social, and economic factors within which Hitler rose to power, those that fail to give the decisive role to Hitler himself do not have eyes for that which was new and entirely unprecedented—his role in creating a political faith which in the final analysis must be examined theologically in order to be understood.

### The Logic of Mein Kampf *Is Theological*

In one of his infrequent references to *Mein Kampf* J. S. Conway suggests that there was very little connection between the actual campaign carried out by the Nazi propagandists and what he refers to as the "rambling prognostications of *Mein Kampf.*"[4] Of course, no particular propaganda program was prescribed by Hitler, but the logic that lay behind the Nazi persecution of the churches was as clearly expressed in *Mein Kampf* as was that for the persecution of the Jews. It accounts for not only the underlying relationship between these persecutions but also why some version of modified or German Christianity was in the last analysis totally unacceptable.

The basic logic of *Mein Kampf* is one that, when reduced to a brief formulation, horrifies the beholder. Then it fascinates him with the question of how such a logic could have captured the minds of so many people and left most of Europe in shambles before it had run its course. It can be reduced to the following propositions:

1. In his *Kampf*, his struggle, Adolf Hitler learned the basic laws of life to which a people must adhere if they are not only to survive but also to be a truly great people in history.

2. In the course of his struggle through the dregs of society in Vienna he learned the right political implications of these basic laws

of life while at the same time discerning a fundamental sickness at the heart of European, but especially Austrian and German, society.

3. These political lessons enabled him to discern with clarity the true fundamental causes for the capitulation of Kaiser Wilhelm's regime. It rotted from within.

4. By displaying in his work this basic insight into reality and into the real causes for Germany's collapse, Hitler commended himself as the physician qualified to correct the ills he had discerned and to formulate a political doctrine that would unite the German people on a genuinely national basis, and unleash their true creativity to deal with all their social and political problems in a manner that would allow them to rise to a heretofore unknown level of greatness.

5. Thus, properly understood, Hitler's personal struggle was really Germany's struggle for recovery, and so he was worthy to be the leader because he fought not for himself but for the whole people.

In propositions 1 through 3 the basic reference is to the *Weltanschauung*, the world view based on reality because it was learned from experience. Propositions 4 and 5 refer to the charismatic leader, the one blessed with insight and the *talent* to formulate the world view into a viable political faith and to create by his ingenious propagation of it a fighting movement among the German people. There was thus a logical circle between Hitler's world view and his own claim to charismatic leadership. The world view authenticated his leadership because only that leader would survive the struggle for power in the party who was most gifted in political acumen and who could create a broad following with his voice. The charismatic leadership validated the world view by political success, that is, by transforming it into effective institutional realization through the political power achieved. Thus was forged the strange, mystical relationship between the leader and the people, the true national community (*Volksgemeinschaft*), first in Hitler's mind, and then in the minds of the masses when Hitler's propaganda efforts took hold.

The first volume of *Mein Kampf*, entitled "An Accounting," presented the story of his struggle and how he came to his world view. In Hitler's political faith this account constituted the *fides quae* or the content of the faith. Volume 2 on the "National Socialist

153

Movement" spells out the relationship between the world view and the movement. It was the *fides qua* or the faith by which the movement believed what it believed. Let us now consider these in turn.

### *The* Fides Quae *of Hitler: The World View Derived from Experience*

By his own standard of validity, namely, that of visible success (p. 571),[5] Hitler's world view was true because he was able to create a mass movement by means of it. This cannot be lightly dismissed, if for no other reason than because it brought so many people to accept the principle of total war. Surely it had some contact with reality, it must have been in some respect matched with reality (*wirklichkeitsgemäss*), or it would have lacked all power to persuade. That basis was nature, posited by Hitler as ultimate reality.

For him the basic law of nature is eternal struggle. It is ultimate wisdom to know that nature remains mistress of all things, especially of men and nations. Not to realize this meant according to Hitler to suffer delusion like those poor half-educated souls who believe that man is the master of nature (p. 267). Because no special laws govern men, their highest realization and achievement must come about according to the law of eternal struggle: "In eternal struggle mankind has become great—in eternal peace it would perish" (p. 149).

It is interesting to note that Hitler made a distinction between an ideology and a world view (p. 316). Each is in its own way idealistic and dogmatic. But ideologies, like pacificism, are born of man's attempt to be detached from nature. They start from abstract thought and so they create artificial boundaries unknown to nature and end up distorting reality. A genuine world view, on the other hand, derives its ideas from nature and so gives free play to the forces of life. Should it come to a struggle between a world view and an ideology, there was no doubt in Hitler's mind as to which would prevail. Ideologies move intellectuals, but world views move the masses.

From this basic view of nature as eternal struggle Hitler took two laws that governed his political faith from beginning to end—the law of heredity and the law of self-preservation. In his view nature operates with "all means" (p. 311) to prevent the mixing of the separate species in reproduction and to preserve the strongest while eliminating the weakest. She is utterly ruthless in following the shortest, most efficient route to select the strongest for survival (p. 313). Walther Hofer aptly described Hitler's ideas as an "application of vulgar-Darwinian thought" in which "the life of men and nations becomes an unending mortal struggle."[6] Brutality, aggression, the idea of using "all means" with a maximum of force were for Hitler self-evident principles that should be applied directly to all human institutions and especially to politics (p. 268).

The concrete picture of historical reality that Hitler filled into the forms furnished by these basic laws of nature is well known. His world view was precisely his uncritical impressions of life and reality formed in the course of the years he spent in Vienna from 1907 to 1913, when he was sixteen to twenty-three years of age. No better illustration has been furnished by history for Ortega y Gasset's mass man.[7] Hitler assumed that his impressions of life were wholly true and ultimately valid. The result was that when he thought that he had discovered a great sickness in society, namely, the presence of Jews, he fell into the greatest illness of his society, Antisemitism. He wrote of his adoption of Antisemitism in terms that suggest a conversion experience (pp. 59-63). But the great insight came when he "learned" that social democracy and its press were really Jewish enterprises (p. 54), that Marxism was a Jewish idea (p. 67), and that parliamentary democracy was a Jewish device (p. 98). All of the enemies of Pan-Germanism were basically one enemy—the Jew.

Here the reader of *Mein Kampf* is confronted with the basic anomaly of Hitler's personal convictions. Alan Bullock put it this way: "The baffling problem about this strange figure is to determine the degree to which he was swept along by a genuine belief in his own inspiration and the degree to which he deliberately exploited the irrational side of human nature, both in himself and others, with a shrewd calculation."[8] On the one hand, Hitler presented as a matter of genuine, even painstaking discovery that Jews were the single great enemy in European society. The following statement is typical of his thinking both for his speeches throughout his career as well as for *Mein Kampf:*

The Jewish doctrine of Marxism rejects the aristocratic principle in nature; instead of the eternal pre-eminence of force and strength, it places the mass of numbers and their dead weight. Thus it denies in man the value of the person, disputes the significance of nationality and race and thereby deprives mankind of the presupposition for its subsistence and culture. It would, were it the basis of the universe, finally result in the end of every order conceivable to man.

If the Jew by the aid of his Marxist confession of faith conquers the peoples of this world, then his crown shall be the funeral wreath of humanity, and once again this planet will move through the ether without men as it did millions of years ago. [P. 691]

Here the Jew is characterized as the enemy of life itself. But, on the other hand, Hitler could go on to write in the same volume:

But really the art of all truly great national leaders in all ages consists primarily in this, not to scatter the attention of the people, but rather always to concentrate on a single enemy. It belongs to the genius of a great leader to make quite different enemies appear to belong to a single category, because the knowledge of many enemies all too easily brings weak and unsure characters to begin doubting the rightness of their own cause. [P. 129]

Alan Bullock found little reason to question the basic sincerity of Hitler's Antisemitism, and, as is typical of many scholars writing on the subject, he described it in terms of the Jew as the universal scapegoat.[9] Hannah Arendt more profoundly plumbed the phenomenon of Nazi Antisemitism when she described it as an expression of the identity crisis of the atomized masses. In her words:

This gave the masses of atomized, undefinable, unstable and futile individuals a means of self-definition and identification which not only restored some of the self-respect they had formerly derived from their function in society, but also created a kind of spurious stability which made them better candidates for an organization.[10]

Leon Poliakov, a noted authority on Antisemitism who wrote a number of books on Jews under the Nazis in several countries of Europe, came closer to the significance it had for Hitler as a political principle when he described it as the doctrine of a single enemy, which he then explained in these terms:

According to this doctrine, then, the support of the masses could be gained only by confronting them with a single enemy, who on the one hand is absolutely bad and hateful, but on the other hand is tangible and accessible.[11]

But none of these scholars focused precisely on the anomaly before us: Hitler's description of the Jews as the unnatural destroyers of human order offered, as his own genuine discovery, side by side with his doctrine of one enemy, a calculated measure to maintain control over the masses. How far did Hitler's Antisemitism go? In view of the

Holocaust this question is utterly absurd, for it is self-evident how far it went. But I mean, did he really believe that the Jews were involved in a conspiracy that had even the remotest possibility of conquering the world? When we consider his own aspiration to be the great Führer and when we consider that he himself claimed that "it belongs to the genius of a great leader to make quite different enemies appear to belong to a single category," then we have reason to think that he himself made distinctions between enemies that he would not allow for his followers. Certainly this would account for his well-known ambivalence with regard to England.

But more importantly, it shows that Hitler was at least as aware of the dynamics of prejudice as, say, Gordon Allport, who wrote: "Whether successful or not, the demagogue is at bottom advocating a totalitarian revolution following the pattern of fascism."[12] In Hitler the world had to do with a totalitarian revolutionary who uncannily knew enough about the dynamics of prejudice to employ them in his self-conscious effort to establish total control over society. When you stop to think about it, it was truly an ingenious doctrine. If a man believes that he has many enemies, he will be forced to develop an economy of hatreds, to make discriminate judgments about who is most and who least dangerous. But if he hates all enemies with the full fury that he feels for his worst enemy, and if he places that fury at the disposal of the state, then he is, to say the least, a highly motivated citizen.

Considered from the standpoint of calculation, Antisemitism was the most predictable, most virulent hatred running through society. By feeding that hatred, whipping it into white heat, Hitler had, as it were, a supply of energy-hate that could be turned against anyone who stood in his way. It could be turned against Gentiles, for Gentiles could be turned into Jews simply by the Führer's imprecation. There were, as the totalitarian mind inevitably says in some form, "the Jewish things to do" and "the Jewish things to say," just as today in America we hear about the "white" and "black" things to do and say. Interestingly, in Hitler's world view black people were placed in the same category with Jews as degenerates. In 1928 he complained, "Racial degeneration continues apace. The bastardization of great states has begun. The Negroization of culture, of customs—not only of blood—strides forward."[13]

On the basis of the doctrine of one enemy as applied by a state committed in principle to "all means," no one in Germany and no one in the world could in principle be excluded as a potential target of that hatred. In Hitler's totalitarian society every individual who for any reason acted against the interest of the people as defined by the Führer became in that moment a Jew. For this reason no one was more Jewish in Germany than Dietrich Bonhoeffer and his comrades in the German resistance.

Richard Rubenstein was quite correct, I believe, when in his essay, "Religion and the Origins of the Death Camps," he characterized Nazism as a religious rebellion against a Christianity whose history had furnished the raw material for its own hate and prejudice.[14] But when he discussed the *origins* of the death camps themselves, he overlooked, I believe, the contribution made by Hitler himself in refining that raw material and turning it into the most effective psychological mass terror ever known. The death camps were not the logical conclusion of religious Antisemitism, for which Hitler held the Christian Socialist Party of Austria in utter contempt (p. 130 f.), but rather they were the product of Hitler's own secularized, National Socialist Antisemitism, of which he was only too proud. For Nazism the death camps were another application of the doctrine of all means to establish totalitarian terror as it spread throughout the Third Reich. Hitler's world view and his interpretation of the laws of nature constituted the origin of those camps and nothing else!

But this is not to disagree with Richard Rubenstein's basic assertion that National Socialism was itself a religion. It is precisely because it was a self-consciously intolerant faith that no syncretism, no mixture, no hybrid religion of "German Christians" could be made official; but J. S. Conway has documented that story. Hitler's discussion of the causes of the collapse of Kaiser Wilhelm's regime reveals most clearly the religious character of his world view. It amounts to nothing less than a total explanation not only for the loss of the war but for every evil that he could identify in German society. Again, there is reason to think that this was deliberately attempted for the sake of its propaganda value.[15] Hitler wrote: "The inquiry into the causes of the German collapse is therefore of decisive significance, especially for a political movement whose goal is to be the overcoming of the defeated" (p. 247). At the outset of his discussion of the causes of the collapse, Hitler introduces the idea of a fall, suggesting the protology of the myth of the races which comes in the following chapter. "The depth of the fall of any body is always measured by the distance from its momentary location to the one it had originally. The same applies to the fall of nations and states" (p. 245). After rehearsing many different signs of decay—cowardice in the ranks, complaints from the home front to soldiers in the field, incompetent leadership, and outright treason, which is the only interpretation that Hitler would allow for the general strike of 1918 and the November Revolution—Hitler turned to the deeper underlying cause. He described Germany as suffering from a spiritual and physical disease, the toleration of which had criminal implications. The whole body politic of Germany stank with rottenness, cowardice, and half-heartedness (*Faulnis, Feigheit,* und *Halbheit* [p. 250]). The people had forsaken their national ideals and had come to worship money after the manner of the corrupt leaders of international finance capital—the Jews (p. 255). These Jews were in a secret conspiracy with their apparent opponents, the Marxists, also Jews, to undermine all national loyalty and health. Everywhere these men were in evidence. They were responsible for prostitution and the spread of syphilis, of which he wrote: "The sin against blood and race is the original sin of this world and the end of that humanity that gives itself over to it" (p. 272). But for Hitler "all of these signs of decay were in the last analysis the result of the lack of a definite, generally acknowledged, world view" (p. 292), which also accounted for the lack of judgment and resolution on the part of the leaders. Germany really suffered from lack of leadership in its hour of trial. But how did that come about? Germany had fallen into a general condition of moral and physical weakness because, Hitler informs his reader, it had failed to recognize "the race problem and its significance for the historical development of nations" (p. 310).

It was in this context that Hitler presented his own world view as that which was needed for Germany to recover, and thereby commended himself as the right kind of leader. At the same time he accounted for the generally bad condition of German leadership. He did it with the myth about the Aryans, the great culture founders of history, and their life with the culture bearers, the lesser races of men who were conquered by the noble, blond Aryans. Under the leadership of the more intellectual Aryans great cultures were formed lasting for centuries. In the beginning stages the Aryans married only with their own kind and in this period the cultures flourished. But in the latter stages the conquerors violated their own principle of purity of blood and they began to intermarry with the lesser bearers of culture, which resulted in a corresponding decay in the health of the culture (p. 319) as the impure, mixed blood spread its weakness and cowardice and half-heartedness. Hitler actually offered this as the reason why Germany lost World War I. He called it "blood poisoning." This was also the great insight that he had to offer for the proper basis for Germany's recovery. If the cause of all Germany's ills is this impure blood in the veins of the people, then the only thing to do is to have a state in charge of a leader with this "great insight" into reality who will see to the establishment of a national program of biological regeneration, breeding out the bad blood and breeding in the good blood. Had it not been actually attempted, one could simply be amused instead of being horrified.

This then was Hitler's *Heilsgeschichte* (holy history). Its protology was the myth of the Aryan race and their rise in history through the great cultures of the past and their fall by intermarriage with the lesser races. The present age of wrong was understood as alienation from one's own racial heritage. Salvation was to be the recovery of that heritage through the national program of biological regeneration. This would result in the new age of the master race, the race of men and women who would create a new culture for the future—one that would last a thousand years. Such was Hitler's eschatology.

What is striking here is that this *Heilsgeschichte* from beginning to end operates within the limits of time, even if quite mistakenly with regard to the so-called Aryans. It amounted to a resignation to the conditions of finitude, while at the same time asserting total power for itself within those conditions. This is what makes the logic of *Mein Kampf* theological. By asserting total control within the limits of finitude, Hitler deified himself and made himself into the savior of the German people. It was in this respect that he thought of himself as the child of providence. It may come as a surprise to many that Hitler could have written: "Even we are not so simple-minded as to believe that an infallible age could ever be achieved. This does not release us from the responsibility of fighting known error, of overcoming weakness, and striving to attain the ideal" (p. 487). I am not suggesting that Hitler ever had the slightest inclination to self-criticism, but rather that his world view amounted to the deliberate decision on the part of mass man to live within the limits of finitude without either the moral restraints or the hopes of traditional religion—in this case, Christianity. That is the final implication of the content of the *fides quae* of Hitler. The challenge to Christian faith could not have been more direct.

## The Fides Quae *of Hitler; or the Faith Formulated by the Charismatic Leader*

Hitler's faith was a nature religion because its content was drawn from nature as interpreted by Hitler. But it was a religion because when he set out to express his world view as to its character and place in human subjectivity, he drew all of his analogies from religion—to repeat, religion—as he understood it.

For Hitler a world view takes shape in that place in human subjectivity above political compromises where awareness of human needs and weaknesses and the consciousness of human possibilities and strengths intersect. That was one reason why, I believe, it appealed to the philosopher Martin Heidegger. As Hitler put it, "Political parties are inclined to compromise, world views never. Political parties reckon with opponents, world views proclaim their infallibility" (p. 507). It is clear from this statement that the very idea of the National Socialist party was only a temporary expediency, as indeed it turned out to be. The sad history of 1933, in which all other political parties were effectively eliminated while the governments of the several states were successfully coordinated, is evidence again of Hitler's fundamental consistency with the ideas expressed in *Mein Kampf*. National Socialism was a world view which was intolerant by definition.

Far from being embarrassed by this state of affairs, Hitler justified it by drawing lessons from the history of Marxism as a fighting world view and from the history of Christianity. Marxism had to criticize existing conditions for some seventy years in order to prepare the way for its revolution and its own task of construction (p. 505). World views cannot be content with being one party beside others, Hitler argued, any more than Christianity in history was content just to build its own altars. It also proceeded to destroy the heathen altars (p. 506). Such intolerance is necessary for the "formation of an apodictic creed":

It may pain the individual today to state that with the appearance of Christianity the first spiritual terror entered into the much freer ancient world. Nevertheless he cannot deny the fact that the world has been oppressed and dominated by this compulsion since then, and that force can only be broken with force, and terror only with terror. [P. 507]

This statement not only draws its justification for terror from church history but also implicitly suggests that Christianity can expect no better for itself than that which it meted out to others. If that were not indication enough of Hitler's basic antagonism toward the churches, the context contains the explicit call for adherents of the world view consistently to undermine all that tends to contribute to "an existing condition" (p. 505), as he put it. One shudders to think how much the history of the Church Struggle from 1933-45 bears witness to Hitler's success in undermining the churches and their influence on their own people.

As for the propagation of the world view itself, Hitler was not ashamed to draw freely on the idea of religious dogma—again, as *he* understood it. For example, the concept of *völkisch* is patently vague and subject to many different interpretations, as are the religious ideas of the "indestructibility of the soul, of eternity and its existence, the existence of a higher being, etc." (p. 417). But when they become formulated as part of a creed with apodictic force, which for Hitler meant when the highest ideals of a man are acknowledged and bound to the deepest needs of his earthly life, then there is no disputing about, or questioning of them (p. 416). So, too, must the ideas of a world view be accepted by the followers: "From general conceptions a political program must be formed, and from a general world view a definite political faith" (p. 418). And this can happen, Hitler taught his readers, only when "one man" steps forward out of the masses, formulates "granite principles," and proceeds to fight for their sole authority in the land (p. 419). Here Hitler could scarcely have avoided thinking of himself as the founder of a political faith with a total claim on all German society. Here a whole new dimension is added to the claims for the world view. Whereas one could say that it is *wirklichkeitsgemäss* because it is based on nature, now one can say that through the effectiveness of the charismatic leader and the fighting organization of obedient followers, the world view becomes a *wirklichkeitschaffende* force, a power to create a new reality.

Here again the logic is theological and at this point soteriological, as Hitler laid claim to the role of savior of the German people. Again, it is difficult to conceive of a more direct challenge to Christian faith.

### IV. What Can We Learn from the Impact on History of Hitler's Faith?

I should like briefly to suggest some lessons that I think are important for American churches and for theologians in particular.

Call it idolatry, call it utter perversion, National Socialism is a powerful reminder of the strength of an aroused mass movement. We must, I think, face up to the weakness of the churches if ever, in some situation of extreme national crisis, "the American Way of Life," as Professor Will Herberg called it, should be utilized by an effective demagogue and turned against the churches. Frankly, I do not expect that it will happen, but I would be foolish to say that it could never happen here, especially since the discrepancy has been so well documented between what most Americans believe is the American Way of Life and what the churches proclaim it to be.[16] Demagogues we have had and do have as well as underground fascist movements. But the state of America's mass faith is at present relatively benign, though there are some signs of restiveness.

One thing is fairly certain. A revolution from the left in this country would never receive mass support, any more than it did in Germany. The women's liberation movement has more chance of success than the extreme political left. But it is conceivable that nihilist revolutionary types could incite illegal repressive measures on the part of the so-called Radical Right by acts of violence. This is precisely what some would like. For this reason I believe that theologians and pastors should be very circumspect in their preaching and teaching, especially about the so-called theology of revolution. I know of nothing that could do more to deepen the alienation between the churches and the masses than that. This is not to suggest capitulation to the masses in their desire either for a comfortable status quo or for a faith that they do not have to think about.

If there is one lesson for theologians and pastors to learn from the Nazi experience, it is, I believe, that the idea of an invulnerable area for theology, which became current with the publication of Martin Kähler's *The So-Called Historical Jesus and the Historic Biblical Christ* in the 1890s, has in the light of the Nazi persecution of the churches to be laid to rest.[17] None were untouched by guilt, even in their theologizing during that period. Kähler's attempt to separate theology from historical inquiry by the device of distinguishing between *Geschichte*, as the realm of historical significance and effectiveness, and *Historie*, as that which is subject to historical investigation, has been rendered most dubious. The history of National Socialism shows that something may be highly significant in history, may have an enormous impact, and yet be poles away from truth.

Further, the history of this period and the response of the churches under Hitler indicate, I think, that we in America should seriously consider resources other than preaching for combating mass faiths. The relatively recent tradition of *kerygmatic* theology has easily justified its lack of impact upon the churches on the basis that only God can communicate God's Word. I am prepared to concede that as a theologian I must be open to the church's witness to the presence of God in Jesus Christ, but I do not believe that the sermon is the only or even the primary witness to the self-communicating activity of God for our time. Let us look again to the tradition of *didache* in church history and develop a dialogical theology of teaching as a necessary complement to preaching. And as we do so, let us look to the relationship between church and university. Recent history forces me to ask the question: Can the churches be free if there is no freedom in the state and no freedom in the universities? Can we separate the question of faith from the question of truth?

Last and most important, because of the Holocaust and because we have been challenged in all seriousness by the example of a man like Richard Rubenstein in his work *After Auschwitz*, I believe that theologians of the church should come down out of the Barthian "above" in theology and pursue with historians all along the way the truth question in regard to the whole history of the church, but especially the historical Jesus and the relationship of a chastened Christianity to Judaism. This is to say that we theologians should stop speaking "as though" we had a special noetic access to the history of Jesus and the primitive church not available to the working historian as historian. Let us talk about faith within the limits that make faith intelligible as faith, namely, the limited perspectives entailed by the fact of our finitude, of our acknowledged creaturehood before God.

# III
# Theological Implications

# 10

# Troubled Self-Interpretation and Uncertain Reception in the Church Struggle

Eberhard Bethge

In May 1967 Karl Barth, the patriarch of Basle, wrote to me thus:

It was new to me that Bonhoeffer [as I read in your biography of him] in 1933 viewed the Jewish problem as the first and the decisive question, even as the only one, and took it in hand so energetically. I myself have long felt guilty that I did not make this problem central, at least public, in the two Barmen declarations of 1934 which I had composed. In 1934, certainly, a text in which I said a word to that effect would not have found agreement either in the Reformed synod of January 1934 or in the General synod of May at Barmen—if one considers the state of mind of the confessors of faith in those days. But that I was caught up in my own affairs somewhere else is no excuse for my not having properly fought for this cause.

In 1918 political action was my theme too (as can now be seen in Bonhoeffer's path from faith to action), after I had left theological liberalism behind me; and it took the shape of Swiss Religious Socialism. But the theme fell into the background when the *Römerbrief* came, and I went to Germany in 1921. To German audiences and readers I then became less known for Religious Socialism than for my new attempts to reinterpret the Reformation and make it work again. Unfortunately the Germany of 1921, burdened with its problematic Lutheran tradition, suffered precisely because of the lack of what I silently presupposed to exist or because of what I failed to emphasize properly, namely: ethics, common humanity (*Mitmenschlichkeit*), the church serving the under-privileged, the cost of discipleship, socialism, peace movements—and, in all of this, just politics. From the beginning Bonhoeffer apparently felt this lack strongly and the necessity to fill the gap: later he sharpened ethics and in the end brought it into the discussion on a wide scale. Such discussion was and is the long overdue and, I hope, decisive supplement to Christian thinking in Germany, which Bonhoeffer so strongly represented. And so the mystery of the impression

Bonhoeffer represented, of his becoming a martyr just for this reason, is explained.[1]

Whether that gap has been filled is very much to be questioned right now. On the contrary, there are signs that the gap is widening again. At present there are groups of men who try to learn how to explain that theme of ethics and politics, and there are others who resist this emphasis with great effort and many old weapons. The studies of the Church Struggle, of its self-understanding, and of its new reception confront us with new urgency. We should look at the Struggle with great care and try to iron out our differing perspectives.

These are the headings under which I want to look at the German Church Struggle, in a general way, and perhaps speak even more as a partisan than as an objective scholar. The reason for doing this is so that scholars can be given yet another opportunity to look at the objective details.

The periods of German Church Struggle were as follows:
1. 1933-1935: The struggle was understood solely as a Church Struggle, with the opportunity for nonconformism.
2. 1935-1938: The Church Struggle became an unwanted political struggle, pressure being exerted toward disobedience.
3. 1938-1945: The Church Struggle disintegrated as a mismanaged political struggle; the alternatives became secret resistance or truce.
4. After 1945: Reinterpretation followed, half of it directed toward Church Struggle, half toward resistance, accompanied by confusion of interpretation as either a fight for obedience to Christ or a fight for freedom of mankind.

I

No doubt the Protestant opposition, which organized itself slowly in the Confessing Church of the Barmen and Dahlem synods, in the first years called its fight strictly a Church Struggle and nothing else. Certainly it was not conceived as a political struggle; as such it would have been understood as a betrayal, politically wrong and theologically weak, of the church cause. And, we should remember, adherents of the opposition considered the fight the struggle of a *Weltanschauung*, an escape from the real issue; they pointed at people who, stressing their general duty to carry on the *Weltanschauungs* struggle, in the long run evaded every concrete and dangerous church allegiance and thereby avoided the real risks. The combatants of the Confessing Church emphasized their fight for the "pure Word of God," for the confessions of the Reformation, and against the new heresies inside the church which destroyed pure doctrine and the uncorrupted preaching of the gospel. They were therefore anxious at all costs not to appear to be political reactionaries, internationalists, or degenerate Western democrats—as one clearly can see from the first statements in the summer of 1933 of the Young Reformers *(Jungreformatoren)*.

In articles, sermons, or addresses of those first years—and they were meant to be "unpolitical"—one will therefore find expressions like "years of darkness" in reference to the Weimar Republic. You will find the "joyful yes" to the new German antiliberal state in the great appeal of the Young Reformers, and a greeting to the "national rebirth" in Martin Niemöller's new edition in 1934 of his book *From U-Boat to Pulpit (Von U-boot zur Kanzel)*. This is not to say that everyone had become a National Socialist. Yet the attitude was not one of expediency, but—except for a few people like Barth, Dehn, and Bonhoeffer—the Young Reformers wrote with real enthusiasm about Germany's being finished with the Weimar experiment.

Therefore one cannot find any written or published protest by any Confessionalist against the destruction of human and political rights by the German legislation of March 1933:

1. None against the decree of the Reich President "for the protection of Nation and State," limiting the freedom of speech, press, assembly, the secrecy of post and telegraph, the protection of house and property. (This decree, by the way, was used with von Hindenburg's name and authority to dissolve Bonhoeffer's seminary in 1937 and was suspended only on March 8, 1945.)
2. None against the *Heimtücke* legislation, which identified all opposition to the government with hostility to the nation, by which—for instance—links of the Confessing Church to the foreign press became most dangerous.
3. None against the *Ermächtigungs* legislation, the authorization

of the government to free itself from clauses of the constitution and to get rid of parliamentary control.

4. None against the decree "for the restriction of civil service," which banned Jewish Germans from offices, including—for instance—professors of Jewish descent from theological faculties of the state universities.

All this was manipulated in a seemingly democratic and legal way, and we were not prepared to resist. For many reasons this self-castration was greeted with relief by most Protestant Germans: 1) as deliverance from liberal decay, 2) as deliverance from the communistic threat, 3) as a conservative philosophy of legitimacy (Carl Schmitt), 4) as consistent with Lutheran theology emphasizing the "orders of creation" (anti-Western, anti-Calvinist), 5) as a turn against "political Catholicism" (Bonhoeffer was quite an exception, voting in March 1933 for the Center party though a Lutheran pastor), 6) as a result of the shock of the Versailles Treaty and its consequences, and 7) even as evidence of an Antisemitism still alive in the church opposition, although the opposition was soon to be fighting the application of the Aryan paragraph to the church. The spirit was summed up by Gogarten: "When a nation which has gone so far from orderly form must be brought back into form, then it must first be put into a uniform again."[2]

That there was no reaction by the church when the first great wave of emigrants went into exile is therefore understandable. No protest was heard when the liberal and pacifist theologian Fr. Siegmund-Schultze, banned by Hitler himself, had to leave Germany in June 1933. Bishop Heckel later in 1934 used a sharp and effective weapon when he reasoned that the opposition pastors would be reckoned among the Prague Emigrants if they continued their fight against Reichsbishof Müller; by using one of the worst of invectives and the worst of threats he warned that opposition pastors would be labeled as fellow-travelers with left-wing and Jewish politicians who had been exiled in Czechoslovakia.

The church itself in those first years produced no emigrants at all. Paul Tillich and Karl-Ludwig Schmidt left the country as members of left-wing political groups and as university professors, and they did not hope or even count for any support from the churches. With Barth—later—it was a different matter. He counted on the Confessing synods in 1935 and hoped for something to come from the Confessing Church. But this church considered his political case such a burden that they were quite relieved when he did not appear at the Synod of Augsburg (1935). And they did not offer him a post at one of the church seminaries either, but let him return to Switzerland.

In this context of a self-limiting self-interpretation, a closer look into the problem of the ecumenical language—in letters, reports, and statements about the Church Struggle in those days, and in foreign press coverage of it—could throw some light on the very different approaches of the time. We cannot do that now. Sometimes the differences of interpretation inside and outside the Confessing Church seemed nearly insurmountable. The Brethren Councils reacted in a very embarrassed fashion and considered the humanistic or political approach a misrepresentation of their case—or, more than that, an unwanted distortion of it and a danger to their very existence. Even Barth in Basel and Bonhoeffer in London tried very hard to interpret the essence of the fight to their ecumenical friends as a strictly theological case against heresy. They were afraid that the humanistic interpretation would completely weaken the kernel of the opposition and contribute to its collapse. They might have been right. The opposition at Barmen and Dahlem would never have taken so firm a stand on the basis of humanistic and liberal—or even democratic—reasoning. It had no idea of using resistance on such a basis.

But this is only one side of the story, easily enough described with the advantage of hindsight. The actual participants and onlookers saw the other side of the story, which was quite different.

Yes, they understood themselves as fighting a Church Struggle. In this struggle under the attacks of "German Christian" doctrines they experienced an amazing rediscovery of the Reformation Confessions. And in this act of confession an unexpected partnership with the so-called former liberals and orthodox positivists emerged. Under the pressure of the Führer principle in church government and synods they experienced a rediscovery of the unity of spiritual and organizational matters under the Kingship of Christ, and led the opposition church by means of Brethren Councils. And this purely confession- and church-oriented opposition in its totalitarian surroundings became not only a witness for but even an organized stronghold of freedom. It was in fact an island of nonconformism. Parts of the population understood this at once. People who had forgotten that there was such a thing as "pure preaching of the gospel and confession" came to Church. Every Sunday morning liberals, artists, politicians, and others came, and church collections in Dahlem and other places suddenly increased at a previously unknown rate.

This means that present characterizations of the structure and theology of the Confessing Church as antiliberal, introvert, dogmatic, monolithic, authoritarian, and diastic to the world are only partly justified. Such judgments can only be made in situations which are utterly different geographically or historically. It means, also, that the unchanged continuation of Confessing Church doctrine and practice under different historical and geographical circumstances must lead from an essential nonconformism to a poisonous conformism. And this is just the opposite of what the Church Struggle, understood solely as *Church* Struggle, really has been: a room to breathe in or a roof to live under, free in the midst of a system of terror. The exclusive interest in ecclesiology of those days was in fact an act aimed at a relative human freedom.

## II

The basis for this self-understanding of the Confessing Church suffered a decisive shock in 1935 when the Nazi regime changed its policy from indirect influence on or occasional interference in church matters to state legislation which openly and directly interfered with church administration and the freedom to proclaim the gospel.

I do not of course overlook the fact that there had been interference before. One instance was Hitler's decree for church elections in July 1933 and his speech on the eve of that Election Sunday. But throughout the time of Ludwig Müller's and even Kommissar Jäger's administrations the Confessing Church leaders could more or less maintain the interpretation or fiction that the conflict was one inside the church in which they asked for disobedience within the law, and that they were fighting not National Socialism or government authorities, but heretics and church usurpers.

And I do not overlook the fact that long after 1935 some Confessionalists still continued to interpret their actions as a struggle purely of the inner church, claiming sometimes that they understood the men of the Third Reich politics better than they understood themselves—and this because of those leaders' longtime Lutheran education as to the relation of state and church—a view which they could not change overnight.

But there is no doubt that from that point on, a noticeable and deep change took place, which speedily resulted in a remarkable decline of memberships in the Barmen-Dahlem opposition and in deep and fatal cracks inside the general Protestant front itself.

Just when the Confessing Church seemed to have come to a peak of success—1) revealing the obvious fiasco of Ludwig Müller and his practices of "German Christian" church government, 2) building up its own emergency church legislation and organization (Dahlem synod), 3) hoping even to get the much wanted legal acknowledgment by the state authorities for their offices and officers—precisely then came that change in state policy and legislation which finally undermined and crushed their spirit and the organization of ecclesiastical self-determination.

Three decrees, signed by either Göring or Hitler, provided the instruments to turn near victory more and more into defeat and to cause a hopeless splintering of the opposition groups.

1. In March 1936, the harmless looking finance departments were imposed on the church administration for the purpose of controlling all movements of church money.

2. In June 1936, law departments for church cases were established in order to end the independent courts, which usually decided favorably for Confessional officers and their claims.

3. In July 1936, the Ministry for Church Affairs (under Kerrl) was instituted, and subsequently the most powerful decree for the "securing of the German Evangelical Church" was issued, the law which nearly brought the Confessing Church to her destruction by its many individual implementing ordinances.

As a result of this state legislation it became ever more clear that whoever continued to follow the line of the Barmen-Dahlem synods and continued to follow the emergency church government in the form of the Brethren Councils was openly disobeying the decrees and laws of the state. The claim to fight heretics inside the church and their distortion of the image of the church became difficult to maintain. Whenever one disobeyed the state decrees, he continued to emphasize that he wanted to fight politically not state legislation itself but misguided state legislation which had illegally become church legislation. But the enemy to be fought was now revealed to be the state itself. At first nonconformism and, at this juncture, disobedience showed themselves to be two very different steps along the path of resistance.

To carry out this disobedience no one was well prepared. To criticize anti-Christian practices in press and education, in occasional single actions like the *Denkschrift* (memorandum) of 1936 or other proclamations from the pulpit which made headlines abroad was not the same as consistently to disobey valid laws, which, being uninteresting, nobody reported abroad. The usual Lutheran interpretation of Romans 13 had not previously allowed an oppositional consciousness to develop. Reluctance to believe that one was really governed by a criminal government made it difficult for individuals to accept the situation. And the very emphasis up to that time on a merely inner church and not on political resistance now led to embarrassing arguments.

These years were therefore heavily loaded with long, weary discussions in synods and pastors' conferences of what to make of the state measures, of how perhaps to reconcile them to old state-church relationships and patterns. At the same time all kinds of police actions suddenly occurred, and the intercession lists for imprisoned pastors became longer in 1937 than ever before or ever again. Some candidates of the Confessing seminaries, many pastors, and even members of the leading Brethren Councils in different church provinces left the ranks of churchmen.

Small minorities still persisted in open disobedience. Their avowed reason was again the theological commitment to the Barmen and Dahlem declarations. They were now accused by the majority of risking the whole structure of the organized church and carrying on activities which would eventually lead to their being driven from the pulpit and forfeiting the preaching of the gospel every Sunday. The minority in synodal decisions still did not reason with humanitarian or political arguments; they were even less inclined to do so than before. They argued for changes in church politics, but not for another government: to do so would have been considered useless suicide by everyone. So there was unequivocal resistance, but it was resistance lacking any political concept of an alternative Germany; that is, the resistance had no program for political freedom.

Through this kind of resistance, freedom was certainly achieved in those groups, but there was no program. There was little thinking and writing about the ethics of freedom—perhaps this was not possible—and not much elaboration of the relation between faith in Christ and human liberty—which at the present time we painfully try to establish convincingly. Perhaps it was not even necessary at that time. The more dogmatically firm in those days the Christocentrism of the men was, the more self-evident became the awareness of Christ's freedom in and of itself.

Such awareness was a well-documented experience that, today, sometimes makes old men who have survived homesick for golden days of faith and obedience, days of remarkable freedom within that inner circle. But sometimes they forget that under changed circumstances, old stories frequently repeated create not freedom but only boredom—or even indignant rebellion.


## III

The self-interpretation of the Confessing Church in its struggle ran into its deepest crisis with the Crystal Night (*Kristallnacht*) of 1938 and the brutal preparations for and implications of the imminent war. Perhaps the crisis was greatest just before it was realized to be such.

The already difficult step from nonconformism to disobedience toward the government was not followed by the further, definitely harder, step of active political resistance. (Dietrich Bonhoeffer was the exception.) There were some men who just jumped into the third level of resistance without ever having belonged to the groups of the first two levels of resistance; Gerstenmaier—a most disturbing example now, and more so after the war—was such a person.

Up to 1945 there remained a group having its own inner rules and still assembling and speaking in synods, speaking the language of Barmen and Dahlem, risking life and salary, free movement and reputation, the future of and the education of its children—attracting much more attention from the authorities and from ecumenical friends than their number would suggest.

But this courageous group entered deeper and deeper into a kind of schizophrenic double life. They continued to fight and even to suffer imprisonment to carry out their claim that to follow Barmen and Dahlem, they had to teach and ordain candidates independently of the official Nazi governed church. But the candidates who were still loyal to Barmen had nearly all disappeared from sight in the front lines, having perhaps been decorated or become officers in the battles of Dunkirk or Leningrad.

The breach between Karl Barth and the Brethren Councils came into the open when in 1938 he clearly stated his case in political terms. First there were his lectures on the interpretation of the Scottish Confession and his *Rechtfertigung und Recht* [Justification and Law], pointing clearly in the direction of opposition to all Lutheran tradition about the political ministry of the church. This was the kind of theology which a central figure of the Brethren Councils such as Asmussen had for some time opposed. But the alienation came to an open, declared breach when Barth's letter to Hromadka became known. The Brethren Council was forced to separate itself from this hopelessly democratic Swiss. After Crystal Night Barth wrote:

Many of the best men in the Confessing Church still close their eyes to the insight that the Jewish problem and even more the political question, in particular and in general, have today become a question of the faith.[3]

The key events were: 1. the oath of loyalty sworn in 1938 (Anschluss) as a birthday present to the victorious Hitler, not only by "German Christians" and neutrals but also by nearly all Confessing pastors; 2. the case of Barth's letter to Hromadka; 3. the denunciation by the Lutherans of the pastors who—in the manner of so-called high treason—drafted the famous prayer during the Prague crisis; 4. the total silence of the churches after Crystal Night. All of these events excluded the Confessing Church from any relevant deliberations about its attitude to the war, or any commentary about all breaches of faith and breaking of treaties.

At the beginning of the war Barth wrote to the *Manchester Guardian* protesting that the news of Niemöller volunteering for Hitler's army could not be true. But it was true. Of course there were different men with different motives who followed that example of Niemöller. They had at least three reasons: 1) to escape the imminent danger of being killed, which was expected by many inmates of concentration camps; 2) to manage things so that men of integrity could perhaps reach positions of influence—for the sake of a *coup d'état* (members of the organized conspiracy like Bonhoeffer thought so); 3) simply to fight for the fatherland. The last was certainly not out of the question. That many officials of the Confessing Church actually volunteered for the army in 1939/40 was not surprising.

When Bonhoeffer during his cross examinations in the summer of 1943 had to cover up the ongoing conspiracy and also tried to attempt to divert the prosecutor's attention to his loyalty to Hitler's Germany in war, he gave a written description to Dr. Roeder which he could assume would sound convincing because there was some truth in it:

It is very difficult for me to see how the earlier conflicts with the Gestapo, which, as I profoundly believe, emerged from a purely church attitude, led to my being held capable of such a grave offence against the obvious duties of a German towards his people and his country. . . . If people want to know my idea of the Christian's duty of obedience towards authority, they should read my interpretations of Romans 13 in my book, *The Cost of Discipleship*. The call to submit to the will and demands of authority for the sake of Christian conscience has probably seldom been expressed more strongly than there.[4]

As for the strong wish of the Confessing Church to serve the nation in war: the hundreds of young confessing pastors who volunteer information today speak with sufficient clarity, and especially about the high rate of casualties among the men in their ranks. I have never talked to one of them who had not accepted his draft card as an experience of inner liberation from his guilt which arose from his severe embarrassment at being considered politically suspect just because he was a member of the Confessing Church; who had not accepted the draft card as the long-sought opportunity to prove his inner national conviction and to sacrifice himself for the nation as a soldier. They agree that the volunteering of Pastor Niemöller at the beginning of the war had its noticeable effects in the Confessing Church. I am really permitted to tell you this, because I know the young generation of confessing pastors and have had contact with them as only a few other clerics have had.

If there were some men in the Brethren Councils and in the ranks of the young pastors who knew that their reasoning was deceptive, they did not have the instruments, assistants, or doctrines—or the occasions—to express themselves. Karl Barth alone—soon after the war—in his *Christengemeinde und Bürgergemeinde* [Christian community and political community] showed them how a theological doctrine of political resistance and uprising could be thought out and verbalized. The earlier Confessing Church lacked all presuppositions for so acting. The current self-interpretation of the Barmen-Dahlem declarations even worked as a barrier to a change of mind, because the diastic elements in it were more effective than the elements directed toward the world. What shaped the self-understanding and the troubled reactions of those men in this extraordinary period of German history?

In the nineteenth century in Germany there was for a time a parallel cultivation of the two strong European forces: liberalism and nationalism, interest in human rights and interest in national independence with unity. But in Germany nationalism won the field. Since the days of Bismarck, Christians in Germany were fascinated by a strong national foreign policy and therefore by all efforts to strengthen unity. This weakened enthusiasm for inner policy (*Innenpolitik*), for domestic struggles like that of the trade unions, for personal, electoral, and parliamentary rights. The once strong liberalism and its domestic claims were shoved behind in favor of national unification and a strong foreign policy.[5] This remained the case in the Weimar Republic. Many churchmen who later became strong members of the Confessing Church considered the failure of that Republic was its inability to change the priority from an inner policy to a strong foreign policy. Therefore in the beginning they hailed Hitler's efforts in that direction.

This diversion of civic self-consciousness from the concept of inner (domestic) liberties to the concept of outward, national freedom promoted . . . strong orientation toward success abroad; and this stunted the capacity for constructive opposition which is the basis for a democratic state.[6]

Now Hitler's Germany again fascinated the Christians (as it did most Germans) with the old concept of absolute inner unity, of unification with the lost territories (in opposition to the provisions of Versailles), of the rightness of suspending for that purpose all personal liberties—all of this apparently being threatened by the Western Allies and later by the Soviets. The anticipation of unification was too much, and it was now too late to change and develop both of those long neglected inner political virtues of resistance and opposition. The latter could now only be pursued in conspiratorial form. But to do so seemed identical with betraying one's own identity.

Few Christians did so. A first change might have occurred when some personally came into dreadful contact with pure terror against, for example, friends or Jews. Or some might have entered circles where exact information about new Nazi plans and cruelties was available. Or some might have had actual contact with conspirators—as in the case of Bonhoeffer. But then you did not make these connections as a churchman: you were entirely alone.

The Confessing Church was careful not to include in the intercession lists individuals who suffered imprisonment for so-called purely political reasons. Bonhoeffer knew the situation perfectly well and did not expect his church to include him on the list. But he might have expected that there would be a learning process later, a process from which would emerge an ethic of civic opposition or even of revolutionary resistance.

## IV

This disorganized state of affairs was not suitable for an eventual calm and useful reception of the heritage of the Church Struggle after the collapse of 1945.

John Conway has recently given a vivid account of how the confessors of faith, so long silent, had to tell their story after the war—of course along the line of their self-interpretation, of their having fought the Church Struggle. This story was now told by men who perhaps had been put back into the offices of a church which—on the whole—had just resumed the role and organizational structure it had prior to 1933; they called the church's "time of disgrace" in those twelve years a passing episode instead of the new starting point which young utopians like Bonhoeffer had believed in. And this story was told by men who suddenly appeared as members of "the resistance" without clearly defining what kind of resistance was meant. But the blame for this lack of clarity was not entirely theirs. When the Allies, not having beforehand the best information about the real character of the Church Struggle, sought out people whom they could trust, they made of us churchmen the kind of resisters we actually had not been. The time came when we were inclined to believe them, to believe that we had been political resisters. The Stuttgart Declaration of autumn 1945—though it had its own interesting history of formulation, especially in the correspondence between Barth and Niemöller, and encountered certain difficulties because of the hesitation of persons present—was a true confession of the fact that there had not been a clean record at all of resistance for human rights. But without further elucidating the real problem of political and ethical theology, Stuttgart with its Declaration remained a foreign body in German church history.

So today we find ourselves in a confused situation; on the one hand, the old combatants now in important positions appear as resisters, without our rethinking the self-interpretation of the Church Struggle. On the other hand, there are the experimenters, who in the new Evangelical academies or in the *Kirchentag* movement developed new social-ethical models—a movement which did not change the churches very much and, on the contrary, even provoked a strong conservative reaction.

In 1949 Heinrich Forck, one of the radical and courageous members of the second church administration up to the end of the Church Struggle, on behalf of the still existing Brethren Councils of the Protestant church composed an official memorial book for the martyrs of the Confessing Church. In the introduction he said:

The difference from the political Resistance movement is that the starting point of the struggle was not based on politics but exclusively on the Confession of Faith of the Church. All of the men we speak of in this book, and with them all men and women who suffered and were troubled like them, underwent their suffering, not because they were in disagreement with the policy of the Third Reich or because they noticed a disaster for our nation in this policy, but only and quite exclusively because they saw the Confession of Faith of the Church attacked and out of their loyalty to Christ wanted to protect it, even if doing so meant risking their lives.[7]

The book also contains an article about Bonhoeffer, but of course it must have been written with deep-seated misunderstandings. The picture given is wrongly colored and far distant from reality which simply has not been perceived. To illustrate the problem I will mention that the German reviews of my 1967 biography of Bonhoeffer usually stop short of the third part, the political chapter. They simply omit any mention of it. And Bonhoeffer's old combatants or enemies still alive have not said a word in public about this chapter, nor has any professor or church leader.

In the trial in 1952 of the neo-Nazi leader Remer, the man who had crushed the uprising against Hitler on July 20, 1944, Ernst Wolf and Hans-Joachim Iwand handled beautifully the question of revolutionary resistance from a Lutheran point of view.[8] Their statements found their way into all new Protestant encyclopedias, but they did not enter the general consciousness of the church. In the church were lodged the sayings of witnesses in the trial of Remer who as Christians dissociated themselves totally from the so-called high-treason activities of Bonhoeffer.

Political resistance by a Lutheran Christian which carried the brutal consequences of high treason, deception, and plotting—all remained, at the very least, very unpopular themes among the churches. To attack your own state—and this during a war—was and is not really acknowledged to be a civic right or duty, even when that state rides rough-shod over all morals and human rights. Human rights still have the smell of the fruits of the Enlightenment and the French Revolution, and they are by that fact alone doomed to be met with mistrust. The fight between an authoritarian state and a real democracy is going on in Germany even today.

Neither the Weimar republic nor our second Democracy can tie itself to a secured and established state- and civic-consciousness (*Staats-und Bürgerverstand*). Therefore the heritage of the Third Reich remains ambiguous: it either relapses into the protective measures of the *Obrigkeitsstaat* or bursts out into radical anti-establishment movements, in which latter situation the polarizations of the Weimar Republic are coming back.[9]

Edmund Schlink summarized the situation in his book *Der Ertrag des Kirchenkampfes* [The harvest of the church struggle] (1947): The Church Struggle led to the recovery of the Word of God as normative for the Church; subsequently the Confessions of Faith again became the binding center for the provincial churches and made clear that structural matters cannot be separated from spiritual ones: Schlink directed this against that "German Christian" who, in a deteriorated discipleship to Sohm's liberalism, wanted structural and spiritual matters to be separate. Therefore some churches afterwards organized their governing bodies so as to unite in one way or another the ministries of a bishop, a president, and a chairman of administration. The difficulties resulting from these attempts and from reducing control are obvious now. Schlink of course emphasized how the concentration on the "Word of God" turned against the liberalism of the 1910s and 1920s and helped to overcome *Kulturprotestantismus* (Protestant culture-religion). And, to be fair, he shows as well how the church out of its new understanding of the Kingship of Christ came to discover a new responsibility toward the world. But he adds also that a stand against totalitarianism, the persecution of the Jews, and the dehumanization of men was taken rather faintheartedly.

Walther Künneth, who wrote his analysis of the Church Struggle *Der grosse Abfall* [The great apostasy] in the same year, sounds yet another note. For him the Church Struggle was a great triumph over liberalism: the Confessing Church eliminated liberalism. Künneth, having in the twenties always been close to Lutheran national ideas, drew too clear a line between the so-called autonomies of the French Revolution and the Enlightenment, on the one hand, and the theonomy of the Church, on the other.

So the results of the Church Struggle were handled chiefly in the fields of theology and ecclesiology. No wonder that old liberalism with its humanitarian, political, and social-ethical problems, on the one hand, and with critical, historical research, on the other, came back in full strength so soon. The latter appeared first: it did not seem to demand personal involvement and change as much as the first. But then the first came over us like a flood, everywhere overflowing all attempts to canalize its thrust.

These understandable reactions, resulting from the unresolved dissensions of the Church Struggle, provoked a new Confessional Movement in Germany which declared a new Church Struggle, more bitter than before because, as it is said, a "second Enlightenment" threatens. Künneth is its academic leader, but this movement does not help to solve the problems at all: it will perpetuate them to continue them, again unresolved. They say, "No other gospel!" They refer to Barmen, and they even have their new Dahlem: let us build up our own educational institutes and ban certain teachers from the examining of candidates! And already they are trying to expel the "liberals" and the "forces of decomposition," i.e., the new humanistic heretics.

A new fight about the interpretation of the Church Struggle certainly is imminent, and therefore it is time for new and very careful studies. The Roman Catholic J. B. Metz says: "The modern rights of freedom of men are still not integrated into the fundamentals of Canon Law." He speaks on the interesting theme, "Reform" and "Gegenreformation" today![10] The head of the Church of the Rhineland, Joachim Beckmann—great old fighter of the Church

Struggle and leading theologian—last Christmas tried to interpret the Barmen declaration for our time. He wrote, "Here [in Barmen] the spirit of the Enlightenment and of Nationalism was abjured." The essence of Barmen—he thinks—is to be seen today in the new attempt to overcome the Enlightenment; again we have to fight against a theology of adaptation, against the doctrine of a second source of revelation, against all the sins of "German Christians." Geneva says, the world writes the agenda, and so repeats 1933!

But I suggest that there are changes which make all the difference.

1. In 1933/34 the heretics held the positions and all the power in the churches. Now the defenders of that faith are still the holders of government.

2. It is not the same whether racism and nationalism or humanism writes the agenda. The gospel includes humanism, but not any doctrine of the superiority of groups of men.

3. Barmen would never have been what it was if there had not been a rather clear and obvious agenda written by the world which made the formulas for friends and foes understandable at once. There is no real Barmen without that agenda.

4. The Declaration of Barmen was not only a verbal happening: it was linked with the cries and actions of and for dehumanized groups of men. (I think all genuine confessions have been linked with fights for suppressed people.) Dogmatics and humanism were bound together, and those confessions of faith had to be confessed in the face of great personal risks. Today the inflated imitations of Barmen remain completely in the realm of safe verbal exercises: there is no risk, nobody suffers, nobody cares whether I agree with him or not. Moreover, the "new champions" of Barmen refuse to link their efforts expressly (*expressis verbis*) to any humanitarian actions or partisanship.

5. Thus, as we have seen, though Barmen at the time was not intended to be a political declaration, it was such in fact, and became more and more politically charged—and it was more and more betrayed, even by the Brethren Councils, when they did not live up to those political implications. The new version of "Barmen" is deliberately meant to be a depoliticization of the gospel.

6. The diastase of world and church during the time of Barmen was in fact a strong attack on that world and was understood as such by that world. That diastase just happened; the new diastase is manufactured with much artificial anguish.

7. The confession in 1934 of the Kingship of Christ as the sole source for proclamation and for the ruling of the church had the obvious effect of opening up pluralistic realms in totalitarian surroundings and of giving people room to breathe, though the effect seemed to be monolithic. The fundamentalist repetition of Barmen today fights pluralism—and we are left without much room to breathe in. The classical *solus* in the confessions of faith becomes totalitarian, antidemocratic.

8. The old enemies of the Declaration of Barmen, the "German Christians," made the church particularistic, nationalistic, and provincial; the so-called new enemies, the humanists, make the church at least universal, part of one humanity.

9. "German Christian" adaptation-theology or the doctrine of a second source of revelation: which of these did Bonhoeffer have in mind when he wrote on July 16, 1944 (it was when I felt unable even to preach in my military unit in Italy!): "One has to live for quite a time in a community in order to understand how Christ is taking shape there"? But it is usually this Bonhoeffer, the old radical fighter for Barmen, who now—according to the new Barmen-Confessionalists—is one of the most effective destroyers of Barmen.

Does not the study of the self-interpretation and the reception of the Church Struggle show us most convincingly that the exclusion of certain theological, social-ethical, political, and humanitarian kinds of problems will not do, whatever the reasons may be, and that they will come back to us with full force and with an alarming threat to the message and the societies we are living for?

Hans-Joachim Iwand, one of the best men of the Confessing Church, a few years after the war said:

Have all the good spirits left us to think that fanaticism [he talked about confessionalism!] is the only heritage which we must save for the next generation out of that disastrous time? With the password—against Liberalism!—so much mischief has been aroused to warn us not to make it our polestar again.

We wanted to cancel that which the Enlightenment had given us. It was the beginning of all that followed, and that beginning happened a century ago.[11]

# 11

# The Message of Barmen for Contemporary Church History

Arthur C. Cochrane

I

In 1934 representatives of Lutheran, Reformed, and United churches, of free synods, church assemblies, and parish organizations met at Wuppertal-Barmen and constituted the first Confessional synod of the Evangelical church in Germany. On May 31, 1934, the synod unanimously adopted the Barmen Theological Declaration in order to withstand the errors of the "German Christians" and the Reich church government. It became the theological basis of the true Evangelical church, commonly referred to as the Confessing Church. It was the point of departure for the deliberations and resolutions of subsequent synods held in Dahlem (1934), Augsburg (1935), and Bad-Oeynhausen (1936). It was binding upon the church's Council of Brethren and its administrative boards in their conduct of the practical work of the church in its struggle against the Reich church bishop, the Reich church committees, and the Ministry for Church Affairs appointed by the National Socialist government under Hitler.

The Barmen Declaration was adopted by the Second Free Reformed Synod in Siegen, March 26-28, 1935, and is now numbered among the historic confessions of the Reformed church in Germany. In the constitutions and church orders that have been issued since 1945 by the Evangelical church in Germany, the United Evangelical Lutheran church in Germany, the Evangelical United church, and by thirteen of the established churches, the Barmen Declaration has been incorporated with varying degrees of acceptance. In the constitution of July 13, 1948 of the Evangelical church in Germany, Barmen was not adopted in the confessional preamble but was included in article I, section 2, as follows: "With its member Churches the Evangelical Church in Germany affirms the decisions reached in the first Confessional Synod in Barmen. As a confessing church, it recognizes that it is obligated to implement the insights gained in the Church Struggle concerning the nature, task, and order of the Church."

Perhaps even more significant is that in May, 1967, the United Presbyterian Church in the U.S.A. adopted the Barmen Declaration in its Book of Confessions along with the Nicene and Apostles' Creeds, the Heidelberg Catechism, the Scottish and Second Helvetic Confessions, the Westminster Confession and Shorter Catechism, and the new Confession of 1967, thereby affirming that Barmen is to be numbered among the great creeds and confessions of the ecumenical church.

I have been invited to speak on "The Message of Barmen for Contemporary Church History." With this topic our conference on the Church Struggle and the Holocaust moves into a new phase. With the exception of Franklin Littell's opening lecture, for the most part we have been looking backward to the history of the Church Struggle. We have been inquiring about its history and historiography. We have been asking about what occurred and did not occur during the years 1933-45, and about the political, economic, cultural, philosophical, and theological explanations of those events. Now we are invited to look to the present and to the future, and to ask specifically what the Barmen Declaration has to say to the church today.

Involved in our topic is a hermeneutical problem. As a theologian and expositor of Holy Scripture, I am naturally grateful to textual and historical criticism for what it has been able to contribute to our knowledge of the meaning of what the prophets and evangelists wrote in their day and of the situation (*Sitz im Leben*) in which they spoke and wrote. However, as Karl Barth complained in one of the prefaces to his early commentary on the Epistle to the Romans, most modern commentators stop there and, unlike Luther and Calvin, do not go on to ask what the text has to say to us in our quite changed situation. Similarly we are grateful to men like Karl Bode and Wilhelm and Gerhard Niemöller for their labors in recovering the text not only of the Barmen Declaration but also of the Minutes of the Synod, and for the labors of a host of historians for their investigations into the message of Barmen in 1934, into the situation in which it was proclaimed, and into the impact it had at that time.

But 1970 is not 1934. We are faced with the task of letting Barmen come alive and speak to us, even as the Augustana, the Heidelberg Catechism, and the Ten Theses of Berne came alive and spoke powerfully during the Church Struggle. As a matter of fact, the Barmen Declaration represented what the Synod of Barmen believed to be the message of the Reformation Confessions for the Church in 1934. It stated: "Precisely because we want to be and to remain faithful to our various Confessions, we may not keep silent, since we believe we have been given a common message to utter in a time of common need and temptation." Barmen let the message of the Reformations Confessions be heard without being a parroting of the sixteenth-century confessions.

I confess that the task of letting Barmen speak to us is much more difficult than a recapitulation of the history of 1933 to 1945. Indeed, it can be fulfilled by a theologian only "according to the measure of grace" that is given to him. How much easier it is to attempt—with the detachment and objectivity of the historian—to reconstruct the political, economic, cultural, and theological situation at that time, in order to hear the concrete message Barmen delivered thirty-six years ago; to assess the degree to which that message had been accepted and acted upon by the church in Germany; and to show that, as Armin Boyens has done in his important book, *Kirchenkampf und Ökumene 1933-39. Darstellung und Dokumentation* (1969) the message of Barmen was—in spite of all shortcomings and failures—far better understood by the church in Germany than in all other countries. And let not the churches outside Germany excuse their failure to hear the message of Barmen in 1934 to 1939 because they had no crisis situation in their churches! The same blindness that had befallen the Christians in Germany had come upon Christians in other lands. I know whereof I speak. For I returned from Germany to Canada and attended the meeting of the World Presbyterian and Reformed Alliance in Montreal in 1937 and had the well-nigh hopeless task of trying to interpret Barmen to that body. If in the intervening years our eyes have been opened a little bit and we now have a somewhat better appreciation of the theological issues at stake at Barmen, we owe much to the translation of the works of those two teachers of the Confessing Church—Karl Barth and Dietrich Bonhoeffer.

My task, then, is to try to say what I believe is the message of

Barmen for the church that stands at the threshold of the 1970s. May I be excused if I refrain from trying to say what the message of Barmen is for contemporary *German* church history?[1] I will confine myself to its message for the ecumenical church and for the church in the United States of America. I am sure that Dr. Theodore Gill will ably supplement what I have to say in his concluding lecture of this conference: "The German Church Struggle: What Can America Learn?"

Nineteen-seventy is not 1934, we said. Since the end of World War II we have seen the world divided by an Iron Curtain between East and West. Armed with the atomic bomb, the United States pursued a policy of containment against Soviet Russia until Russia, subsequently equipped with nuclear weapons, forced a stalemate at the Cuban crisis. Yet the "balance of terror" continues with both camps stockpiling nuclear, chemical, and biological weapons of mass extermination sufficient to destroy the population of the globe many times over. Meanwhile we have seen the emergence of Red China, apparently hostile to both Russia and the United States. And we have witnessed that "miracle of history"—the establishment of the state of Israel after nearly two thousand years of the history of the "wandering Jew." Gradually there has arisen the so-called Third World—the underdeveloped nations of Asia, Africa, and South America seeking liberation from economic, political, and racial imperialism from the East and from the West. At the same time the United Nations has been as helpless as the League of Nations to prevent the outbreak of war or to achieve peace in Korea, Vietnam, the Middle East, Africa, and Latin America. Hand in hand with an astonishing technological revolution, culminating in the landing of men on the moon, we have witnessed an increasing disparity between the rich and the poor nations, and between rich and poor within nations. Frustrated and embittered, the poor and the black are in revolt, resorting to both nonviolent and violent tactics. In Germany, France, the United States, Japan, and elsewhere, there has been a remarkable rebellion of youth against military, industrial, and educational establishments and against the mores of an older generation—followed now, it seems, by the backlash of a sullen, silent majority. Meanwhile governments are seized by a strange paralysis, unwilling or unable to rid mankind of the scourges of poverty, war, and racism.

And what has transpired in the church during the 1950s and

1960s? Meetings of the World Council of Churches have been held in Amsterdam (1948), Evanston (1954), New Delhi (1961), and Uppsala (1968), the last preceded by the Geneva Conference on Church and Society. Conversations are underway that may lead to the inclusion of the Roman Catholic church in a council that already includes the Orthodox churches. Unquestionably the ecumenical movement has contributed immensely to greater understanding and cooperation among the churches of the world and among churches within particular nations—even if it has not led to a reunited Christendom. More spectacular and more unexpected has been the renewal within the Roman Catholic church under the leadership of Pope John XXIII and the Second Vatican Council. The new stance that that church has taken not only toward Protestant and Orthodox churches but toward the non-Christian world, even Communism, has opened the way for encounter, dialogue, and cooperation—the fruits of which it is not yet possible to foresee. In the field of theology, Catholic scholars have been extraordinarily industrious and for the most part have been concerned with the substance of the Christian faith. One cannot say the same thing about Protestant theology in general. Although the theology of Karl Barth and Dietrich Bonhoeffer is by no means a spent force, there has been, since 1945, a sort of rebirth of nineteenth-century liberalism, beginning with existentialist theology, followed by a secular meaning of the gospel and a new morality which ended logically in the "God is dead" movement, only recently relieved by a revived interest in eschatology and a theology of hope.

This, then, in broad outline, is the contemporary world and the contemporary church for which Barmen, we believe, has a message. But this only raises the other side of the hermeneutical problem. Who is able to discern the signs of his own times? Unlike some historians, for whom hindsight is easier than foresight, I have always marveled that the men of Barmen were able to read the signs of their times and were given a decisive word to utter. The years 1933 and 1934 were full of immense confusion and blindness—a time when the church, to use Ernst Wolf's phrase, stood *zwischen Versuchung und Gnade*, ("between temptation and grace"). Perhaps in this respect 1934 and 1970 are alike. If so, then it will be God's grace if we hear the message of Barmen for our day. Perhaps here is where we may begin. For if Barmen has anything to say to us it is first and last that—in the midst of the darkness and confusion of our times and amid the babble of many voices around us—we may hear Jesus Christ.

## II

The message of Barmen is that Jesus Christ is God's message, God's Word, and that we are permitted and granted the *freedom* to hear him, the *freedom* to trust him completely, and the *freedom* to obey him and confess him at all times and under all circumstances (art. I). "Through him befalls us a joyful deliverance from the godless fetters of this world for a free, grateful service to his creatures" (art. II). Perhaps there is nothing we need to learn more from Barmen than what it has to tell us about freedom. We live in a day when the word *freedom* is on everyone's lips. It is the catchword not only of liberals but of arch conservatives, such as the members of the John Birch Society in this country. The peoples of the underdeveloped nations are striving for freedom from economic exploitation and political imperialism. The black, brown, and yellow peoples demand freedom from white racism, the freedom to discover and to affirm their own identity. The poor strive to throw off the shackles of poverty, disease, and ignorance. Millions long to be free of the scourge of war. The younger generation wants to be free of the hypocrisy and false values of its elders. And in the churches, especially in the Roman Catholic church, there is a new demand for freedom from authoritarian, hierarchical structures, from unexamined, time-worn dogmas, liturgies, customs, and traditions.

Now it is true that Barmen opposed political totalitarianism and ecclesiastical authoritarianism. In art. V we read: "We reject the false doctrine, as though the State, over and beyond its special commission should and could become the single and totalitarian order of human life, thus fulfilling the Church's vocation as well." And in art. IV: "We reject the false doctrine, as though the Church . . . could or were permitted to give to itself, or allow to be given to it, special leaders vested with ruling powers." It was this aspect of Barmen's protest that led English-speaking historians to view the Church Struggle as "The Struggle for Religious Freedom in Germany" and as "The Church-State Struggle in Germany." But this did not and does not get to the heart of Barmen's understanding of freedom. As a matter of fact, on June 29, 1933, nearly a year before Barmen, a gathering of ministers in Bielefeld vigorously protested the appointment of a state commissioner for the Evangelical church of Prussia and demanded "freedom for the Evangelical Church, freedom from the State Commissioner, freedom to preach, also in the press and in the radio, freedom for the Church to rebuild itself." But true, necessary, and courageous as the Bielefeld statement was, it did not get at the real issue that faced the church then and, indeed, always faces the church. It stopped at the point of insisting upon the church's independence from the power of the state, of demanding civil religious liberty—freedom of speech and freedom of assembly. If I may be pardoned for saying so, the Bielefeld statement sounded terribly American, terribly democratic. Barmen was concerned about a deeper dimension of freedom; about the freedom of God's Word in its midst, the freedom to hear, trust, and obey God's Word, the freedom to hear the Voice of the Good Shepherd and not to listen to the voice of strangers—of "other events and powers, figures and truths, as God's revelation."

At the same time it is a gross misunderstanding of Barmen to say that it was only concerned about the church's own religious existence and was indifferent to political, economic, and academic freedoms. Nothing could be further from the truth. The truth is that Barmen was concerned with the freedom of the Word of God and the church's freedom under that Word as the ground and guarantor of all psychological, personal, social, economic, and political freedoms. Barmen knew that the church's freedom is founded upon its "commission," as art. VI states, to deliver "the message of the free grace of God to all people in Christ's stead." Barmen understood what Paul wrote to Timothy, namely, that when the church suffers and is imprisoned, "the Word of God is not fettered" (2 Tim. 2:9). It had learned from Karl Barth's famous pamphlet, "Theological Existence Today," that the real issue was not the freedom of the church from political pressure or from the opposition of the "German Christian" party—but the freedom of the Word of God in preaching and theology—a freedom that had been generally threatened long before the rise of Hitler and the "German Christians." "Once this freedom was grasped," he wrote, "there would then be no talk about all being favorable if Church politics won, or of all being lost if it were defeated."

And now, was it not entirely in keeping with the message of

Barmen when in his book, *Ad Limina Apostolorum*, Karl Barth addressed some of his most critical questions to that document of the Second Vatican Council—the "Declaration on Religious Freedom"—which was so widely hailed in both Catholic and Protestant circles? He asked:

When or where did the witnesses in the Old and New Testaments demand a legally assured scope for their life and the proclamation of their faith, and for the presentation of other religions?

When or where did they defend their freedom to act by reference to the natural dignity of the human person?

When or where did they commend this freedom to the authorities as being in their own best interests?

When or where did they react to the threats of oppression which the ruling powers raised against freedom in any other manner than by resisting and suffering?

Why does this Declaration (except for the final sentence in 15, 5) have nothing to say about the true freedom for which the Son makes us free (John 8:36), which is there where the Spirit of the Lord is present (2 Cor. 3:17), and nothing about the liberating "law of the Spirit of life in Christ Jesus" (Rom. 8:2), into which the Church continuously looks (James 1:25) and which is itself judgment (James 2:12)? In short, why does it say nothing about the "glorious liberty of the children of God" (Rom. 8:21)?

Could not the Church, which is called to this freedom (Gal. 5:13) and stands in it (Gal. 5:1), by speaking to and for itself have given more powerful testimony to governments and to all mankind about "religious" freedom than it did in this Declaration?[2]

However, "the glorious liberty of the children of God" to hear, trust, and obey Jesus Christ is not, according to Barmen, restricted to the church's own faith and life, its own liturgy and order. On the contrary, Barmen expressly declares (art. II) that Jesus Christ is "God's mighty claim upon our whole life." It rejects "the false doctrine as though there were areas of our life in which we would not belong to Jesus Christ, but to other lords—areas in which we would not need justification and sanctification through him." The freedom to hear, trust, and obey Christ means freedom to hear, trust, and obey him as the Lord of all governments, states, principalities, and powers, Lord of race, family, and marriage, Lord of business, commerce, education, art, and recreation, and that He has come to set men free "from the godless fetters of this world." Moreover, Barmen confessed that "the State has by divine appointment the task of providing for justice and peace."[3] In this sense Barmen is a truly revolutionary document.

That even the Confessing Church itself did not hear and did not fully carry out this aspect of the message of Barmen has been readily conceded by the leading theologians and church leaders of the Confessing Church since 1945. In keeping with the Stuttgart Declaration, they have been the first to confess—not the sins of the Nazis but their own sin against Israel—their failure to condemn all subtle and not so subtle forms of racial discrimination and persecution, their failure to condemn Hitler's suppression of the liberties of all German citizens, their failure to condemn his remilitarization and rearmament of Germany, and his foreign policies.[4] The fact is that the Confessing Church stands condemned by the message of its own Barmen confession. "And for this," as Karl Barth has written,

it has been properly and improperly reproached: properly—in so far as a strong Christian Church, that is, a Church sure of its own cause in the face of National Socialism, should not have remained on the defensive and should not have fought on its own narrow front alone; improperly—in so far as on this admittedly all too narrow front a serious battle was waged. . . . In proportion to its task, the Church has sufficient reason to be ashamed that it did not do more; yet in comparison with those other groups and institutions (the German universities and schools, the legal profession, business, theater and art, the army and the trade-unions) it has no reason to be ashamed; it accomplished far more than all the rest.[5]

Our task, however, is not to sit in judgment upon the German church under Hitler. Our task is to ask whether we in our quite different day have heard the message of Barmen: that we may and must hear that Jesus Christ is the Liberator and Deliverer of all men and that we are free and therefore bound to confess him in all areas of human life. And Barmen asks *us* whether we have accepted and made use of that freedom.

### III

We have been speaking about the formal aspect of the message of Barmen, of the freedom to hear and confess Jesus Christ. The accent has been upon freedom—upon the gift and exercise of freedom. But freedom is not license, not arbitrariness. It is freedom to obey. It has a quite definite content. It is freedom to confess that "Jesus Christ, as he is attested for us in Holy Scripture, is the one Word of God" and to "reject the false doctrine, as though the Church could or would have to acknowledge as a source of its proclamation, apart from and besides this one Word of God, still other events, and powers, figures and truths, as God's revelation" (art. I). It is the church's freedom "to testify in the midst of a sinful world, with its faith as with its obedience, with its message as with its order, that it is solely his property, and that it lives and wants to live solely from his comfort and direction in the expectation of his appearance." It is never freedom "to abandon the form of its message and order to its own pleasure or to changes in prevailing ideological and political convictions" (art. III), or to "place the Word and work of the Lord in the service of any arbitrarily chosen desires, purposes and plans" (art. VI).

These articles were directed against the *theologia naturalis* of the "German Christians" who held that, in addition to Jesus Christ, God was revealing himself in the history of the National Socialist revolution, in Germanic blood, race, and soil, and in the messianic personality of Adolf Hitler. However, the crudity of a syncretism of the gospel and National Socialism ought not to blind us to the fact that the heresy of the "German Christians" was the ripened and rotten fruit of an error that had long prevailed in modern Protestantism and has reared its ugly head again in much post-World War II theology. In his commentary on the Theological Declaration (also adopted by the Synod of Barmen) Hans Asmussen declared: "We are raising a protest against the same phenomenon that has been slowly preparing the way for the devastation of the Church for more than two hundred years. For it is only a relative difference whether, in the church along with Holy Scripture, historical events or reason, culture, aesthetic feelings, progress, or other powers and figures are said to be binding claims upon the Church." Prior to Barmen, Barth had insisted that "the resistance has to go further and be directed against the ecclesiastical-theological system of modern Protestantism which in no way is embodied in the 'German Christians' alone."[6] "Because the teaching and conduct of the 'German Christians' is nothing else than an especially striking consequence of the whole development of modern Protestantism since 1700, the protest is directed against an existing and spreading corruption of the whole evangelical Church."[7] What Barmen condemned was a *theologia naturalis* which, under the influence of the rediscovery of stoicism in the so-called humanism that was contemporaneous with the Reformation, first gained an entry into the confessions of the Reformed church in the French Confession of Faith of 1559, article II, and spread to the Belgic Confession of 1561, articles II and III, and thence to the Westminster Confession of Faith of 1643.[8] Not until the Barmen Theological Declaration of 1934 was natural theology categorically rejected and the original witness of the Reformation confessions of the early sixteenth century reaffirmed. It affirmed that Jesus Christ is the one Word and work of God, the one justification and sanctification, the one light and life of the world, the one Lord and Savior. He is not merely one light among many, one truth among many, one word among many. He is the one Word of God. Neither the Bible nor church tradition is that word. All other words, truths, and lights can only bear witness to him Who said: "I am the way, the truth, and the life" (John 14:6).

But now—in and with this *confitemur* and this *damnamus*—the Synod of Barmen claimed to be the one, holy, catholic, and apostolic church. In the confession of Jesus Christ and in the condemnation of the heresy of other lords, saviors, and revelations, the oneness and the catholicity of the holy church was defined. It is superficial to characterize Barmen as "Barthian orthodoxy." In the Theological Declaration is heard not just the voice of an individual theologian, of a theological school, or of a particular denomination, or even of a group of denominations, but the voice of the one, holy, catholic church. It speaks as the whole church to the whole church. This, of course, is not to be understood in a sociological, legal, or statistical sense. From this standpoint no confession, not even the so-called ecumenical creeds, was ever produced by the whole church for the whole church. The ecumenicity of a confession is grounded in the fact that it undertakes to confess the one Lord and the one faith attested in Holy Scripture and given to the whole church.[9] The Synod of Barmen made this claim when it declared "we are bound together by the Confession of the one holy, catholic, and apostolic Church." Moreover, the synod dared to speak in the name of the one church in spite of or, rather, because it was composed of "the representatives of Lutheran, Reformed and United Churches." Here, incidentally, we have something else to learn from Barmen, namely, that the existence of many denominations and schools of theology is not an insuperable barrier to a confession speaking in the name of the one, holy, catholic church. Barmen, or some such confession, could become the confession of the one church even amid the religious pluralism of these United States. But this will happen only when the churches are concerned exclusively for their confession of Jesus Christ and not for ecumenism and church union as such.

## IV

Now this intransigent, uncompromising stand of the Synod of Barmen has been from its beginning and continues to be a serious question addressed to all other churches and to all ecumenical and church union movements. It asks whether they are and want to be the one church of Christ precisely in the affirmation of this specific dogma and in the negation of this specific heresy. It asks whether apart from it there can be any truth unity of God's people, and any genuine reformation and renewal of the church. The question, of course, can be ignored. It can fall upon deaf ears. I would venture to say that since 1945 the question has not been squarely faced by the churches of the world, including the church in Germany. Nevertheless, the question remains. It constitutes *the* message of Barmen for the contemporary history of the ecumenical movement. It was that young man Dietrich Bonhoeffer who recognized and articulated the question as early as August 1935. I refer to a much neglected paper entitled, *"Die Bekennende Kirche und die Ökumene."*[10] He saw that "the German church struggle marks the second great stage in the history of the ecumenical movement and will in a decisive way be normative for its future,"[11] and that "the future of the ecumenical movement . . . depends upon the question being taken up."[12] I propose to consider the question as Bonhoeffer stated it and the extent to which it has been taken up by the World Council of Churches and by the Plan of Union drawn up by the Consultation on Church Union in the United States and recently sent to the churches for their study and action.

Bonhoeffer contended that there was a "reciprocal questioning" by the Confessing Church and the ecumenical movement. Inasmuch as the Confessing Church and the heresy of the "German Christians" no longer exist, I am concerned here with the crisis into which the ecumenical movement was led by the Confessing Church. Bonhoeffer insisted that the Confessing Church confronted the ecumenical movement with the question of the confession of faith in such a way that neutrality was impossible: the ecumenical movement could not maintain relations with the Confessing Church and with the heretical "German Christian" church at the same time. Bonhoeffer admitted that this was "an un-heard of claim." But he said that "if the Confessing Church departed from this claim, the church struggle in Germany (and with it the struggle for Christendom) would already have been decided against her."[13] With the question of the confession the ecumenical movement is asked about the authority with which it speaks and acts. "Is the Ecumenical Movement, in its visible representation, a Church?"[14] Or is it merely an association of Christian men and women gathered together for non-binding theological dialogue with one another, that is, conversations which are never intended nor expected to result in a judgment or decision in matters of doctrine and ethics?

Bonhoeffer observed that "ecumenical work now has largely the character of theological dialogue." (Is such not still the case today?) He warned that dialogue may not be carried on among uncommitted Christian individuals, and that it must be carried on only with the intention of arriving at responsible, legitimate decisions of the church in obedience to Christ's promise and command. The church is not a debating club, not a theological society, not even a conference such as we are presently attending. The only justification for such ecumenical conferences and consultations is that the participants press for a decision between true or false teaching in the church.

Bonhoeffer anticipated the objection that, if this were to become the presupposition for ecumenical work, the ecumenical movement would collapse and its unity and peace would be shattered. But he asked: "Who knows whether simply because of this task of breaking the peace the ecumenical movement will not come out of the struggle strengthened and more powerful? And even if it must go through a severe collapse, are not the commandment and the promise of God strong enough to bring the church through, and is not this commandment more sure than a false rest [peace] and an illusory unity, which one day must come to grief?"[15] Bonhoeffer also anticipated what he referred to as "the dogma of the ecumenical movement" which exercises an astonishing attraction, namely, the notion that the existing churches are branches or parts of the one, holy, ecumenical church, each bringing its own special gift and service to the riches and harmony of Christendom as a whole. But this "romantic, aesthetic, liberal idea of the ecumenical movement," Bonhoeffer contended, "does not take the truth seriously and thus offers no possibility of making the ecumenical movement comprehensible as a church."[16]

And now we ask: Does not Barmen raise a serious and basic question for the Plan of Union drawn up by the Consultation on Church Union (COCU) in this country? The Plan provides that "the united church . . . will from time to time confess and communicate its faith in contemporary language and new forms. . . . Such an affirmation will be prepared after the united church is formed so that it will arise out of a shared life together." COCU has made room—legally and constitutionally—for a future confession but here and now it has nothing in particular to confess. The churches are being united not in a confession of faith but in an ecclesiastical arrangement *for* a possible confession. First union, then confession. But it never happens that way. The scriptural sequence is: "We believe, therefore we speak." The Barmen Declaration did not "arise out of a shared life together" of the German churches; on the contrary, their shared life together arose out of their confession and the confession was precisely that which they had in common and which bound them together with bands of steel. Barmen said: "We . . . declare that we . . . are bound together by the confession of the one Lord of the one, holy, catholic, and apostolic Church" and "we believe that we have been *given* a *common* message to utter in a time of common need and temptation. We commend to God what this may mean for the interrelations of the Confessional Churches."[17] That is to say, first the confession and then—and only then—questions of ministerial orders, sacraments, church structures, and government. The message of Barmen for contemporary church history is that church union per se, that is, an institutional or organizational merger in itself, is not necessarily a manifestation of the one, holy, catholic church. Rather the church has its very existence and its true unity in its fulfillment of the divine commission to bear witness to Jesus Christ, and therefore in its confession of Him.

The same question may be addressed to the World Council of Churches. It is asked whether it seeks to be the church, to be not a council of churches but an ecumenical church council; whether it will dare to speak to and for the whole church in a trust in Christ's promise and in obedience to his command. If it does so, it will not be enough to make acceptance of our Lord Jesus Christ as God and Savior a condition of membership; it will have to declare what concretely it means today to accept Jesus Christ as God and Savior. Just how concretely may be gleaned from the concluding paragraph of Bonhoeffer's article.[18]

Whether the hopes laid on the Ecumenical Council of Evangelical Christendom will be fulfilled, whether such a council will not only bear witness to the truth and the unity of the church of Christ with authority but also be able to bear witness against the enemies of Christianity throughout the world, whether it will speak a word of judgment about war, race hatred and social exploitation, whether through such true ecumenical unity of all evangelical Christians among all nations war itself will become impossible, whether the witness of such a council will find ears to hear—all this depends on our obedience towards the question which has been put to us and on the way in which God will use our obedience. What is set up is not an ideal, but a command and a promise—what is demanded is not our own realisation of our own aims, but obedience. The question has been raised.

The great advantage which the Second Vatican Council has had over the meetings of the World Council of Churches is that it spoke as a church council. No doubt this is one reason why the deliverances of Vatican II have received greater attention than those of the World Council of Churches. Yet having said this, it should be added that Barmen remains a question for both the Roman Catholic church and the World Council of Churches and for their interrelations, namely, whether there can be any true unity of Christ's church on earth save in the confession that he is the one God (Nicaea), the one justification of sinners (Reformation), the one Word and revelation of God (Barmen). This does not mean that in an ecumenical council of the one church there must be uniformity in doctrine, liturgy, and polity. Nor does it imply a doctrinaire acceptance of the Barmen theses. It is fortuitous that Barmen did not confess against Anglicans, Free churchmen, or against Rome. As Bonhoeffer wrote, it confessed *in concretissimo* against the "German Christian" church and against the neopagan divinization of the creature. The antichrist did not sit in Rome or Geneva but in Berlin.[19] The Synod of Barmen confessed the sin and error of its *own* church. But just for that reason its message deserves to be heard and acted upon by all churches which confess that they are not just a part of but are, in truth, the one, holy, catholic, and apostolic church.[20]

## V

We have been considering the message of Barmen for contemporary church history in terms of what Barmen has to teach about freedom and about what it means to be the one, holy, catholic church. But what message has Barmen for the history of the church in relation to Israel? On a surface reading, Barmen has little or nothing to say about Israel and the church. The church is defined in article III as "the congregation of the brethren in which Jesus Christ acts presently as the Lord in Word and Sacrament through the Holy Spirit"—without any reference to Israel. To be sure, the one Word of God which we have to hear, trust, and obey is Jesus Christ as attested in Holy Scripture, and that means the scriptures of the people of Israel in both their Old and New Testament forms. Moreover, article VI declares that "the Church's commission . . . consists in delivering the message of God's free grace to all people" and therefore to Jew and Gentile. Nevertheless, there is no direct reference to Israel and the indirect references are admittedly obscure. One might, therefore, conclude that Barmen had no message concerning Israel in 1934 and has no message concerning Israel today. But this is to overlook the historical and theological situation in which Barmen arose and the effect which Barmen has had upon the church's self-understanding in relation to Israel. The fact is that except for Israel there would have been no Synod of Barmen and no Barmen Declaration.

Let me try to explain. In New Testament scriptures we Christians have been taught that "salvation is from the Jews" (John 4:22) and that "the Gentiles have come to share in their spiritual blessings" (Rom. 15:27). Similarly, the recovery of the gospel of God's free grace in the Barmen Declaration came from the Jews. I do not mean that Jews directly contributed to the formulation of the Barmen theses. I mean that the Jews by their very existence, by the hatred and suffering they endured at the hands of a pagan world and a paganized Christendom were the occasion which produced Barmen. For the heresy of the "German Christians," against which Barmen was directed, was their espousal of the Antisemitism of the National Socialist ideology. Or rather, the "German Christian" denial of Jesus

Christ assumed the concrete form of the denial of the Jews as God's chosen people and their right to citizenship in the German nation and, if they desired, to baptism and full membership in the Christian church. The demonic, godless essence of National Socialism was not racism per se but Antisemitism. And because God the Creator has everlastingly bound himself with a holy covenant with Israel, the essence of National Socialism was a rebellion against the God of free grace.

It is a historical question of some consequence just when Karl Barth came to recognize this truth. At first, Barth seemed to regard the "Jewish question" and the Aryan paragraph as secondary and merely symptomatic of the pervading theological sickness. "The protest against the heresy of the 'German Christians,' " he wrote, "cannot begin with the Aryan paragraph, the rejection of the Old Testament, the Aryanism of the 'German Christian' christology, the naturalism and Pelagianism of their doctrine of justification and sanctification, or with the deification of the State in 'German Christian' ethics. It has to be directed fundamentally against the source of all single errors, namely, that the 'German Christians' assert German nationality, its history and its political present, as a second source of revelation *beside* Holy Scripture as the only source of revelation, and thereby show themselves to be believers in 'another god.' "[21] And in the same year—1933—Barth could write that as long as the doctrine and practice of the "German Christians" are not radically called into question, "it would do no good even if the day after tomorrow the wretched Aryan paragraph were completely to disappear from sight."[22]

From a sermon that Barth delivered at the University of Bonn, December 10, 1933, on Romans 15:5-13, however, it is evident that he had come to see the Jewish question as a question of faith in Jesus Christ and that Israel *post Christum* is identical with Israel *ante Christum*. And this was five months before the Synod of Barmen convened! Moreover, Martin Niemöller, his brother Wilhelm (who is present with us at this conference), and Friedrich Müller, who organized the Pastors' Emergency League in October 1933, were fully aware that Antisemitism struck a blow at the heart of the Christian faith. Indeed, it was the one error which they singled out in the fourth article of the pledge to which every member of the League subscribed: "In making this pledge, I testify that the application of the Aryan paragraph within the Church of Christ has violated the confessional stand." Nor should this article be dismissed as having to do only with church polity. It was a recognition and acknowledgment of the indissoluble unity of Israel and the church, of Jews and Christians. Without this recognition and acknowledgment Barmen was impossible. Whatever message Barmen has for the church today or will have in the future has come from the empirical fact of the existence of Israel. "Salvation is from the Jews"—not only two thousand years ago but in every generation as well.

Barmen, in turn, was the impetus for profound theological reflections on the relation of Israel and the church by a host of Christian scholars both during the Church Struggle and since 1945. It dawned upon them that the Jewish question is the question about Jesus Christ, that the spirit of Antisemitism is the spirit of antichrist, and that where the Jews are hated and persecuted, the faithful followers of the Jew, Jesus of Nazareth, will also be hated and persecuted. They realized that in the last analysis the Church Struggle and World War II were waged because of Israel and that in spite of the Holocaust, Israel could not be annihilated.

Thus says the Lord, who gives the sun for light by day and the fixed order of the moon and the stars for light by night, who stirs up the sea so that its waves roar—the Lord of hosts is his name: If this fixed order departs from before me, says the Lord, then shall the descendants of Israel cease from being a nation before me forever. [Jer. 31:35-36]

The new theological understanding of Israel was accompanied by a profound sense of the enormous guilt of Christians against their Jewish brothers. It was learned that if the church is to look to the rock from which it was hewn and to the quarry from which it was digged, it must look to Abraham our father and to Sarah who bore us (Isa. 51:2). And if it is to look to the future, the hope of Israel is the only hope of the church and the world, namely, the faithfulness of God to his promises to Israel fulfilled in the Messiah who has come and who is yet to come.

This, then, is the message of Barmen for the contemporary churches. But have our churches and congregations heard and believed that message? I leave it as a question.

# 12

# Catholic Resistance? A Yes and a No

Gordon C. Zahn

## I. Introduction

If I may begin on a somewhat personal note, this conference represents a most welcome opportunity to me. Not only is it an honor to participate in a meeting with scholars of the stature represented here but it also provides an occasion to balance or correct misunderstandings that may still persist in connection with my earlier research into the scope and nature of German Catholic support for Hitler's wars.[1] When that work first appeared—indeed, more than a year before it appeared!—it was roundly condemned in certain quarters as a vilification of the religious leadership of a desperately oppressed religious community and as a studied refusal to acknowledge and give due respect to the Catholic resistance efforts and the heroic sacrifices they produced.[2] Needless to say, in my view neither charge had any real substance. That they were made and that they received a surprisingly high degree of acceptance, especially in Germany, may tell something of particular interest to this conference.

Following the end of World War II and the total collapse of the Third Reich, the victor nations, in their determination to trace the responsibility for all the horrors that had occurred and to exact appropriate retribution for them, inadvertently cooperated in the creation of a myth, the myth of a total and unrelenting resistance to the Hitler regime on the part of the Christian churches. That there was an element of truth in this, as is the case with most myths, would be impossible to deny. After all, there were the heroes—the Niemöllers, the Delps, the Galens, the Bonhoeffers, and the multitude of others, some still unknown and probably never to be known—who had become symbols of opposition, many of them paying for that opposition with their freedom and, often enough, with their lives.[3] The Catholic church in particular, thanks to its link to the outside world provided by the Vatican, was able to call continuing attention to the increasingly restrictive and oppressive measures being taken against it and to voice its protest to those measures for all the world to hear. All the world, that is, except that part under Nazi domination. This meant that much of the information concerning the interferences with church operations and personnel were better known to outsiders than to German Catholics themselves. As far as they were concerned, and this would be especially true once the prospect and then the actuality of total war became a dominant concern, such things as traditional religious processions and ceremonials as well as the maintenance of a religious press and parareligious organizations could be regarded as luxuries easily to be dispensed with in such times of crisis.

Be that as it may, the churches were pretty much assumed to be "clean" of Nazi taint when the war ended, so much so that clergymen soon became prime sources of the character references and testimonials that enabled others to obtain the much-coveted *Persilscheine* (certificates of being clean of Nazi taint) issued by the Occupation authorities. Such "history" as was produced at that time tended to confirm the developing myth, sometimes through loose and hasty scholarship, sometimes even through careful editing, if not actual "correcting," of the record.[4]

This continued through the recovery period and into the prosperity of the *Wirtschaftswunder* (economic miracle) at which time dissident journalists and authors, together with a new generation of probing historians, began to raise discomfiting questions. As far as the Catholic record was concerned, there were political and theological overtones to this new trend of scholarship. The so-called *Links-katholiken* (left-wing Catholics), most unhappy with the extent to which their church and the Adenauer government were welded together and even more unhappy with the extent to which this combine was committed to Cold War policies and rationalizations, moved into the forefront of what may be described as a period of reassessment and exposé. From relatively quiet "sleeper" studies such as those inquiring into the Concordat negotiations and the dissolution of the Center party, the probes expanded into full-scale and sharply critical (sometimes to the point of being "debunking" exercises) analyses of what Amery, one of their members, was to describe as "the capitulation."[5] My own work, it might be pertinent to add, was eagerly welcomed by writers of this new "school" as a contribution to their revisionist campaign, an evaluation that was evidently shared by their opponents who were so willing to dismiss it out of hand.

The further passage of time and the cooling of ideological passion made possible by the end of the Adenauer era have brought us to the point where it may now be possible to view this whole issue in fuller perspective. Few historians of merit today, I suspect, would endorse the enthusiastic and uncritical defense of the record of the churches under Hitler. Similarly, few would share the accusatory fervor which marked much of the work—and probably accounted for most of the motivation—of the destroyers of the myth. What we should be striving for today is an awareness of the balance between good marks and bad in the record of the major Christian communities for the Nazi years. Some, it is true, may have fewer of the latter than others; but where this is so, it is proper to question if this was due to the purity and courage of their commitment or if it is to be explained in terms of the regime's refusal to grant them the chance to become part of the National Socialist dream. On the other hand, if the final historical accounting, as I am inclined to believe, should show that religion in general and the Catholic church in particular contributed more in the way of effective support than in effective opposition and resistance, this will have to be seen in the context of the fact that the church was about the only social institution to offer any effective resistance at all.

Sociologically, of course, the record could scarcely be otherwise. Religion, like all the major institutions of society, is at one and the same time subject to its control and a potential competitor for the interest or allegiance of the individual members of society. In the case of religion, its declared commitment to a value and belief system of supernatural origin and orientation intensifies that competition, at least in theory, until it can become a source of dissent and disobedience. The particular mix between the support for a given social order by a religious organization and the threat it might pose to social unity and conformity will vary according to such things as size, mode of organization, doctrine, and, of course, situational factors. Thus the Catholic church, the classic model of a society-wide and bureaucratically organized *ecclesia*, with a body of sharply defined dogma and tradition, is normally likely to have a greater stake in establishing and preserving a comfortable, or at least tenable, *modus vivendi* with the greater society and stress the support function of the institution. The small, world-denying and world-despising sect which encourages the spirit-guided free response of the individual believer to his personal religious impulses and inspiration is much more likely to be associated with deviance or to have propensity for deviance.

But when the situation is not "normal," this difference can fade. Because the Catholic church is, or seeks to be, doctrinally stable and because it is so visible, there are times when it will find itself threatened and made a target for persecution precisely because of its "power," actual or assumed, over the believer who is also the subject of the secular authority. Hitler's Germany provided such a situation, and it forced the church and its leaders into a sometimes stridently defensive posture which, whether they intended so or not, undoubtedly inspired some believers to contemplate or undertake deliberate acts of resistance toward the Nazi state. That this was more than was intended in many cases is clearly indicated by the tendency to fashion official church protests according to the letter of Nazi law and proclaimed policy, even when that letter was completely and obviously contradicted by the spirit in which those laws and policies were being applied. The impression one gets today when reading the official church protests and pronouncements is one of a gentlemanly game to be scored according to rhetorical gains and setbacks. The tragedy is that this is not the way it was played; the losses were measured in terms of individual suffering and arrests. Perhaps the losers did in a sense become, what one prelate reportedly called them, "martyrs to their own stupidity" for taking the game so seriously. If so, we can say, three decades after the fact, it was their stupidity that saved the reputation of the church for the post-Nazi world.

I do not propose to review the record of Catholic resistance to Hitler according to the numbers of those who were involved (that could probably not be determined anyhow) or the numbers arrested, imprisoned, and executed: other studies have already attempted to do this.[6] The two or three hundred German priests sent to Dachau, Bishop Spröll exiled from his Rottenburg diocese, the indignities endured by Rupert Mayer, and the martyr-deaths of Max Josef

Metzger, Alfred Delp, and the far too many others—each of these holds importance for us not as a part of some larger category but as an authentic Christian witness in his own right. We can learn much and derive great inspiration from considering them all together; but it is not until we can view them as separate figures in a tapestry and not as units in a tabulation that we will discover their true meaning and importance for the church, then and now.

This paper is based on a limited survey, limited in time and area, of the official Catholic resistance to the policies and programs of the Third Reich (or, more accurately perhaps, to some of those policies and programs). The data were obtained in a rather interesting fashion. A pastor in a small Bavarian town wrote several months ago to comment on the German edition of my book which he had recently read. It developed that his predecessor had saved mimeographed materials circulated by the Munich-Freising chancery to the clergy, and he kindly offered to make them available to me for inspection with the proviso that the parish not be identified. The anticipation of some significant new discoveries gave way to some disappointment when I found that 1) the period covered was from 1934 to early 1938 with but a few items dated later,[7] and that 2) most of these documents were already known to me from published sources, most particularly the Neuhäusler book.[8] Nevertheless, a thorough reading of the almost one hundred fifty documents disclosed some that seemed new and important and, more to the present purpose, gave sharper focus to my review of Catholic resistance to Hitler.

## II. The Catholic Church as Support for the Nazi State

My focus is primarily sociological and only incidentally historical. To return to the formulation of religion as institution with the dual function of providing support for the existing social order and serving, when the situation seems to demand, as a potential source of dissent and disobedience, both can be amply demonstrated by the Catholic experience. Taking the support function first, one finds certain elements which all but assured the ineffectiveness of whatever resistance the church did attempt or might have attempted. Three are particularly crucial: the church's almost fanatical opposition to Communism or, as it was usually named, Bolshevism; the Concordat and its consequences; and, finally, church traditions and rhetoric which served to augment and reinforce the nationalistic excesses which proved to be its undoing.

There would seem to be no reason to question the mutuality of interest between the Catholic church and the Nazi state with regard to Communism. Catholic opposition to all forms of Marxist socialism was a matter of record long before the Nazi party appeared on the scene. Even in those years immediately preceding the Führer's rise to power—years, let us remember, when the church was actively discouraging and sometimes even penalizing Catholic participation in the movement—Hitler's impassioned opposition to Bolshevist forces and doctrines won him some measure of tolerance and even admiration on the part of church leaders. It is not at all surprising, then, that, once the victory had been consolidated, what had been at best a saving feature was easily transformed into the basis for a fundamental partnership. In Catholic rhetoric at least, church and Nazi state stood as the twin bulwarks for the defense of Western Civilization.

This carried over at times into criticism and protest when some action or other taken by party or even state officials brought a stern warning from church leaders against encouraging or endorsing a *Weltanschauung* which, in its antireligious components, threatened to parallel Bolshevism. A somewhat milder version of the same general approach was the argument that the state, by placing restrictions upon religious associations and practices, might weaken the religious commitment and allegiance of the people and thereby make them more susceptible to the insidious lure of that destructive and alien ideology.

When this same line was turned against the church, it provoked a storm of indignation. This is indirectly involved, for instance, in the protest issued by the Bavarian hierarchy in response to the suppression of the Catholic young men's and young women's organizations in January 1938.[9] It was bad enough for the bishops to mark the loss of these channels of church influence and the manner in which this was accomplished, but their particular annoyance is expressed because the action was taken under regulations aimed at Communism. This "bitter injustice" moved the bishops to comment tartly, "If one wishes to defend against 'communistic, state-endangering acts of force,' he would not demand the dissolution of religious organizations but, rather, their support and protection."

An even more galling affront was the engineered rumor that

Rome and Moscow had reached or were about to reach a secret accord so that Catholics and Communists were to be regarded as allies against the Third Reich. An August 1936 pastoral letter of the combined German hierarchy addresses itself to this charge and seeks to refute it by citing the support provided by Catholics and their church to the Nationalist cause in Spain.[10] The same "fairy tales" are taken up by Cardinal Faulhaber in his commemoration of the sixteenth anniversary of Pius XI's elevation to the papacy. There is no *Weltanschauung*, he declared, whose moral teachings reject Communism and Bolshevism as thoroughly as does the Catholic church and that in the name of God. To those who would question why the Pope does not issue encyclicals against those evil ideologies (an apparent reference to the controversy over the issuance of *Mit brennender sorge*), he answered that this had already been done—and he went on to detail the government restrictions which had kept the anticommunist encyclicals from reaching the German public. This was a strong sermon and, after specifying some of the grim facts of the developing persecution of the Catholic church in Germany, he too warned his hearers that it was possible that two ideologies "as opposed as fire and water" could both be enemies of the church and, moreover, could be strikingly similar in the methods they employ.[11]

However much the Nazis may have tried to play down the notion of any "ideological alliance" with the Catholic church against Communism, the repeated claims and references to such alliance by church spokesmen would almost certainly have the effect of predisposing the believer favorably to the regime because of its determined anticommunism. The negotiation and conclusion of a formal concordat between Nazi Germany and the Vatican—and, even more important for the years to come, its continuation in force despite everything—could only validate and confirm that predisposition. There would be no point in recapitulating here the history of how that agreement was fashioned or debating whether or not it should have been negotiated and with such extraordinary haste. It may well be, as many competent commentators hold, that Rome could not have refused to accept the invitation to discuss the kind of treaty it had been so diligently seeking from former regimes. What we are concerned with here is an attempt to reconstruct and interpret its social consequences. However far newly available documentation [12] may go toward resolving the historian's problems on this score, it is not likely to change the sociological implications. By extending this diplomatic "handclasp of trust," the Vatican did bind the German church in a most formal manner to the support of a regime created by a movement and to incorporate an ideology which it had previously been inclined to oppose. Nor can one too lightly accept the argument that this diplomatic link is not to be read as an endorsement: we need only refer again to the indignation with which Faulhaber and his fellow bishops repudiated the mere notion that a similar concordat could possibly be reached between the Vatican and Moscow. As they saw it (or so one can infer from their reaction), such an agreement was unthinkable precisely because it would represent a degree of affiliation utterly inconsistent with the church's established repudiation of Marxism in theory and practice.

In one sense, of course, the issue was not all that important. The Concordat merely formalized the support Catholics would have been expected to give the regime anyway under the long-standing tradition defining obedience to lawful authority as a moral obligation. To say this, however, is not to deny that this formalization added a new dimension. From that time forth it would be difficult to imagine on what basis a believing Catholic could presume to question the "lawful authority" of this particular government recognized as such in a formal treaty with the Holy See, a treaty that we never denounced or abrogated. More specifically, it was the Concordat and its provisions relating to the avoidance of political activity by the church and its official agencies that were to serve as justification for all the measures taken against Catholic professional, labor, and youth societies and for the incarceration in prison or concentration camp of many priests on charges of "misuse" of the pulpit. Again, these things would have happened without a concordat; however, as long as it was in force, it could be used to clothe with a mantle of contractual legitimacy what would otherwise have been recognized as naked repression.

Another important, and certainly unanticipated, effect of the Concordat was the aura of validity it would lend to one of the more persistent charges brought against the church, that of divided (and therefore diminished) loyalty on the part of its members toward the new order. In all the major areas of protest and resistance that were to develop—with the possible exception of the controversies over the sterilization and euthanasia programs—the hierarchy placed great stress upon the rights "guaranteed" under the terms of the Concordat. From the strictly legalistic point of view they were quite justified in doing so and could present a most convincing case. Unfortunately, however, to claim rights and privileges rooted in an agreement with a "foreign power" had to be an extremely weak posture in a society in which reclaimed national values and identity had assumed paramount importance.

To be sure the bishops did not rest their case with appeals to the Concordat guarantees. Instead the proven loyalty and patriotic commitment of Catholics and their contributions to Germany's glorious past provided emotional highpoints for pastoral letters, sermons, and the like. Particular stress was placed upon the battlefield sacrifices of priests and religious during World War I. "It was certainly not the good Catholics who made the revolution in 1918," Faulhaber declared in May 1936, "The good Catholic soldiers were definitely not the ones who turned to desertion." Then, having neatly co-opted one of the Nazis' own rallying points, he moved on to state a general principle that has an immediate bearing upon the problem with which we are concerned: "Good Catholics will never be on the side of the revolutionaries, no matter how bad things may get."[13]

The patriotic motif was prominent in the 1935 announcement of religious retreats to be scheduled for men called into the labor corps or military service. A recommended theme was "Christ and Soldier," and the memorandum advised that valuable material on this theme could be found in a collection of Faulhaber sermons published under the title, "Sword of the Spirit."[14] This information, it should be noted, was prepared for parish and other spiritual guidance centers and not for general edification. Even more illustrative of the point being made here was a similar announcement to the clergy in January 1938 of a new book commemorating the contributions made by seminarians and theology candidates in their military service during World War I. The book was recommended as a most suitable gift for "our youth" who, as the notice had it, were again "privileged" to wear the uniform so that "they may be inspired by the heroic deeds and heroic deaths of the World War to lead a heroic life as good Soldiers of Christ."[15]

We may take it for granted that such appeals to patriotism had a rhetorical and tactical dimension, but it would be unwise to see this as the total explanation. After all, these memoranda were prepared for circulation among the clergy and not for general public or Nazi censors. Faulhaber and the others may have been "speaking for effect," but much of that effectiveness lay in the fact that they sincerely *believed* what they were saying, and that their anguish and indignation over the refusal of the leaders of the new secular order to acknowledge and give due honor to the Catholic record of loyal service and obedience were every bit as sincere. The arrest and imprisonment of Rupert Mayer on trumped-up charges were injustice enough, but that injustice was multiplied several times over in their eyes when his distinguished war record was taken into account. This is as it should be—yet one cannot escape the impression that the war record, not the injustice, was given priority in the protests which followed.

The rector of the Eichstätt cathedral provides a classic example of what I mean. One of the early "indecency" scandals had to do with a young man, a *gymnasium* student, who had described himself as preparing for the priesthood. The controlled press, eager to destroy the image of the priest, exploited this to the fullest. *Dompfarrer* Johannes Kraus took it upon himself to challenge the press reports on the grounds that whatever the culprit's vocational aspirations might be along this line, he had in no sense been accepted for such studies nor was he anywhere near ready to be considered even a potential candidate. He presented as a hypothetical parallel a similar statement of aspiration to enter upon a career of military service. Would we say that the officers' corps is to be tainted with moral suspicion as a result? The logic was sound and should have been effective enough, but the speaker did not stop there. Instead, he unleashed a surge of emotional oratory in which, speaking as a former officer, wounded and decorated in the nation's service, he expounded on how such a slur would offend him—after which he returned to the point at issue declaring that he was equally offended by the equally unjustifiable slur upon him as a member of the priesthood.[16] Protest this certainly was, and probably quite effective too. But, and this is important, it also must have had the effect of reinforcing the listeners' acceptance of the military virtues he praised so highly and deepening their commitment to their civic duty to render obedience to the national state and its leader.

If we have been concerned here with general and principled manifestations of the church as an agency of support for the social order, it is not to dismiss more specific and often more dramatic evidences of these things in their application. It should be unnecessary to elaborate upon the probable effect of such acts as the ringing of church bells tó mark the occasion of Hitler's triumphal entry into Vienna after Anschluss[17] or the celebration of a Te Deum in the Munich cathedral in thanksgiving for his providential escape in the 1939 assassination attempt.[18] All of these can be understood as "obligatory" in their situational context. They must also be understood, as they undoubtedly were by the ordinary faithful at the time, as visible symbols of support for the Nazi regime as legitimate authority.

### III. Protest and Opposition

Hitler came to power in February 1933; the Concordat was formally signed in July; and less than a year later the official Catholic resistance was under way. The June 1934 pastoral of the combined German hierarchy meeting at Fulda was a public and formal protest against the crippling strictures already placed upon Catholic press and organizational activity at the same time that a "new heathenism" was being given free rein to further its cause and win new adherents.[19] Lewy notes[20] that the protest was muted in that it avoided attacking the new regime directly, a tactic that still did not prevent Gestapo action to suppress it. Muted though it may have been, it can be taken as the official opening of what was to become a steady, though largely unsuccessful, campaign of defensive opposition to an equally steady and eminently successful "war of attrition" conducted by the Third Reich against the German Catholic church.

The open battle, such as it was, was waged and lost in the first five years of Nazi rule. Though underground centers of Catholic resistance existed and may even have grown in strength, World War II and the total mobilization of material and human resources virtually smothered all effective protest of a public or official nature. The great exception to this, of course, was the episcopal outcry against the euthanasia program as late as 1940 and 1941; not only was this protest official and public, it was successful. For the most part however, as the struggle developed, the initiative lay with the Nazi rulers. They determined the areas of contest and the timing, and the leaders of the church responded as best they could. As the regime's power became ever more total and more efficiently consolidated, the resistance represented by formal episcopal protest became ever more hopeless.

The 1934 pastoral joined issue with Rosenberg's *Myth* and the German Faith Movement it inspired. This soon escalated into a mortal struggle to preserve the confessional schools and some measure of spiritual control over Catholic youth. Later a blend of calculated attacks upon religious orders and the priesthood in general, coupled with a tightening pattern of interferences with the normal operation of religious services and related activities, made it clear enough, to the bishops at least, that the very survival of Christianity was at stake. The Faulhaber sermon[21] was one of many attempts to bring this grim fact to public awareness and concern. In a memorable passage he addressed himself directly to the question of whether there was a religious persecution in Germany. Praising Pius XI for his ability to "give things their right name by calling white white and black black" (again an obvious reference to *Mit brennender sorge*), he set forth to do the same. "The question as to whether there is a religious persecution in Germany," he said, "should be left in the first place for the *persecuted* to answer, the ones who experience it in their own bodies, and not to the *persecutors*. One hears it argued that no churches here are being burned or profaned. Yet when, in Bavaria alone, eighty-two convent secondary schools serving 15,000 children can be simply taken over with less consideration than that given a condemned man, that is a crueller blow against the religious life than the burning of a couple of churches."

From our vantage point in time it is easy to argue that the resistance mounted by the church was doomed to failure because the bishops and other official spokesmen did not "give things their right name" in the fullest sense. The protests were surprisingly strong as written: in the case of the schools controversy, local officials were excoriated for the trickery and threats by which they persuaded Catholic parents to support the de-confessionalized community schools; in the case of the "indecency" campaigns against priests and religious, there were scathing denunciations of the dishonest and distorted reports in the controlled press, usually accompanied by careful and convincing factual refutations. Nevertheless, strong as these protests were, they were studiously misdirected to the wrong address. There is little reason to assume that the bishops did not know that the ultimate responsibility for these acts of repression lay in the hands of Adolf Hitler himself; yet they chose to exercise the "wisdom of serpents" in their response. Not only did they refrain from making Hitler the direct object of their protest but they also persisted in maintaining the polite fiction that the fault lay with lesser officials and subordinates. Wherever possible they larded their protests with quotations from speeches and published statements to show that the disputed policies and programs were not in accord with the Führer's personal intentions and assurances. Again, there is much to commend this as a tactic. Unfortunately it also provided the faithful with an opportunity—and, let us not forget, given the nature of the controls and sanctions available to the totalitarian ruler it must have been a most welcome opportunity—to make a distinction, an utterly false distinction, between Hitler and his intentions and the actions taken by the Gestapo and the other objects of the episcopal protest.

The resulting confusion clearly served the Nazis' purpose, and there is every reason to believe it was planned that way. Rosenberg's *Myth*, for example, was never officially "adopted" as a party line; it was merely "recommended" for use by all teachers and pupils by the official publication of the Prussian Schools' Curriculum Administration.[22] Its author's base of operations was a party post (albeit as "Führer's delegate").[23] Yet when the church launched its concerted attack upon the book and the "new heathenism" it proposed, the regime saw nothing inconsistent about defining that activity as an assault upon the new order and its philosophy. So defined, it provided the state authorities with the justification for moving to suppress the Catholic Action network of agencies and organizations as a form of "self-defense"![24]

Since the struggle over Rosenberg's "private" book was primarily ideological, the church was able to hold its own at that level, costly as the incidental effects measured in terms of new organizational restrictions undoubtedly were. The real life-and-death struggle centered upon active control over the formation of youth through the schools and the wide network of athletic, social, and religious youth organizations. In the schools controversy, too, the church's "adversary" was a quasi-official group, the *Deutsche Schulgemeinde*, ostensibly a private professional group dedicated to the creation of a public school system to replace the confessional schools. A May

1936 notice issued by the Munich chancery warned parents of school age children against this organization which they, it seems, were being pressured to join. The warning pointed out that the leaders of this organization had described it as a "fighting organization" dedicated to the elimination of Catholic schools. On these grounds the parents were to consider themselves bound by their religious consciences to refuse to join; but, and here a familiar theme enters, they were also forbidden to do so by their civil consciences since those stated objectives were clearly contrary to the provisions of the Concordat and other existing legal provisions and pronouncements of the state.[25] A year later another instruction was issued to warn the clergy against renewed efforts being made to win members for the *Schulgemeinde*, noting in particular that while it was forbidden for Catholic parents' organizations to publish a 1936 calendar, their opponents were permitted to do so (even to distribute them in the confessional schools despite the fact that the calendar contained material attacking those schools!).[26]

This unfair advantage was a small matter compared to what was yet to come. In his pastoral issued in April 1937, Bishop Sebastian of Speyer went to considerable length to detail the frauds, deceptions, and outright threats marking the vote taken on the schools question the preceding month. Instead of the "jubilation" that, according to the press reports, had greeted the victory of the community schools, he testified to the sorrow and tears of the overwhelmingly Catholic population of the area. He spoke of communities in which the vote had gone decisively in favor of the confessional schools—only to be reported as 100 percent against. In one district having more than a hundred eligible voters, only six favored the proposal; extra effort by the local officials succeeded in raising that total to twelve—but this community, too, was reported as 100 percent in favor. Peasant women were falsely assured that the outcome of the vote would change nothing, even that the religious authorities had, in fact, called for support for the public schools proposal. Heads of families had been threatened with the loss of their jobs or necessary state assistance.[27]

One-sided though the struggle proved to be, it was a spirited one while it lasted. An Easter sermon preached by the Bishop of Trier a week after that same vote was a rabble-rouser in the true sense of that term, and, to judge by the congregation's reactions as inserted into the mimeographed text, it had the intended effect. At several points there was "laughter" or "great excitement"; once there were shouts of "Bravo!" making it necessary for the bishop to appeal for order. Nor was this all. In a strikingly symbolic act of protest, orders were given by both bishops forbidding the ringing of the church bells for Easter (also sung masses, organ music, and other normal marks of celebration) "as a mark of the great sorrow on the part of the Church and her local members over the results of the vote."[28]

Of particular significance is the case of one Alois Kober, a priest who dared take a public stand in favor of the public schools. The Munich archdiocese responded to this departure from its official policy by withdrawing his certification as docent and revoking his permission to preach or conduct his regular religious services. He was warned that failure to renounce his error within eight days would lead to his formal suspension from the priesthood. A quite predictable contretemps developed when the Bavarian ministry for education and culture refused to accept the cancellation of his certification, receiving in their turn a chancery response insisting that the issue was no business of theirs since it concerned purely internal matters of the church. The threatened suspension was confirmed in a letter from Faulhaber in which the errant priest was advised to consider the seriousness of the hour and not be misled by the adulation of those who were trying to bring him to apostatize and continue his opposition to the church on this score. "Your last walk will be one you will have to travel alone, and none of those who cheer you on today because of their enmity to the Church will be able to take from you your personal responsibility before the Judgment Seat of God."[29]  If nothing else, it shows how important the schools issue was to the Catholic leaders: where they had the power, they were prepared to use it.

In one sense the whole schools issue was but one part of the broader struggle for control over the minds and spirit of children and young people. The campaign began at least two years earlier when the Nazis introduced a series of restrictions upon Catholic youth organizations and their activities. Places and times of meetings, as well as the kind of activities to be permitted, were narrowly specified; the display of organizational flags and banners, even the wearing of badges, was banned outside of the approved settings. At the same time every advantage was provided for the state sponsored youth groups and activities. Rallies, outings, and the like were so designed and so scheduled as to crowd out all competition. A particular annoyance to religious leaders was the policy of scheduling Hitler Youth events at hours which made attendance at religious services difficult if not altogether impossible. These tactics were met, but one suspects inadequately, by arranging for special services or by dispensing the young people from religious obligation, the first an inconvenient and the second an admittedly risky solution.

In the battle over the schools the decision of Catholic parents was the prize, and once the state applied the full pressure of its totalitarian power, that cause was lost for the church. The broader struggle was, in the event, even more hopeless. In addition to the external and all but unlimited power of the state, the religious leaders now had to contend with the attractiveness of being part of an exciting opportunity to build a new world order. The youth "elite," already assured of a prominent role in that venture through Hitler Youth and League of German Girls organizations, undoubtedly held greater appeal for even Catholic young people than the spokesmen for a discredited older generation—and especially spokesmen who were themselves part of an institution charged with suspect or limited loyalty to that new order. We sometimes overlook this very important factor and explain the success achieved by Hitler, Schirach, and their plans for the youth too much in terms of imposition of external controls. The reverse was probably true. The idealism, fervor, and dedication of the young (the "internal controls," if you will) probably accounted for most of the enthusiasm they displayed at the mass rallies and "on the streets" as well. These were children of parents who had known a humiliating defeat; they had experienced with those parents the harsh realities of economic collapse and privation; now they were offered a vision of a Thousand Year Reich, a millenium of prosperity and world domination.

The church was destined to lose this one, too; but it did not lose by default. A great deal of special attention was given to developing retreat programs specifically designed to appeal to the young men in military service or labor corps. Great pressure was put upon parents to remind them of their inescapable moral obligation to make certain that their children remain true to the faith and regular in its practice. Whatever could be done (and it turned out to be very little indeed) was done to preserve some semblance of organized youth work under church auspices and direction. "Youth Sunday 1938" illustrates the high priority placed on this objective: explicit instructions as to how to prepare and conduct the special services and ceremonies to mark the day covered three highly detailed pages.[30]  That same year's Eucharistic Congress scheduled for Budapest was closed to large German pilgrimages, but the event was used nonetheless as the occasion for a special appeal to young people to join in spirit at least with the international celebration and to rededicate themselves to service to the Faith. Once again the content of the appeal assumes special significance. Much was made of the presence in Budapest of General Moscardo, one of the heroes of the Spanish Civil War, and the application took the form of a direct challenge: "My dear young Christian, are you perhaps a greater hero than Moscardo that you are too proud to bend your knee [i.e., before the Eucharist]? . . . or is it cowardly fear of men? Then learn from the hero of Alcazar not only how one heroically risks one's life for his country and his people but also how one shows those same heroic qualities by committing his life for God in the courage of Faith and out of loyalty to the Faith."[31]

Appeals to courage and perseverance and the other manly virtues may have been standard rhetoric in addressing any audience of young men in the Germany of those Hitler years. But by this point in the struggle one must assume that the stress placed on "manliness" had other defensive overtones as well. The 1934 attacks upon the Catholic church, represented by the "new heathenism" of Rosenberg, tended to be ideological. By 1938 they had long since given way to attacks focusing much more directly upon religious practices and religious vocations. The drive to deconfessionalize the schools (a victory for the state, though sometimes mitigated by adamant insistence upon keeping the crucifix in the classroom) had its counterpart, logically enough, in measures to exclude religious men and women from their teaching posts and, ultimately, the shutting down altogether of religious houses, training institutes, and convent schools. All of these, needless to say, were accompanied by official protests citing violations of the Concordat; but one assumes that by this time these were regarded as ritual responses by the authors of the protests just as they undoubtedly were by those to whom the protests were addressed.

The most vicious attack of all was to be directed against the priesthood (and, by extension, the bishops and even the papacy as well). The issuance of *Mit brennender sorge* in 1937 added new purpose to the drive, but it was already well under way by that time. Sometimes the campaign took the form of attacks upon individual priests and their activities. One such case found Bishop Rackl taking to the pulpit of his Eichstätt cathedral to explain why, in the face of a police order requiring its pastor to leave the diocese within twenty-four hours, he had personally instructed the priest not to comply. The announcement, as the mimeographed text of the sermon duly notes, met with "stormy applause." Rackl's highly emotional defense stressed the priest's war record and rejected any possibility that he could, by the wildest stretch of anyone's imagination, be counted among those who "are marching against the State" as the local press had put it. (Here, too, the suggestion was met with indignant shouts of "Pfui" by the aroused congregation.)[32]

Nor was this the only instance of Rackl's playing upon the emotions of the Catholic populace to get his point across. Less than a month later he was officiating at a funeral at a village church (on the Feast of the Ascension, a major religious holiday!) whose pastor had been exiled from the parish by the Gestapo without any explanation being given. A woman parishioner had died in the meantime and, after unsuccessfully trying to use this as the lever for obtaining the pastor's return, the Bishop decided to conduct the burial himself (getting up from his own sickbed to do so, as he was careful to point out). Since the deceased had been a mother, he chose this as an appropriate theme from which to draw the conclusions he wanted his audience to reach. "If I speak now of mother and mothers' love, of mothers' faithfulness and mothers' care, of the sufferings of mothers and the joys of mothers, then I must think in this moment of that other mother, the Holy Mother, the Catholic Church. . . ." The link thus made, he immediately launched into a telling defense of his priest and of the church, carefully inserting cautions that his words were not to be taken as anything but a message of love. Only at the very end did he return to the ostensible purpose for his being there and conclude with a brief one-paragraph reference to the burial of the deceased.[33]

Several of the other documents surveyed refer to two better known incidents: the arrest and imprisonment of Rupert Mayer, the Munich Jesuit whose cause for canonization is being promoted in

Germany today; and the removal from his diocese of Bishop Spröll of Rottenburg. Mayer's arrest prompted a sermon delivered personally by Cardinal Faulhaber. Its title, "Smoke, the Sign of Fire," is an obvious enough reference to the arrest as a sign of religious oppression and persecution. Like his Eichstätt colleague, Faulhaber left no emotional base untouched. Mayer's distinguished war record, the severe wounds he suffered, the decorations he received—all received the expected treatment. An additional argument of particular significance focused upon Mayer's postwar record of anticommunist activity and the bond this fashioned between him and Hitler himself: ". . . and this German man who wears the Iron Cross as does the Führer; who, shoulder to shoulder with the Führer, took his stand against the Communists in Munich; who has a personal testimonial to this effect written in the Führer's own hand—this man sits today behind prison walls!"[34]

The sermon included a detailed survey of Mayer's religious works to refute the charges that he had misused the pulpit for political purposes, and this was expanded a few weeks later in a full resume distributed by the Munich chancery "for personal information" in which the full sequence of events, including the trial and sentencing, was described. A note added that, though a six-month sentence had been passed, Mayer had been allowed to return to the Jesuit residence where he remained under doctor's care.[35] Two subsequent notices are particularly suggestive. The first took the form of an announcement to be read from all pulpits on the Sunday following its issuance (January 20, 1938) to notify the faithful that Mayer had again been arrested on charges that he had resumed preaching in violation of police orders and that he now had to begin serving the sentence that had been passed the previous July. The announcement referred to the Cardinal's earlier address and his position that such silencing of a priest constituted a violation of the Concordat; a protest to this effect was still pending decision. Mayer himself, the announcement made clear, had decided not to plead for pardon and wished it to be made known that it was his most urgent desire that the faithful preserve their calm, remembering him in their prayers "in true Apostolic fashion."[36] Apparently even this was not caution enough: a postscript to another chancery notice sent out five days later rescinded the instruction to read the earlier announcement from the pulpit. The additional information (again marked "for personal information only") was included that Mayer was being held for the time being in the Landsberg prison.[37]

Surprisingly enough, the Spröll case received considerably less attention even though it represents the most serious step taken by the Nazi authorities against a German bishop. A September 1938 statement issued by the Bavarian hierarchy and devoted to the actions taken against convent schools and teachers carried an addendum with specific instructions that it be read exactly as given. In the text of this appended statement the bishops denounced "as a serious assault upon the freedom of the Church" the order that had been issued against the Bishop of Rottenburg forbidding him to remain in his diocese and, further, his forcible removal from the Württemberg province by the police following his refusal to leave voluntarily.[38] Nothing more. This, together with the rescinding of the public announcement of Mayer's arrest, must be taken as convincing evidence of a policy decision on the part of church officials to discourage active and open reactions against the regime. Whether this restraint was imposed by the Nazis under threat of severe retaliation or whether it reflects the bishops' own commitment to prudence in a difficult situation is not entirely clear. What is clear, however, is a determination to limit the church's opposition to formal protest, still public but decreasingly so, and not encourage or endorse active resistance to Nazi rule on the part of their following.

The harassment and punishment of individual priests who had somehow earned the particular displeasure of the secular authorities undoubtedly had the effect of disrupting church operations and, even more to the point, deterring other individuals from giving similar offense. A much more devastating blow, however, was the campaign of vilification and scandal directed against the priesthood itself. This reached peak intensity in the widely publicized charges of sexual misbehavior supposedly conducted under cover of religious community life and, once discovered, condoned and protected by higher ecclesiastical authority. Ordinarily one might think that charges of this nature might best not be dignified with more than a formal denial on the assumption that not too many of the flock would be likely to "buy" such an outrageous story. In the setting of Nazi Germany—especially, one might suggest, with all the emphasis placed on racial purity and the manly virtues and all the other values which went to prove the superiority of the Aryan *Volk* and its supreme destiny—any suggestion of sexual weakness or deviance could not be permitted to pass unchallenged. So must the churchmen have reasoned at least; for the response to the charges was immediate and charged with emotion.

That the charges were a deliberate attempt to undermine the respect for, and the authority of, the clergy by sullying the image of all who chose the religious vocation is obvious enough. The indecency charges and show trials were not the only devices to be directed to this end. Currency manipulation was another favorite charge; then too, there were frequent (and patently fraudulent) "feature stories" about elderly "priests" and young "wives" or, to turn this around, criticism of celibacy as an unnatural or unworthy denial of manhood. Sometimes, too, there were more sinister references to the confessional as a cover for subversive communications. Nothing, however, seemed to cut as deep as the morals charges. For one thing these had a distinct bearing upon that on-going struggle for the hearts and minds of the youth: any suggestion of "protected" homosexuality or other forms of sexual abuse would obviously jeopardize the desperate effort being made by church authorities to continue some form of organized youth activities.

Passing reference has already been made to the so-called Fall Schülle (Schülle affair).[39] This involved the young man whose "intentions" to study for the priesthood had been twisted in the press reports to suggest that he was well on the road to ordination. He was presented, too, as one of the principal figures in the Catholic youth movement in Baden. Finally, much was made of the fact that his misdeeds had become known to "church circles" through the confessional without the young culprit being turned in to the authorities.

A point-by-point rebuttal was prepared to be read at all services on a Sunday in January 1937 (with the exception of those specifically for children): as a *gymnasium* student, the young man was nowhere near beginning studies for the priesthood and certainly he had not been "accepted" for such study; his involvement in youth activities was at the branch level of organization and his "leadership" post had lasted only six months and that had been two years earlier; as to the final accusation, the sacredness of the confessional seal had to be respected, but this could not be taken to imply approval or condoning of acts which Catholic moral teachings include among the most revolting and unnatural faults to which human nature is prone.[40]

The Kraus sermon picked it up from there and elaborated the issue into a full-fledged denunciation of the press. Kraus began by noting that he had been forced to do battle for the church on but three occasions during that year, the first at his post. There was a protest against the pamphlets and posters of the German Faith Movement; then he felt called upon to rise to the support of Bishop Gröber when he had been brought under attack; and, most recently, he had written to the press to protest and correct its false reporting on the Schülle affair. In the first two instances he had been ignored; the third had led to his being attacked in meetings and in the press. The Schülle affair is one of the three instances of press distortion carefully refuted in this sermon (the other two involve a priest who supposedly expressed Antisemitic sentiments and a priest in Dachau who supposedly represented himself as a go-between in negotiations between Moscow and the Vatican), all three of which, he reasons, were intended to smear all priests and religious. We have already noted the stress placed upon his war record and his pride in his former officer status and how he equated transforming Schülle's aspirations to the priesthood into a slur upon that vocation with what would have been the equally offensive attempt to smear the officers' corps had the unfortunate young man said he had aspirations for the military life. The most impressive thing about this eight page (single-spaced!) sermon, however, is the openness of his denunciation of the abuses perpetrated by the controlled press. As such it stands as an outstanding example of Catholic resistance and, objectively speaking, may have earned its author the punishment he was later to receive.[41]

A more formal rejoinder to the substance of the indecency charges and the manner in which the trials were being conducted took the form of a lengthy letter addressed to Goebbels personally and written by Bishop von Preysing of Berlin. In a thoroughly systematic manner he sets forth three "accusations" he felt were implied against the church and proceeds to counter each, making extensive use of appropriate citations from episcopal statements, news reports, as well as the exchanges of correspondence between protesting ecclesiastics and government officials. In a biting footnote

he contrasts the seemingly unlimited space devoted to these sensa-
tionalized trials with the severe restrictions placed upon the Catholic
press to keep it from making the other side known. "The primary
goal of these reports, headlines, lead articles, cartoons, and the like
can only be seen as the defamation of the Church, the Bishops, the
priests, the convents, the confessional schools, and Catholic youth
work."[42] At another point he brings the comparison even closer to
home by placing the emphasis and unbounded publicity given allega-
tions involving religious and priests in the context of what he terms
the "open secret" that the Nazi state went to great length to keep
the sexual misdeeds and other punishable offenses occurring within
its own ranks from ever reaching public notice. A most telling point
indeed—but it is interesting to note that it was made in a private
communication to one of the top government officials, not in a
sermon or pastoral letter addressed to a more general audience
where, one assumes, it might have had greater impact.

What we have seen then—and these examples could be multiplied
several times over—is that the official church did "resist" the Nazi
state by protesting what its spokesmen regarded as infringements
upon the rights and freedom of religion and, in particular, as violations of the letter and spirit of the 1933 Concordat. For the period
covered by the documents upon which this review has been based,
the major areas of contention between the protesting church and the
increasingly repressive state were the Rosenberg ideological challenge, the deconfessionalization of the schools, the progressive elimination of religious youth services, and, finally, an ever-tightening
noose of restrictions upon church facilities and activities coupled, as
we have seen, with a smear campaign almost without parallel designed to discredit the church by discrediting the priesthood. It is
most unfortunate that the documentation does not extend into the
war period, but it is extremely unlikely that this would have changed
the essential picture. True, the successful resistance to euthanasia
would have to be added to the list, but this positive accomplishment
would be more than balanced by the failure to mount any opposition
at all to Hitler's unjust wars, a failure I have documented elsewhere.[43]

The one issue that, above all others, has troubled the conscience
of mankind since the collapse of the Third Reich, the attempted
extermination of European Jewry, finds virtually no mention at all in

225

this group of documents. The absence seems significant even though the "final solution" did not get under way until a later period than that covered by the data put at my disposal. One might have expected some comment to be occasioned by Crystal Night and its aftermath in November 1938, but none is recorded here. Cochrane's description of the reaction of church leaders to that event as one of "turning a blind eye" is probably accurate as is the explanation he suggests, namely, that "Exhausted and demoralized by their previous efforts, they fell silent even in the face of such outrages."[44] In the several hundred pages of mimeographed material I have reviewed, only three references bearing upon the Jews and their problems were encountered and only one could be said to be at all direct. The first merely indicated the appropriate fees for record searches to establish Aryan descent, and this was included in a thirty-five page summary of laws and regulations bearing upon church and religious activities.[45] The second was not only indirect but negative as well in its implications. In a Faulhaber statement opposing the vote in the schools question, he attempts to counter the argument that it might be well for churchmen to look to Russia and Loyalist Spain before criticizing their own government; his response suggests that the public officials for their part might well look toward France "where even Jews and Masons sit in the government" and where parents were still allowed the free choice of sending their children to confessional schools.[46] The third reference occurs in the Kraus sermon. One of the cases of false reporting by the press singled out by him for detailed refutation was an article in *Der Stürmer* in which the author, representing himself as a Catholic priest, endorsed the Streicher brand of Antisemitism. On the basis of a complete check of the clergy listed for all the dioceses of Germany, Kraus found no priest of the name given in the article; far more important, however, was his insistence that "No Catholic priest may write such things. No Catholic priest could write such things without having first thrown overboard all the fundamentals of Christianity."[47]

Before proceeding to an assessment of why the Catholic resistance to Hitler failed, one further point must be introduced. To focus attention, as has been done throughout this paper, upon the official leadership of the church and the statements issued or actions taken in its name is to overlook the resistance activities of Catholics acting as morally inspired individuals. There is good reason to believe that this resistance, largely still unrecorded, had more tangible effect than all the protests issued from chancery offices or, for that matter, from Rome. Through such resistance lives were actually saved, fugitives hidden and fed, illegal leaflets circulated, and even, at the last desperate stage, overt treason attempted. Some of these activities received secret support from men like Cardinal Faulhaber who—as was recalled by a woman active in the "underground railroad" engaged in spiriting Jews into Switzerland—was generous in his financial contributions to that work (always in untraceable cash, needless to say). No review of the Catholic resistance to Hitler, then, could be complete without some acknowledgement of these efforts. At the same time, however, the point must be stressed that what they did, they (even a Faulhaber!) did as individual Catholics and not as agents of an organized and approved program initiated by the institutional church. In the fullest theological sense, of course, these individuals, especially those who were to suffer imprisonment and death as a result, were "representing" their church, and their actions do redound to the credit of that church. In the narrower sociological sense "the church" acts as a corporate association of believers through its functionaries exercising their formally defined powers and authority. It is with these that we have been primarily concerned here; and it is at this level of operation that a true resistance failed to materialize or, when and where it did, could claim little or no effect.

## IV. Why Official Resistance Failed

It is a relatively simple matter to explain why the official Catholic resistance to Hitler was largely unsuccessful, at least as success would be measured by changes in Nazi policy. The national state will always have a broad array of controls and sanctions available to it that, from the individual's point of view, are more immediately threatening than those available to competing institutions of society. The totalitarian state, by definition, expands this normal advantage to an absolute monopoly of power so that any opposition to its purpose or programs carries serious risks indeed. That the creation of just such a state was the Nazi objective none can deny; that they came frighteningly close to reaching that objective is a matter of record.

The Catholic church, like its Protestant counterparts, was highly vulnerable to Nazi power, a fact that must have been known to its responsible leaders from the very beginning. The protections and guarantees provided by the Concordat might seem to contradict this on paper, but they were respected only to the extent that the state authorities thought some good (for the state naturally) could be achieved—or, at least, no harm done—by respecting them. Public protests unavailing and private contacts with Party and government leaders equally unproductive, the leaders of the church soon were forced to face the reality that a more active resistance, even assuming they would have found it possible to reconcile this with the traditional teachings promoting loyalty and obedience to lawful authority, could open the way to the elimination of the last few vestiges of religious activity and subject the faithful to the open persecution they had thus far, for the most part, been spared. The rhetoric of the protests continued to remind the faithful that martyrdom was a cross that Christians must always be prepared to bear, that the demands of God must always be given precedence over those of the temporal masters. Nevertheless, when it came down to specific issues that might seem to involve this choice, the church leadership always stopped short of calling for the kind of concerted and open resistance that might have led to such martyrdom on a massive scale.

There were several possible reasons for this. Perhaps one may fault the bishops for a failure of vision and commitment, perhaps even for a failure of courage when the chips were down. In strictly pragmatic terms one can see that their decisions in favor of restraint were "dictated" by prudent circumspection. What is more, they were probably quite correct in their pessimistic assessment of the prospects of success for any more determined stand they might have taken or advised. Evidently, and with perfectly good reason, the German hierarchy had come to the conclusion that they could not count on the loyalty of their "troops" in the event of an open and all-out church-state confrontation. The controversy over the introduction of the *gottgläubig* designation as a religious category on personal registration forms was a case in point.[48] This midway designation, between formal and specific religious identification and the "unchurched" classification, was the subject of several chancery directives, and repeated references were made to this as a form of what we would today describe as "chickening out" into apostasy. But those same repeated references testify to the effectiveness of the Nazi rule in that they indicate that a sufficiently large number of

Catholics did make use of the opportunity to stay in the good graces of the secular authority and still satisfy their consciences that they had not actually renounced their Christian faith.

If so, it would follow that any move which would have served to intensify Nazi animosity toward the church and its members would carry with it the prospect of large scale apostasy. For bishops charged with the sacred responsibility to bring the souls placed in their care to salvation, this would be a strong deterrent indeed. And with respect to those who would listen and obey in what even the bishops regarded at best as a futile gesture, for them there would always be the concentration camp and worse. This, too, might give the bishops pause. It is not surprising, then, that even in situations where the "troops" seemed eager enough to follow or even take the lead in contesting Nazi oppression, cautionary episcopal voices were raised to restrain the irate faithful from actions which might invite Nazi reprisals. The aroused Catholics who rushed to the defense of the various episcopal residences that had been attacked by "spontaneous mobs" gave testimony to a potential for active, even organized, resistance. Still, the hard truth of the matter was that after each such event, the Nazis moved in and used it as an excuse to impose new restrictions upon the church under the pretext of discouraging future violence and disruption. With the cards stacked against them, only the foolhardy would entertain any ideas of organizing large scale active resistance. And whatever else the German bishops in Nazi Germany may have been, they were not "foolhardy."

It is possible, of course, that leaders of the church underestimated the potential for resistance. In 1939 the Catholic population of Greater Germany was reported to total more than thirty million.[49] It is strange to think that such a large number could be quite as helpless and vulnerable as the bishops apparently took them to be. Or if these "troops" were too hesitant and confused, too enamoured of Nazi claims and accomplishments, part of the blame for this must be charged to those same religious leaders. Elsewhere[50] I have discussed the "patriotism-and-protest combination" tactic as an important factor in the almost total Catholic support for Hitler's war effort. One can see the same process operating in this broader context of support for the regime itself (or, if one prefers, in the absence of any truly effective resistance to that regime). The pastoral letters, the sermons, all the incidental announcements that we have introduced here as evidence of the church's opposition to Nazi oppression can also be read in most cases as contributions to Nazi morale, especially in their repeated insistence upon unquestioning loyalty and sacrifice to Folk and Fatherland.

To say this is not to deny that their authors' primary purpose in issuing these statements was clear enough: the "patriotic" part of the combination lends force to the repudiation of the insidious charges brought against the church and its organizations and to the reminder of the debt owed by the national community for past sacrifices made on its behalf. As arguments in an on-going debate, they were undoubtedly effective, and one can understand the "unchurchlike" responses they evoked from the congregations when they were presented. But there was another effect that must be considered, and the actual situation in which these statements were issued and the audiences to whom they were addressed are important here too. Every such appeal to patriotic sentiments would in effect serve to reinforce the hearer's personal commitment to the state and the nation "in spite of all." The patriotism-and-protest combination might have made better sense had it carried some implication that the patriotic support would be withdrawn or diminished were the persecution to continue; but it is clear that nothing was further from the intent of the Faulhabers, the Galens, and the others who were making these appeals. We have already cited the Munich cardinal's insistence that the Catholic could never be a revolutionary, no matter how bad things might get. This opinion was shared by the Bishop of Münster who concluded what may have been the most stirring and outspoken protest of all with the words, "Of course we Christians make no revolution! We will continue to do our duty in obedience to God, out of love for our German Folk and Fatherland."[51] The Nazi oppressors, that "enemy in our midst who tortures and strikes us," might have been annoyed (as they were); but they had no real reason to be worried as long as their principal ecclesiastical opponents held to that particular line.

Of all the documents I recently surveyed, two may again be singled out as examples of especially direct and strong denunciations of the Nazi persecution. The first is that April 1937 sermon in which Bishop Rackl defended his cathedral pastor who had been ordered to leave the diocese.[52] He noted that the news report on the case had put into print a charge that had previously been circulated only by word of mouth, the charge that there unfortunately were still "some circles in Eichstätt who imagine they are able to march against the State." To Rackl this was "a declaration of war" of sorts and, in that specific context, quite ridiculous; the congregation's responses indicated that they thought so too. "I take it," he declared, "that someone is suggesting that our *Dompfarrer* belongs to those who are marching against the State! (stormy boos and jeers) Beloved! Let me say it again: one who has served at the Front in the war for four long years—in the very front lines serving Germans' honor and welfare, such a man has never marched against the German State and can never march against the German State. (loud applause) And then if such an officer of the Fatherland later becomes an officer of the Catholic Church, and officer of JESUS CHRIST; one of God's officers, that Fidelity that is inscribed on his banner is a proclamation of fidelity toward State and Fatherland as well." Then the clinching argument: "No one loves his Fatherland as truly as the Catholic priest!"[53]

If this seems excessive, the sermon delivered three months earlier by Johannes Kraus, presumably the priest the bishop was defending, tends to bear it out. References already made to this sermon suggest that this may well have been a major, if not the precipitating, cause of the punitive action taken against him. The bluntness of his denunciation of the smears and distortions published in the press, together with his careful refutations of them, make this a remarkable document. But no less remarkable is the patriotic fervor that colored his ardent defense of the priesthood. One need only return to cite the rousing conclusion: "Everything for Germany, and Germany for Christ! And again: Everything for Germany, and Germany for Christ! And still a third time the pledge: Everything for Germany, and Germany for Christ!"[54] The irony of it all, of course, is that, while the Nazis were not likely to be at all impressed by this display of nationalistic enthusiasm, the congregation was very likely to be caught up as much in the surge of patriotic commitment as by the spirit of protest the sermon was intended to instill and express.

To this extent, the patriotism-and-protest combination would be self-defeating; I would go further and suggest that, in that particular historical situation, it was probably counter-productive. That is to say, it would serve to intensify the listener's identification with and commitment to state and nation—not, needless to say, to those Nazi persecuters but, rather, to that "Germany" to whom all was to be pledged. Which brings us to the most sensitive point of all. I submit that one of the main reasons why German Catholicism and its leaders failed to mount an effective resistance to Hitler is to be found in the extent to which those same leaders were themselves caught up in the uncritically nationalistic mood of the time.

It is far too easy to assume, as some of the critics of my earlier work have, that these fervent affirmations of loyalty and dedication are little more than rhetoric tailored to satisfy Nazi ears so that some measure of stability, minimal but sufficient to maintain communication between bishop and faithful, might be assured for the church and its operations. I do not question that this was a factor, but I would insist that it does the bishops and the other ecclesiastical spokesmen a grievous injustice to inflate this into the only or even the dominant factor. Making full allowance for the exigencies of a situation of extreme stress, I believe the conclusion is inescapable that the bishops said what they did because they sincerely believed in the rightness of what they said. To them it was quite shameful that the state would ignore the loyalty and the readiness to sacrifice that had always been promoted by the Christian Faith; and a good part of their dismay rested upon the fact that loyalty and sacrifice (*military* sacrifice especially) were vested with a kind of sacredness in their eyes: so, too, with their repudiation of revolution as a possible option for the Christian. It was not only because of their fears that revolution would serve the objectives of the hated Bolshevism (though that was certainly an important consideration). It was far more the reason they gave: purely and simply, Christians do not "make revolutions"; Christians *are* always obedient to legitimate authority; Christians *must* "render unto Caesar." If this seems inconsistent with the fact that they did encourage Catholic support for the Franco cause in Spain, the explanation may be because the struggle against the Loyalists would more likely be viewed by them as a "restoration" than a "rebellion." As far as Hitler was concerned, however little love they might have had for him or for his movement, he did become "legitimate authority," and this was ratified by the recognition extended in the Concordat. Once this took place, those theological-ideological principles would apply and this would limit the kind and the degree of resistance the Catholic community might be expected to muster against the Third Reich. Nor is there any reason to believe that the support provided by the church was necessarily a grudging support. The contrary is much more likely to be true. At the beginning at least, the gains and advances in territory and world prestige must have been as gratifying to the leaders of the Catholic church in Germany as they were to the rest of the population. In fact, had the Nazis not chosen to embark upon the ideological campaign against Christianity, one suspects they would have found the Catholic church and most of its members among the most ardent defenders of the Third Reich.

In such an event it is virtually certain that few, possibly none, of the documents I have reviewed would ever have been written. This conclusion follows from the nature of the documents themselves. The resistance and opposition they represent were exclusively defensive in character, and narrowly defensive at that. This was a struggle in which the Nazi officials could, and usually did, choose the issue, the timing of the battle, and the battleground as each phase developed. The only partial exceptions to this rule were, first, the "new heathenism" issue (in which the more aggressive church could claim a kind of victory in that the Rosenberg movement failed to win the widespread support it sought and soon became something of a dead issue) and, second, euthanasia (in which the church, thanks largely to Galen, registered its only major success when that program was quietly terminated). It may be of some significance that the church's response in both instances took the form of an "attack" of sorts and did not limit itself to defensive protests; but it would be too much to conclude from this that similar successes would have accompanied more aggressive action in other areas of conflict which the Nazis might have defined as more critical. The disadvantage of an overly defensive posture lay in the fact that the protests lost much of their force as they became repetitious. Appeals to Concordat protections in particular took on something of a ritual character after they had been ignored more than once or twice.

The narrowness of the defense is perhaps more basic. In none of these documents, with the possible exception of the Kraus reference to the impossibility of a Catholic priest endorsing the *Stürmer* line concerning the Jews (a rather indirect exception at best), do we find the Catholic protests concerned with injustices suffered by other churches or groups. The suppression of Socialist organizations and the arrest and imprisonment of their leaders paralleled and preceded the actions taken against Catholic organizations and religious orders. To take a more dramatic example, the brutal liquidation of the SA drew no public denunciation from Faulhaber or the Munich arch-diocesan officials despite the fact that the "Night of the Long Knives" reached its bloodiest climax in their own backyard. One would hesitate to say that the church officials "welcomed" the removal from the scene of Socialists, Communists, and the revolutionary rabble of the SA; but the fact remains that they did not distinguish themselves *as early as June 1934* as defenders of even the most elementary rights of those who happened to be viewed with political disfavor by the representatives of the new order.

Only when the blow struck nearby were such things as the distortions of the controlled press or the excesses of the Gestapo brought to the attention of the Catholic faithful by their spiritual leaders. The same reticence marked the behavior of the other Christian churches as well; no one, it seems, was overly anxious to borrow trouble with the Nazis. In the case of the Catholic church, however, there was another reason. Any attempt to protest actions taken against non-Catholics would certainly have been received by the regime as precisely the kind of "political" activity explicitly forbidden to the church under the terms of the Concordat. Here, again, we may have grounds to question the wisdom of entering upon an agreement which included such a limitation in the first place, if only because of the opening it gave for too complete a distinction between the "political" and the moral realms of behavior. But behind it all was the failure to recognize or find common cause with others not of their fold; they simply did not see that the Communist war veteran denied a job or sent to a concentration camp for his beliefs was a victim of injustice fully as deserving of their concern as the priest evicted from his pulpit, Iron Cross and all.

If there is any single overriding lesson to be learned from this, it would seem to be that the religious community must never become so enmeshed in its support for a given socio-political order that it loses its potential to be a source of dissent and disobedience. In other, more familiar terms, the church must recognize that it has a stake in maintaining a separation of church and state as that separation is defined from its own perspective. It is a serious mistake to see that separation, as Americans are so prone to see it, only in terms of protecting the purity and independence of the secular order from unwarranted intrusions or domination by the spiritual. The problem as it developed in Germany (and as it may exist here to a greater degree than we are aware!) is also one of preserving the purity and independence of the spiritual community and its teachings from domination by the national state with its definitions of situational needs and priorities. The traditional readiness to grant "the presumption of justice" to "lawful authority" no longer suits the needs of a world where the secular rulers increasingly respect no guides but the maximization of power and expediency in determining their policies and programs. If mistakes are to be made, it might be better for the churches to err in the direction of being too critical of state authority, too ready to oppose policies and programs which carry even a remote threat of departing from or ignoring moral rights and obligations. This should hold true even when, especially when, it is not their own personnel or interests that are at stake. This may make for greater tensions between church and state at times, but at least it will make it less likely that the church and its leaders will go along in easy conformity until, quite suddenly, they find themselves locked into the kind of helpless situation Nazi Germany came to represent.

The whole sad history of the Third Reich from its beginnings as an extremist fringe movement to its final collapse, just when it seemed to be on the verge of gaining the world domination it sought, was an event *sui generis*, a supremely traumatic experience which the world is not likely to have to suffer in the same form again. It would be a serious mistake, however, to write it off, as some have done, as a completely accidental (or, as others prefer, diabolical) constellation of circumstances having no real bearing upon more "normal" situations. Rather, we must recognize the unpleasant truth that, unique though it may have been, it arose out of human potentialities and tolerances for evil which carry the grim promise that something like it could happen again anywhere and against which reasonable men must always be on guard. It is extremely important, then, that we be alert, even somewhat hypersensitive perhaps, to anything that might indicate we are again moving in that direction or that may already have arrived.

Our religious communities have a special advantage and a special responsibility in this regard. They should be the best equipped to recognize these signs and the most determined to prove that they shall not fail again when leadership and effective resistance are required. Saying this, I must go on to confess that I have seen little to justify any confidence that they are ready to assume that task. While preparing these concluding observations, I took time off to read Daniel Berrigan's defendant's-eye-account of the trial of the Catonsville Nine,[55] and it occurred to me that this report on Catholic resistance to Hitler would be much different were it possible to include the story of a similar group of Catholics—priests, religious laymen and laywomen—taking it upon themselves to break into some government office to destroy the lists of Jews scheduled for deportation to Auschwitz. Nor is the comparison as far-fetched as it may seem at first glance: to Fr. Berrigan and his co-defendants the draft records they destroyed were also "potential death certificates" both for the men who might be sent to their death and for those they would be sent to kill. But the more I thought of it, the more convinced I became that there would not be too much change in this report after all. In the case of the hypothetical "Frankfurt Nine" we can be sure that their bishop and religious superiors would have hastened to dissociate themselves publicly from their rash and destructive act; the point would have been made that most Catholics were, as always, ready to do their duty in love and obedience to Folk and Fatherland; and one may be certain, too, that the bulk of the Catholic faithful would have found it difficult if not impossible to understand what the culprits were trying to do or say. All of which describes the reaction of the general American Catholic community to Catonsville.

Other comparisons, equally disturbing and perhaps not quite as controversial, come to mind. Was the silence of the German hierarchy over the war atrocities committed by the Nazi armed forces that much more complete than the silence of the American Catholic hierarchy over My Lai and, long before that, the widespread use of napalm and chemical warfare against a predominantly peasant population? I am afraid not. Furthermore, the German bishops come out looking better on this score since they could at least claim ignorance, whereas the American bishops presumably can read the full details with their breakfast coffee. Protest and opposition there have been—but these have come from journalists, politicians, individual citizens, and even generals while the Catholic bishops, whether individually or through their organization presided over by the bishop in whose diocese we meet today, have remained silent. The anniversary of My Lai is upon us this week, but they have not even done so much as to order the silencing of church bells as a sign of penance and reparation.

There are other "parallels" deserving at least some passing thought and comment by the responsible spokesmen for our religious communities. I am thinking of high government officials choosing to attack the news media in terms reminiscent of a Goebbels; a judge whose conduct of a trial might well have won a nod of approval from Roland Freisler; charges brought in that court which bear more than a faint resemblance to those that put Rupert Mayer in prison. Some, perhaps all, of these "parallels" may be forced, but it should not be too much to expect that the official Catholic leadership might at least be included among those who have criticized these things, if not, indeed, be leading them. The fact is, needless to say, that neither is true. And I, for one, choose to conclude from this that the lessons of the Nazi era have not been learned.

My sociological conscience warns me that these observations have been too value-tainted, but I will let them stand without apology. My justification lies in the nature of this gathering and its purpose. We are here as a group of "experts" looking back upon a historical period in which values that should have been recognized and insistently proclaimed lost much of their force because those who had major responsibility to see that they were translated into human behavior spoke too softly or too ambiguously or waited until it was too late to speak at all. It is for us to do what we can to assure that this need not happen again.

# IV
## Personal Reflections

# 13

# On Nazism and the Church Struggle

## Ferdinand Friedensburg

It is with some reluctance and with a heavy heart that I have come here from Berlin to speak to you about a problem on which I cannot claim to be an expert. I am neither a theologian nor a man of the church in the proper sense. In the struggle of the churches against Hitler or of Hitler against the churches, I have not been in the front line, within the Confessing Church—the fighting body of the German Protestants—an organization about which we are going to hear more in my address to-day. I have been a humble member although one of the men in the critical hour. Because of my political reputation as an adversary of the Hitler regime—perhaps a reputation not quite undeserved—I should have been an embarrassment for my clerical friends, who tried to remain outside the purely political field. During the struggle itself, therefore, I had to be more an observer than a combatant, and the theological aspects of the conflict were not my concern. As a German patriot, however, I was deeply, terribly ashamed of what was going on in our Christian country, and if I was more an observer than a combatant, I certainly was a very passionate observer.

Apart from my lack of immediate competence, I must ask you to understand a rather complicated matter, which escapes clear and systematic explanation. In a dictatorship, citizens are generally kept entirely uninformed about everything which does not please the dictator. Knowledge depends upon chance, upon rumors which often are distorted or completely false. News transmitted by newspapers or radio is neither complete nor always reliable. The information from other countries is not always helpful. During the first years of National Socialist rule, most foreign countries followed a policy of appeasement very similar to today's general inclination to appease the Soviet government; and, quite naturally, news detrimental to the objectives of such efforts was less favored than news which favored them. In the beginning Hitler and his men liked to obscure their aims and even their actions under an impenetrable cloud of propaganda, of distortions, and often enough of cunning lies, with the result that neither in Germany nor abroad could an exact knowledge or a comprehensive review of developments be achieved. Hence, a good deal of what has happened in this dark period of our history may be explained and even partly excused by the ignorance of a great part of the population. Certainly, to understand such a situation is difficult for men who live in a democracy with its characteristic abundance of information.

But we have to recognize the effect of this lack of accurate news and we have to understand that this difficulty has, to a special degree, influenced the opinions of true Christians who are under the obligation to love their neighbors, even their enemies, and to look for the good in everything. Cut off from sufficient and correct information, a great number of church people were inclined to believe the best of the new movement, until the overwhelming proof of Hitler's antireligious spirit and of the terrible crimes became only too evident. Later we will have to investigate the true character of this ignorance which was not entirely due to the policy of the state authorities.

We have to consider also that Hitler rose as a champion against Bolshevism, the atheistic nature of which the Russian Communists proclaimed quite frankly. At the last election in Germany before Hitler came to power, not less than one sixth of the voters were Communists, but after 1918 there had been continuous danger of a Communist revolt. In the choice between the two opponents, the decision for Christian people was only too obvious. In the beginning, Hitler liked to simulate a certain degree of Christian mentality and respect for the churches. No wonder that the clergy, especially, succumbed to the temptation to see Hitler also as the defender of the faith, or at least to regard him as the lesser of two evils. Since in many ways the path for future development had been laid in the first year of the National Socialist regime, to change the route which many men in the clergy had taken in good faith at the beginning proved to be very difficult. On the whole, it is important to recognize the fundamental changes which took place within the short period of twelve years between 1933 and 1945. Stimulated by personal experiences or better information, by the impact of successes and failures, few institutions or single men remained so steadfast and unchangeable as later they may wish they had been. Reviewing this twenty-five years later, we have to resign ourselves to an honest and sober representation of the ups and downs in the development, even if it is difficult to understand.

When Reich President von Hindenburg, in January 1933, called Hitler to form a new cabinet, Germany was an overwhelmingly Christian country; 97 percent professed to be Christians, practically two-thirds Protestants, one-third Catholics, nearly 1 percent Jews, and those without church membership 1.4 percent. While the forty million Protestants were divided into some dozens of regional churches and denominations, the twenty million Catholics, as is true everywhere, formed a solid unity under the supremacy of the Pope in Rome. This link with a distant power, withdrawn from the influence of the National Socialists, gave the Catholics a certain reserve of power and therefore a certain independence during the whole period—all the more so since Mussolini, Hitler's ally and in some ways his model, ruled over purely Catholic Italy and always tried to remain on good terms with the Pope. Quite the contrary, the Protestant churches lacked unity, and their traditional dependence upon the local and regional authorities made them weak and exposed them to the arbitrariness of a secular government. Moreover, the Catholics controlled a strong political organization in the Center party which, in 1932, held 12 percent of the seats in the Reichstag. It is true that in the spring of 1933 the Center party voted with all non-Socialist parties for the bill giving Hitler extraordinary power. Shortly afterwards, the Center party was dissolved with the rest of the parties. But before this happened, the party leaders succeeded in inducing Hitler to conclude a concordat with the Holy See, the concordat which, for twelve years, gave the Catholics unassailable support, a support which the Protestants with their scattered and loose organization grievously lacked. On the other hand, the Catholic church, because of its apparent strength, was in a position to be more flexible, less fundamentalist, more obliging about carrying out the orders or wishes of the state; this had the not quite desirable result that this leniency led to a weaker resistance in the conflict, which sooner or later unavoidably involved the Catholic institutions too.

After all, it is difficult to speak of the Christian churches in the situation of that time as a solid force, compared with the force represented by the National Socialist movement. This secular political force, moreover, had the advantage of being free of moral scruples to a degree that again and again surprised and finally deceived its adversaries.

This is neither the time nor place to analyze more profoundly Hitler's character and the nature of National Socialism. For our review, however, it is decisively important to recognize that Hitler was entirely devoid of moral considerations and not less devoid of principles of any kind. He was fanatically ambitious, and the only key to his actions was his will to power. To this dominating passion he subordinated everything, and for this dominating passion he used moral or intellectual considerations as tools whenever and however they suited his plans. I am even disinclined to believe in the genuineness of his Antisemitism. It was not a question of principle. A genius of demagoguery, Hitler instinctively perceived the advantage of mobilizing the aggressive instincts innate in most men, instincts which for centuries and in not a few countries have been traditionally directed against the Jews. Like so many other propagandists, he suffered the fate of becoming a victim of his own propaganda, and his fanaticism drove him to the escalation of the anti-Jewish terror. I refuse to consider him a lunatic. He was an evil genius, all the more powerful in that he had no human obligations.

For our problem we have to start from the realization that Hitler was entirely indifferent about religion and church. His attitude toward both was strictly dominated by their usefulness or their noxiousness for his political plans. No wonder that his utterances sometimes changed accordingly. I have the impression that the fanatical adversaries of the churches were to be found more among Hitler's followers than in the person of the Führer himself, who was rather pragmatic in all problems of ideology. At the beginning, Alfred Rosenberg, in publishing his famous book *Der Mythos des zwanzigsten Jahrhunderts* (*The Myth of the Twentieth Century*), attempted to create some sort of National Socialist religion, which would of course be entirely free from Christianity. But his doctrines were too intellectual to inspire the rank and file of the party, and at the end of the Third Reich Rosenberg was nearly a forgotten man.

Instead, the brutal principles and slogans of the black formations, the SS, increasingly penetrated all party institutions and organizations. Here too it is difficult to discover anything of a systematic ideology. The crude emanations of these ideas in speeches and articles have found very little formal articulation or definition. There is no doubt, however, that the SS was not only technically but also spiritually a real adversary to Christianity. And perhaps the most violent hatred of Christianity arose not from the leaders—Himmler, Heydrich, Heissmeyer—but from the men second in command, the sergeants of the SS corps, from the men who later supplied all the hangmen and mass murderers at Auschwitz, Dachau, Bergen-Belsen, and other places. Here were the real, conscious, and resolute enemies of the church, the men who not only were rid of all moral considerations but were possessed of a certainly vague but very passionate antichristian feeling. In order to commit crimes for which they had received orders, they were obliged for the sake of their own moral self-preservation to develop a substitute for the traditional commandments—or better, to find an antidote to all the principles they had known since their childhood. A vicious circle set in: in order to exonerate their Christian conscience, they had to invent a new antichristian *Herrenmensch* philosophy, the philosophy of the mastership of a certain elite race and certain chosen persons, the doctrine of the inferiority and unworthiness of other races and people. In this way, the inadequacy of the Christian faith developed into antichristian radicalism; crime further created more malicious crime. However superficial and vague this philosophy may have been, it proved a terrible force, bringing about the deaths of thousands and hundreds of thousands.

On such a dark background, we have to contemplate the relationship between National Socialism and the churches. On the one hand, we see the leaders totally indifferent toward religious problems, moved by nothing other than pragmatic and tactical considerations in their fight for power, accompanied by growing antichristian fanaticism in the lower ranks. On the other hand, there was a divided collection of church organizations, single clergymen and laymen, some heroic fighters, some weaklings, even some traitors, most of whom were uncertain, irresolute, often disappointed and deceived people, thrown to and fro by changing events and by personal experiences and impressions. Under these circumstances, the fight was unequal from the beginning, and only owing to God's grace and to the indestructible nature of the foundations of Christianity have the churches survived at all.

As to the human side of the problem, we are bound to reflect more precisely on the cruel dilemma in which many good Christians found themselves during the war when the very existence of our fatherland was at stake. Our sons, our brothers, our fathers, our husbands, our friends were on the front, fighting and dying. Our cities with their churches and their universities were being bombed. The terrible threat of Bolshevism came nearer and nearer, certainly provoked by the National Socialist aggression—but no less dangerous therefore—and certainly not coming as a champion of Christianity. On the other hand, because information increasingly leaked out about the mass murders, the knowledge that the war had been planned and initiated by our so-called government and the growing conviction that only after Hitler's total defeat could the rescue of Christian institutions in our country be hoped for put us into a terrible situation, forcing upon us a clear choice between our loyalty to Christ and our loyalty to our country.

I do not like to quarrel with the men, not even with the faithful members of a Christian church, who had neither the courage nor the strength to decide to be unequivocally against a man whom they recognized more and more as the Antichrist, but who represented after all their country and their nation. And, as you know, even the Western nations for a long time took pains to persuade Hitler to compromise his aims and they were continuously disinclined to encourage resistance within Germany, despite many efforts made by German clergymen to mobilize their friends in London and Rome for support of the clandestine anti-Hitler movement in our country. Sometimes we, the German patriots and followers of Christ, were really in despair, in view of the blindness and the lack of understanding in London and perhaps still more in Washington.

I have been obliged to be as circumstantial as possible in describing the general conditions under which the struggle of the churches against Hitler took place. Those who have never lived under a dictatorship, especially under a belligerent dictatorship, can hardly understand the tremendous moral and psychological difficulties of such a struggle.

At the beginning of the National Socialist movement, when

Hitler had to strain every nerve to conquer public opinion, he also made great efforts to win over those who consciously and actively clung to the Christian faith. In the first program of the National Socialist party of 1920, Hitler proclaimed in article 24: "The Party stands up for a positive Christianity without binding itself to a particular confession. It fights against the Jewish materialistic spirit inward and outward." But in the same article he said: "We postulate religious freedom in the state as long as its stability is not endangered, and the moral feeling of the Germanic race is not offended." Here we find the ominous ambiguity in Hitler's church politics. He tried to conciliate the Christians with his affirmation of "positive Christianity" while he withheld all practical consequences of this confession by establishing a clear subordination of religion to the interest of the state and to the vague concept of Germanic morality. And the interpretation of the terms *state-interest* and *Germanic morality* was entirely left to the whim of the Führer, demonstrated again and again in the following years. The much disputed infallibility of the Pope is mild compared with what Hitler claimed and what was conceded to him in the right to decide absolutely, without any chance for contradiction, what was right and what was wrong.

To keep this statement of 1920 in mind is of special importance. Its wording gives the best clue to the whole development of the coming struggle between Hitler and the churches. Hitler made efforts to subjugate the churches to his political aims without breaking entirely with them. The churches, however, were forced to follow a similar line: they had to respect the existing authority of the omnipotent state and to show homage to it in order not to endanger the very existence of the churches in Germany. Simultaneously, they tried hopefully, sometimes perhaps credulously, to use as far as possible the treacherous elbowroom assured to them for Christian speech and Christian activity. That neither side ever succeeded in attaining its conflicting aims was due to the nature of this conflict, and it was certainly—unfortunately—due to a large degree to the human weakness of not a few of us.

Hitler's formula of 1920 for the relation of his party to Christianity gives us also some idea of the tremendous difficulty churches and clergy were in. What should they believe? What should they expect? What could they hold to? Similar assurances to quiet distrustful elements in the clergy had been published, it is true, in

Hitler's famous book *Mein Kampf,* distributed by the millions in Germany and abroad. Furthermore, when Hitler became head of the government in January 1933, he declared: "The new government is going to give its firm protection to Christianity as the foundation of our entire morality." And later: "The concern of the government is turned toward honest cooperation between church and state."

While great effort was made in the same declaration to affirm that Hitler's fight against evil forces within Germany would also be to the good of the churches, Hitler affirmed once again the threat of thirteen years earlier, that membership in a certain religious community would never be tolerated as a privilege if there was opposition to his will. Since he personally decided what was law, this announcement could only mean that Hitler would never tolerate any opposition on religious grounds. There was constant vacillation between suppression and some sort of tolerance. Disturbed because of misgivings in certain church circles, Hitler even went so far as to dismiss one of his most ardent followers, the *Gauleiter* Arthur Dinter, when this man founded a new German People's Church (*Deutsche Volkskirche*) based upon the myth of race and soil. Hitler remained a formal member of the Catholic church (a remarkable fact), no doubt without practicing his faith in the usual form (participation in the Mass and Confession), but paying the church taxes until his death in 1945. He may have despised the Protestant clergy for their lack of unity and organizational strength, but many of his utterances prove that he felt a good deal of respect, perhaps blended with hate and jealousy—but I repeat: a good deal of respect—for the Catholic church. His followers, having a more instinctive aversion to the churches than Hitler (who was, as noted earlier, entirely indifferent in religious affairs), did not have enough spiritual or intellectual training to elaborate a new religious conception based upon race and soil, heroism and hate; their notions were by no means uniform, and were often changed depending on the criticism and opposition they experienced in dealing with the churches.

No wonder that, in those first years, only small forces of religious or moral or technical resistance developed within the churches, and that the churches were generally unprepared for the slowly intensifying struggle with their powerful adversary. Moreover, during the first two years of National Socialist rule there was a remarkable rise of church activity in both confessions, statistically evident in the number of church weddings and baptisms. Even the number of people leaving the churches declined significantly.

In view of the apparent weakness or compliance of all the older authorities and institutions, and with the growing resolution of the new men to extend their domination to the point of totalitarianism, a gradual change took place. More and more the slightest remainder of free talk or thought or action not prescribed by the party appeared incompatible with the character of the new state—even in the field of religion. Perhaps it was more the tyrannical ambition of the leaders in the lower ranks than the wish of the government itself that attempts were made to coordinate (*gleichschalten*) Church and party. In order to exalt the party doctrines to some kind of divine will, the *Gauleiters* and *Kreisleiters* (district and county leaders), the heads of the regional party organizations, demanded from the clergy the inclusion of Hitler's person and of the party's doctrines in ecclesiastical lectures and sermons. God in his grace, so they said, had sent the Führer to save the German people from utter downfall. His words were to be regarded as part of the divine revelation and the Bible had to be cleared of all obsolete un-Nordic notions and doctrines.

If such challenges did not suffice to rouse opposition—and unfortunately they did not in many cases, often enough being contrived and pronounced by National Socialist clergymen, especially Protestant clergymen—it was the Jewish problem which revealed in inexorable seriousness the incompatibility of Christianity with the new pseudoreligion. Here evasion became impossible. Even the most superficial connection to Christianity could not tolerate the idea that a baptized Jew be excluded from the parish; that Christian persons of non-Aryan origin be suspended from their offices—not to speak of the horrible things which happened later on. Little by little criticism arose within the churches, at first from a few conscientious individuals—clergymen and laymen—in the anonymous parishes who were perhaps in a stronger position than those pastors who were more exposed to the ubiquitous watch of the secret police. It became the rule that the sermons of all clergymen who were regarded as unreliable in the political sense were surveyed by inconspicuous men, and even prayers were scrutinized. Even if these spies were—often enough—unable to understand the religious meaning of what had been said, and even if the authorities were for a long time reluctant to intervene against the church services, these actions were not without consequences. I remember how much my clerical friends in the Confessing Church were annoyed and disquieted by the regular call to the police station after every Sunday service; how much time was wasted and how much it hampered the honest communication with the faithful members of the parish, who were so anxiously expecting guidance and encouraging words from their pastor in those troubled times.

Unfortunately but understandably, serious conflicts developed within the Protestant church itself—already divided by so many differences in organization and confession. Many clergymen, perhaps the great majority, came from the same sections of the population which had acclaimed Hitler so enthusiastically; by tradition and education these men were conservative and nationalistic, and the rise of the Third Reich appeared to them to be the long hoped-for deliverance from the Red nightmare. So they were only too willing to overlook the dangers to Christianity, which today are so conspicuous to all of us, in the doctrines and in the attitude of the National Socialist movement. *Credo quia absurdum*, they wished to believe in spite of all warnings of reason and conscience. So we cannot avoid admitting the regrettable fact that in the summer of 1933, half a year after Hitler's advent to power, more than two-thirds of all Protestant clergymen voted for National Socialist representatives in all church institutions. The foundation of the later ill-famed organization of "German Christians" also proved initially to be a tremendous success. However, a German proverb says: "Wenn die Not am grössten ist Gottes Hilfe am nächsten." ("When need is greatest God's help is closest.")

The triumph of the so-called German Christians did not last long, and it was their own wantonness and puffed up behavior that brought about their end. On the occasion of the first synod, two-thirds of the members had appeared in brown shirts and high boots; their first leader greeted them as the SA "assault battalions of Jesus Christ." They adopted the so-called Aryan paragraph—the National Socialist regulation which excluded persons of non-Aryan origin from all official employment—for the entire church area, and they agreed with the elimination of all Jewish words from the service except Hallelujah and Amen. In many cases, opposing clergy were imprisoned or ill-treated or both. The youth organizations of the churches were forcibly incorporated into the political formations of the party.

This conduct removed the last excuse for everyone who had up to now been inclined to believe in the good of the new movement; slowly, but more and more vigorously, criticism, opposition, and even open resistance broke out. I do not need to name all the faithful ones who took the initiative. But I cannot help citing Martin Niemöller who, in September 1933, founded the first genuinely opposing body, the Pastors' Emergency League. Karl Barth, then still in Germany, raised his voice in his book *Theologische Existenz heute*, a book in which he condemned in the most severe terms disobedience toward God and pragmatic compliance with the secular demands of the day.

The real turning point of the conflict proved to be a big demonstration of the "German Christians" in November 1933 in the Berlin Sportpalast, during which the unchristian forces within this organization threw off the last mask and proclaimed an entirely new church. At this point the confessing movement, which at first had shown some inclination to compromise, had no other choice but to raise the banner and to organize for open fight. The Confessing Church met in spectacular synods at Barmen and at Berlin-Dahlem; it gathered nearly one half of all clergymen still in office, and a great crowd of laymen, and frankly proclaimed the duty of disobedience to all unchristian doctrines and orders.

The most immediate anxiety now was the education of the younger generation of clergy. The problem was solved with astonishing success by the foundation of clandestine academies which gave examinations according to regulations, held training colleges for preachers—in short, constituted a regular well-functioning church organization.

The formation of such an outright opposition was only possible, of course, because Hitler was uncertain how to deal with it. Being entirely uninterested in religious affairs, he considered the events for the time being as a typical example of a superficial quarrel between clericals. In this conviction he was strengthened by his "German Christian" advisers who were disinclined to admit the full extent of their failure, advisers whose inadequacy Hitler himself certainly recognized. He even temporarily withdrew his favor from the "German Christians," hoping that thereby the opposition might be appeased, especially since a good deal of the fighting spirit of the confessing movement had been created by the incapacity and even by the moral unworthiness of the leading "German Christians," especially the ill-famed Reichsbischof Ludwig Müller. Hitler limited himself to directing his customary ruthlessness against single persons: Niemöller was sent to the concentration camp at Dachau; Karl Barth fled to Switzerland, where he continued his warnings and exhortations. Not a few clergymen went to prisons and concentration camps, sometimes on the strength of a judicial sentence, sometimes on the strength of an administrative warrant, sometimes without either. From my own captivity in the cellar of the Berlin Gestapo, I remember meeting clergy from both churches who were entirely uninformed of the reason for their arrest. But the number of clerical prisoners always remained limited, partly because many clergy—quite apart from the "German Christians" themselves—accommodated themselves to the relentless violence and learned to speak in the veiled language, so familiar in all reports of the time, and partly because the State endeavored not to alienate the majority of the population, whose Christian mentality had remained unbroken.

This indulgence was especially advisable during World War II, which covered nearly half of the Hitler period. Hitler knew that most Germans went into this war without enthusiasm—contrary to their attitude twenty-five years earlier—in order to fulfill their military duty. It seemed essential even to Hitler, Goering, and Himmler to keep as many Germans as possible in good temper. But many testimonies are available which show that Hitler concealed his bitterness and rage against church resistance only temporarily: to his confidants he spoke frankly on several occasions about his resolution to settle the account with the churches after the war. He said that a man could be either a good German or a good Christian: he could not be both simultaneously. Still more outspoken about the coming reprisals were his followers, and there was no doubt that the real test for the churches was still to come. The details of this *Endlösung*—final solution to the church problem—were already much discussed in Hitler's clique. The churches had to be eliminated entirely from public life and the population had to be definitely dechristianized. By depriving the churches little by little of their financial resources, Hitler expected to bring all church activities to a standstill.

What I have just explained is mainly true for the situation in the Protestant world. As I stated previously, the Catholic church had been from the first in a different, somewhat more favorable situation. The organization of most Catholics in the always rather influential Center party had prevented most members from joining the nationalistic forces of the right wing groups, from which the National Socialists drew most of their recruits. Their clergymen were also less exposed to blackmail and bribery than their Protestant brothers, since celibacy gave them no wives and children for whom they had to care. (In the actual fight of the churches in the Communist occupied part of Germany we today observe the same situation respecting the greater independence of the unmarried Catholic clergymen.) In the Third Reich, their initial compliance with the new rule, bought or bribed by the famous Concordat, had given way in the summer of 1934 to a more critical attitude, after Erich Klausener, the head of the Catholic Action in Berlin, had been murdered by SS men in his office. Although the strong anticommunist feeling of Pope Pius XI and his good relations with Mussolini weakened somewhat his fighting spirit against Hitler, it cannot be said that he favored Hitler. Several German archbishops and bishops took a still firmer stand— sometimes even openly—against the National Socialist crimes, and we should not forget the name of Clemens Count Galen, archbishop of Münster, who proclaimed his criticism against the deeds of National Socialism with exemplary courage. So there is no doubt that Hitler and his clique began to hate Catholicism as much as Protestantism, and that the fate of the Catholic church would, had Hitler been victorious, have been not much different from that of the Protestant churches.

Taken as a whole, the development of the relationship between the churches and Hitler makes it no more excusable, but perhaps a bit more comprehensible, that the churches failed so lamentably in the face of the crimes committed in this dark period of our history. I have always taken a strong line in this respect, and I am not inclined to renounce my conviction before this audience. But since our conference has to deal with this special problem separately, I shall limit myself to a few remarks. Crimes of such terrible scope in time, in place, and in the number of victims were practically possible only with the more or less ready collaboration of many thousands, perhaps hundreds of thousands of functionaries—policemen, soldiers, technicians, doctors, workmen—and with the tacit acquiescence of millions more. I feel terribly ashamed to admit that this has been possible in a so-called Christian country! Moreover, I am disinclined to believe in the usual excuse, that most people had been unaware of what was going on. Of course, those who willfully closed eyes and ears were afterwards able to assert that they had neither seen nor heard anything. Those who wished to know were able to collect information practically from all sides, including broadcasts from foreign countries. On the other hand, it is true that there were always courageous voices of protest like those of Cardinal Archbishop Galen and Cardinal Faulhaber who raised their voices against violence and lawlessness. The famous *Buro Grüber* in Berlin worked more silently, but therefore perhaps more efficiently, in a practical way to save victims of lawlessness. With the help of a number of friends in the Protestant clergy, and for several years without interference from the authorities, Grüber succeeded in saving more than a thousand Jews by arranging for their escape to foreign countries, which regrettably did not do much to facilitate this humane and Christian work. If God in the Old Testament promised Abraham to spare Sodom and Gomorrah if only ten righteous men could be found, then the world may have to be reluctant in the condemnation of our country too.

In the final balance, the German Church Struggle is, despite everything to the contrary, not without a few positive items.

First, the churches have survived. They have neither been destroyed by antichristian secular authorities nor spiritually estranged from the true faith by weaklings or deserters or traitors within their own ranks. And this result may mean something in view of the terrible force arranged against them. The enemy possessed, in the words of Martin Luther, "Gross Macht und viel List" ("great power and much cunning")—more dangerous than power. The resistance and final rescue have certainly been possible only by the grace of God; it would, however, be unjust not to appreciate with respect and gratitude the action and attitude of thousands of clergymen and laymen in both churches. That the Christian spirit was still living and vigorous, even under the most violent persecutions, was already evident from the great caution with which Hitler dealt with the church opposition, a caution which he certainly found very trying. That the ominous final solution of the church problem planned by Hitler and his men for after the war was not realized was chiefly due to the timely arrival of Eisenhower's and Montgomery's armies. These armies discovered still strong and healthy Christian churches upon which a new and better future could be built.

Second, the courageous resistance of a considerable portion of church members and the special performance of individual champions have helped us in a dark hour to maintain some residue of self-reliance and therefore some hope for a better future. Our nation has not been *una massa perditionis*—in the saying of the Fathers of the Church, a mass of perdition. We have had the ten righteous men in our midst and so there is still hope.

Third, the long and bitter struggle has forced many of us, clergy and laymen, to reflect more deeply and more seriously about our faith, to perceive our weaknesses and to search our consciences. I may dare to assert that even today there are some hopeful symptoms visible as the consequences of that black time. Perhaps the churches have not gained much and, after the disappointment of their deplorable failure under Hitler, they could not expect better. But in general our people have become more tolerant, more peace loving, more liberal than they had been before in their human relations and with their European neighbors, even with those who do not respond to them in the same spirit. A visible and remarkable sign of this new spirit in Germany is the passionate pro-Jewish feeling with which the overwhelming majority of the German public follows the events in the Near East. This feeling is not influenced by reason or interest; it is indeed of an unselfish character. I trust that this somewhat startling change in German mentality will sooner or later develop for the benefit of the Christian churches!

However, I do not wish to conclude my address with a statement which might be regarded as too optimistic or perhaps even as an expression of a new haughtiness. This would not be becoming after the review of such a terrible period in our history. So let me rather conclude with a reminder, by quoting the words of the first declaration of the Protestant churches after the war, proclaimed at Stuttgart in 1946:

We accuse ourselves because we have not confessed courageously enough, prayed faithfully enough, trusted joyfully enough, loved ardently enough.

# 14

# Some Perspectives on Religious Faith after Auschwitz

Richard L. Rubenstein

One of the oldest tasks confronting a father in the Jewish tradition is that of deciding what he will hand down to his children. Personality is very largely a distillation of memory. A very significant part of the personality children take with them is dependent upon what they receive from their father. I therefore begin this discussion of theology by sharing with my audience some things that have happened to me within the family circle. I do so because of my conviction that theology can no longer be an interpretation of the received Word of God. It may have been that at one time. Since Sören Kierkegaard, a certain subjectivity has entered the discipline. The theologian must share with his readers his own personal religious existence. It is no longer possible for the theologian to be primarily the spokesman for or the defender of institutionally defined faith. If one wishes to be a theologian in our time, one must begin with the personal equation.

In the summer of 1960 I visited Europe for the first time. I spent the summer partly in Amsterdam and partly at a Dutch North Sea resort, Wyk aan Zee. I had just completed my doctorate and wanted to visit my wife's native land. She was the same age that Anne Frank would have been had she survived. She had escaped from Holland during the four days of the German invasion of May 1940. Her family was among the very few Dutch Jewish survivors of the Holocaust. We wanted to visit her childhood home as well as to come to know those of her relatives who had been fortunate enough to survive.

At first it did not occur to me that I might have any interest in meeting Germans or visiting Germany in spite of the fact that Germany was only a few hours away. Then I began to notice German visitors, especially at Wyk aan Zee. There were signs everywhere in German advertising *Zimmer frei*, "room available." I remember my first contact with a German. An elderly man thought I was Dutch and asked me for directions. I did not know whether to be courteous or react in rage. At the time I could only see Germans as cold-blooded, mass murderers of my people.

Things became more complicated on the beach. My children often played ball with their Dutch cousins. Occasionally, the ball would roll near a German family. They would invariably return it. Eventually, I had to face the question: Could I permit my children to play with Germans? This may seem trivial, but the question had great existential import for me at the time. And, I was not able to resolve it satisfactorily.

In August of that year, I took my eleven-year-old son Aaron into Germany to see the country that had caused our family and our people so much horror. When I first crossed the border, I had the distinct feeling that I was entering enemy territory. The town we first visited was Düsseldorf. By accident we met Dr. Hans Lamm and the editors of the *Allgemeine Wochenzeitung der Juden in Deutschland.* Through Dr. Lamm's good offices, we were invited to attend a briefing which was being given by the *Bundespresseamt*, the Press and Information Office of the Federal Republic, in Bonn. This followed the season of the *"Schmiererei,"* the defacing of synagogues which had just taken place throughout West Germany.

My son listened intently during the briefings. He was understandably very curious. As we drove back to Holland, he began to ask me questions about Auschwitz. They were not the kind of questions I had expected. I thought my son would ask me about the Germans. He did not. He took it for granted that the murders had been the will of the German people and their legally constituted government. Most of his questions were about the United States.

"Daddy," he said, "didn't the Americans know there was an Auschwitz?"

"Yes, they did," I replied.

"Well, if that's so, couldn't they have done anything about it?"

"I'm not sure."

"Well, didn't we have any German prisoners of war?"

"Yes, we did."

"Couldn't they have been used as hostages to make the Germans behave?" he asked.

I couldn't answer and I would not today suggest that we could have effectively held German prisoners hostage to Nazi good behavior. What is important was that my son perceived that more was involved in the Holocaust than the Nazis and their victims. As I wrote in *After Auschwitz*, a shadow of alienation entered that eleven-year-old boy which has never left him. One of the most important effects of my taking my son into Germany was that both of us had to face the question of what kind of human community might be possible for him—not only with Germans but also with his fellow Americans. Both of us had to ask ourselves what sense of community we might have with our fellowmen, especially since we refused to delude ourselves that only the Germans thought the world would be better off without Jews.

Above all, I did not want him to hate Germans, not for the sake of Germans but for his own sake. I understood that hatred is a poison which eats away at the soul. If hatred cannot be directed against an external object in realistic action, it will sooner or later turn against the subject who possesses the hate. It was not my wish to see my son grow up possessed of a hatred against Germans which he would be compelled to expend against himself.

Nor did I want his image of himself as a Jew to be controlled by that of the helpless victim going up in smoke. There was nothing in any way dishonorable or degrading about those who were compelled to become victims. Nevertheless, it was not an identity which any man ought to be compelled to choose if he were not compelled by fate so to do.

The problem of my children's developing identities was further intensified by the fact that they knew that their mother had literally escaped by the skin of her teeth. One day during that 1960 sojourn, I chanced upon my nine-year-old daughter Hannah. She was walking near the Westerkerk opposite the Anne Frank House. I noticed that she was reading and was oblivious of everything around her.

"What are you reading, Hannah?" I asked.

"Anne Frank's Diary."

In June 1969, nine years later, I again visited Germany, this time to take delivery of a new Volkswagen at the factory in Wolfsburg. We were visiting Paris at the time. The day before I was scheduled to go, my younger son Jeremy who was then eleven, the same age his older brother had been nine years before, asked,

"Daddy, can I come with you?"

After thinking it over, I replied, "Yes, Jeremy, you may."

The two of us took the night train to Hanover and thence to Wolfsburg where we picked up the car. We were impressed by the enormous industrial chimneys which towered above the Volkswagen plant, but somehow they made us think of the chimneys of the crematoria of yesteryear. We returned to Paris by way of Cologne where we spent the night. While in Cologne, Jeremy began to ask me almost the same questions his brother had nine years before. Jeremy was aware of the family history. His reaction was, however, slightly different.

As we stood in the plaza before the great Cologne Cathedral at about nine in the evening, Jeremy suddenly turned to me and shrieked.

"Daddy, get me out of here. I don't want to be near these people."

I understood his reaction. It was a shudder of utter horror when he realized the enormity of what the people around him had done. Nevertheless, as a father, it was my responsibility to help him mature as an individual who was beyond both hatred and resentment, the fruitless aggression of the powerless, so that he could deal realistically not only with Germans but with all non-Jews in the years to come.

Regrettably, there is more to the problem. I am not unaware of the history of the Nazi period. Although I would certainly defer to historians of the period for some precise details—I am painfully aware of the relations between both the Evangelical and the Catholic Church and the Nazis. There were, of course, individual and group resistance; but, in general, the record of the Christian Church towards the specific issue of the extermination of the Jews was less than heroic. The mystery of Pope Pius XII's reaction to the events remains a painful question to this very day. It is clear that the Pontiff knew in great detail what was happening. For considerations which remain a mystery to this day, he was unwilling to utter any protest. How shall I interpret this to my children? Shall I simply say that the fraternal bond, problematic as it has been throughout history, between Jew and Christian broke down completely? Could I encourage my children to look for a reconciliation some day based upon Christian repentance and Jewish acceptance of the Christian confession? To look for such a result would be neither realistic nor even desirable. Were Christians made to feel guilty, they might someday be driven to justify the very thing that made them feel guilty. Any human encounter based upon the idea that one side bears some kind of mark of Cain and must forever do penance to the other precludes genuine reconciliation, especially between rival religious traditions.

Another way of handling the problem might be simply for Jews to avoid, wherever possible, all relations with Christians. One important Jewish theologian is reported to have declared that he will abstain from dialogue with Christians until they repent. It is difficult to take such a position seriously. The theologian in question has willingly accepted many invitations to appear before Christian audiences. Such speaking is already an act of dialogue and encounter. The man's actions simply belie his words. It is no more possible for Jew and Christian to break off dialogue than for the various segments of the family of man to become totally exclusive, non-communicating atomic units. It simply will not work.

The question of what I, as a father, can hand down to my sons and daughter involves another visit to Germany, one which I describe in *After Auschwitz*. On August 15, 1961, two days after the DDR (*Deutsche Demokratische Republik*) erected the wall between East and West Berlin, I arrived in Bonn from Amsterdam to survey political and cultural trends in West Germany. At the urging of my hosts, the *Bundespresseamt*, the Press and Information Office of the Federal Republic, I decided to fly immediately to Berlin.

On August 17, 1961, at 4:30 in the afternoon, I had a two-hour conversation with Probst Dr. Heinrich Grüber at his home in Berlin-Dahlem. Dean Grüber had been the only German to testify in Jerusalem against Adolf Eichmann at the celebrated trial earlier that summer. He had a distinguished record in the defense of Jewish rights, or at least, the rights of Christians of "non-Aryan" origin, during the Nazi period. He had himself been a concentration camp inmate. We talked under almost apocalyptic conditions. American army tanks rumbled outside his home. He was pastor of a church in East Berlin. Living in West Berlin he was very upset that he was cut off from his flock. He began to use the imagery of the biblical theology of history to describe what was happening.

God was punishing a sinful Germany, he declared. He asserted that God was making Germans refugees as the Germans had made others homeless. Having commenced with his biblical interpretation of recent history, he could not stop until he asserted that it had been God's will to send Adolf Hitler to exterminate Europe's Jews. At the moment that I heard Grüber make that assertion, I had what was perhaps the most important single crisis of faith I have ever had. I recognized that Grüber was not an Antisemite and that his assertion that the God of the Covenant was and is the ultimate Author of the great events of Israel's history was no different from the faith of any traditional Jew. Grüber was applying the logic of Covenant Theology to the events of the twentieth century. I appreciated his fundamental honesty. He recognized that, if one takes the biblical theology of history seriously, Adolf Hitler is no more nor less an instrument of God's wrath than Nebuchadnezzar.

If I were a fundamentalist Christian I might be tempted to say to the Jewish community, "See here, you deluded people. When are you going to see the light? When are you going to stop being punished by God and accept his supreme gift to you, by confessing that Jesus Christ is the Redeemer of Israel?"

Nor do I regard such a question by an evangelical Christian as Antisemitic. If one accepts the doctrine that God is distinctively involved in the history of Israel, the fundamentalist Christian may indeed be right in asserting that the sorrows of the Jews have been inflicted upon them for rejecting Jesus. Whether one is a fundamentalist Christian or a traditional Jew, it is impossible to regard the sorrows of Jewish history as mere historical accidents. They must in some sense express the will of God as a just and righteous Creator. Either such a God is a sadist who inflicts pain because he enjoys it or he has a reason for the misfortune he inflicts. The only morally defensible motive for a superior to inflict pain on an inferior would be punitive chastisement which has as its purpose altering the victim's mode of behavior. If one takes Covenant Theology seriously, as did Dean Grüber, Auschwitz must be God's way of punishing the Jewish people in order that they might better see the light, the light of Christ if one is a Christian, the light of Torah if one is a traditional Jew.

I have often stated that the idea that a God worthy of human adoration could have inflicted Auschwitz on what was allegedly his people is obscene. But, notice the terrible price one must pay if one rejects the God of the Covenant. If the God of the Covenant exists, at Auschwitz my people stood under the most fearsome curse that God ever inflicted. If the God of history does not exist, then the Cosmos is ultimately absurd in origin and meaningless in purpose. We have been thrust into the world in which naked amorphous life proliferates, has its hour, only to disappear amidst the further proliferation of life. As human beings we are divided by historical and geographical accident into the tribes of mankind, to no ultimate reason or purpose. We simply are there for but a moment only to disappear into the midnight silence of Eternal Chaos. Like Kierkegaard, I have had to choose between a world without the biblical God and the leap into faith. I have had a slightly different either—or than he. I have had to decide whether to affirm the existence of a God who inflicts Auschwitz on his guilty people or to insist that nothing the Jews did made them more deserving of Auschwitz than any other people, that Auschwitz was in no sense a punishment, and that a God who could or would inflict such punishment does not exist. In other words, I have elected to accept what Camus has rightly called the courage of the absurd, the courage to live in a meaningless, purposeless Cosmos rather than believe in a God who inflicts Auschwitz on his people.

I have done so as a rabbi and a theologian in the full knowledge that my choice has been rejected by my people. Nevertheless, I would rather be rejected by my people than affirm their guilt at Auschwitz.

Nor does the Six Day War of 1967 alter that judgment. It might be argued that the same God who delivered the Jews to the ovens also gave them Jerusalem in 1967. When I stood at the Wall for the first time during the summer of 1967, people who knew me came up to me and asked,

"What do you think now? God has given us all of Jerusalem!"

"God is not on the side of the Jews," I replied, "nor is he against the Arabs. The Jews and the Arabs both love this place and consider it their own. We have a terrible conflict. But, to treat the Arab as *villain* rather than *enemy* is to misconceive the nature of the conflict. I refuse to say *Gott mit uns* under any circumstances."

*The Six Day War, tentative as its conclusions may have been, is no royal road back to the God of History.*

Nor can I make sense out of Auschwitz by regarding it as the latest of a long series of Antisemitic acts inflicted upon Jews by Christians. Auschwitz represents something novel and materially distinct from previous Jewish misfortunes. There is, for example, a difference between the "civilized" Antisemitism of earlier ages and what must be called the Antisemitism of the technological barbarians of the twentieth century. As bitter as was the hostility of Ferdinand and Isabella against the Jews, they must be seen as civilized Antisemites. They reigned at a time when 781 years of Islamic presence was coming to an end on the Iberian peninsula. Once the Moors had departed, the monarchs had to face the problem of whether they had achieved the religious unity for which their people had fought. As long as there were non-Christians in Spain, that nation's sacred consensus eluded them. At the time, the idea of a secular society was totally unthinkable in Spain. There were several hundred thousand Jews in Spain. The way the monarchs dealt with them highlights the difference between civilized Antisemitism and modern Antisemitism.

They gave the Jews three options: The first was to be baptized and become part of Christian Spain; the second was to leave the country if baptism was impossible. Jews who left were permitted to take what they could carry with them. The choice was a harsh one, but it is crucial that we understand that Ferdinand and Isabella had no interest in exterminating Jews simply because they were Jews. Their interest was in the creation of a Christian Spain, not the extermination of the Jews.

The Jews had a third, tragic option: they could remain on Spanish soil as Jews, but they would be killed if they did so. Nevertheless, this option of extremity was not without dignity. Let us imagine a Jew saying to himself, "I can neither leave this place which I love nor become a Christian."

Such a man had in fact elected martyrdom. His death was freely chosen. It served as a witness both to his love of place and his Jewish faith. This is in stark contrast to what took place in the Nazi death camps. One of Hitler's greatest victories was that he deprived the Jews of *all* opportunity to be martyrs. There can be no martyrdom without free choice. In the camps it made no difference whether you were Dr. Edith Stein, who had become a Carmelite nun, or a Hasidic

263

decency has any real credibility to *any* group of people any longer. This is no longer primarily a Jewish problem. Human rights and dignity can only be attained by membership in a community that has the *power* to guarantee those rights. Regrettably, the word *power* must be underscored.

Paradoxically, this insight has made it possible for me and, hopefully, my children to encounter the non-Jewish world, especially the Christian world, without anger or resentment: *we could only be angry or resentful if we expected some standard of conduct from the Christian world which it failed to observe.* But if Auschwitz has taught us anything, it is that in times of stress rights and dignity are operative only within one's primary or kinship group, if indeed they are operative at all. I earnestly wish it were otherwise. It is my conviction that in pre-modern societies it often was otherwise. Nevertheless, I do not see how one can escape the sorrowful conclusion that he alone has rights and dignity who has the power to enforce those rights or belongs to a group that possesses such power. The possession of power is indispensable for human dignity.

In 1967 there was disappointment and even anger in the Jewish community that most Christians did not share their fears for Israel's survival. It was my conviction that the Jewish attitude was fundamentally mistaken. Because of my background and religious commitments, the fate of Israel was of overwhelming importance to me. Nevertheless, I had no right to expect that what was decisive for me had to be decisive for Christians as well. Neither I nor any other Jew had any claim on the Christian world. The only issue for Israel was whether it had the capacity to survive. Reluctantly, I have come to the conclusion that Israel will survive only if it has the capacity to do so unaided by any other power. Without such a capacity, there will be no credible moral deterrent to the extermination of its Jewish population by the surrounding Arabs were they ever to be victorious.

As bleak as this view may seem, it nevertheless makes human fellowship possible for me and, again, hopefully, for my children. I have no unrealistic expectation that human beings will act contrary to their nature. I believe in the psychological reality of the Fall. I am neither disappointed nor resentful when people behave in a way which is both predictable and consistent with their nature. In times of stress, it is unrealistic to expect much virtue or magnanimity from the generality of men, no matter how praiseworthy such behavior may be when it surfaces unexpectedly.

This does not mean that Hitler was right in his leadership of the German people. On the contrary, had Hitler really taken power seriously, he would have recognized the *limits* of German power. Had he acted more circumspectly, Germany would not today be a divided country caught between Russia and the United States. It is because Hitler did not have the ancient pagan understanding that all action which overreaches itself—all *hubris*—is sooner or later defeated by Almighty *Nemesis*, that the German catastrophe reached the limits it did.

The German catastrophe was, I believe, largely due to the fact that Nazism was never a *genuine* paganism but a kind of Judeo-Christian heresy. In *After Auschwitz* I cited an insight of Jean-Paul Sartre in his biography of *Baudelaire* which is relevant to this point. Sartre contends that the priest who celebrates the black mass, thereby inverting Christian ritual and belief, is by no means indifferent to Christianity as might be a genuine pagan. He hates Christianity, but he is dialectically related to its religious system which he both accepts and rejects at the same time. Nazism cannot be seen as neopaganism, as it has been by one well-known Jewish theologian. Nazism was dialectically negated heretical Christianity. Had the Germans been true pagans, the ancient pagan virtues of moderation and respect for limits would have been far more operative among the Germans than they were.

In conclusion, I would like to offer my own confession of faith after Auschwitz. I am a pagan. To be a pagan means to find once again one's roots as a child of Earth and to see one's own existence as wholly and totally an earthly existence. It means once again to understand that for mankind the true divinities are the gods of earth, not the high gods of the sky; the gods of space and place, not the gods of time; the gods of home and hearth, not the gods of wandering, though wanderers we must be. Though every single establishment Jewish theologian rejects this position, the Jewish people have given their assent—with their feet. They have gone home. The best part of that people has ceased to be wanderers. They have once again found a place of their own on this earth. That is paganism.

In spite of the fears of establishment Jewish theologians, paganism does not mean the rejection of one's people's ancestral dance, its distinctive rituals, nor its ancestral story. Both the dance and the story have their place within the renewed affirmation of earthly existence. Before the return to Israel, the story seemed to point to a linear progression of the Jewish people in exile. In reality, the story was always about a cyclical movement. Exiled from their land for two thousand years, after Auschwitz they have come home. Auschwitz was indeed the terminal expression of exile. After Auschwitz the Jews had no viable alternative save homecoming if they were to survive with dignity. The deepest and the most profound of all strivings in the individual and the group may indeed be the striving to return to one's place of origin. Theologically that striving may be conjoined with a return to the archaic gods of the place of origin.

I should like to conclude with an anecdote about my maternal grandmother. She came to the United States as a girl from Lithuania. She was an Orthodox Jewish woman who never learned to speak English. Once settled in New York City, she never moved from what was then the Jewish ghetto in the Lower East Side.

I remember one day as a twelve-year-old, I went to visit her alone. This was difficult because I could not speak Yiddish. Our communication was, of necessity, almost completely non-verbal. While at her home, I accidentally opened a drawer where I discovered a paper bag filled with dirt. On the outside of the bag, there was the stamp of the British government of Palestine. The bag, with its dirt, had been sent to her from the Holy Land. My own Jewish training was exceedingly limited but I had the good sense not to ask her any questions about the bag. I shut the drawer and did not see the bag until twelve years later. As they lowered my grandmother's coffin into her grave, her oldest son took that paper bag containing the earth of Palestine and poured it on the head of the coffin. At that moment I understood something about my grandmother for the first time. My grandmother was a wandering Jew all of her life, but she did not want to wander forever. Somewhere deep within her psyche, she wanted to go home. Her way of going home, at least symbolically, was to return to the earth of her ultimate place of origin as a Jew, the Holy Land. She was a child of earth. In death she wanted her dust to mingle with the dust of the home of her ancestors. I am also convinced that she was returning to the Great Goddess of that earth. In her own way, my grandmother was as thoroughgoing a pagan as I am.

# 15

# Talking and Writing and Keeping Silent

### Elie Wiesel

[On Wednesday evening of the conference, the distinguished novelist, Elie Wiesel, was to speak on "The Literature of the Holocaust." As Mr. Wiesel indicates in his opening remarks, he chose not to speak on the announced topic but, instead, to address himself in part to the lecture previously given by Dr. Richard Rubenstein and in the large to the more basic questions about the Holocaust: What can be told, what can be written, where must silence be kept, what can be witnessed only by living? Ed.]

In truth, I think I have never spoken about the Holocaust except in one book, *Night*—the very first—where I tried to tell a tale directly, as though face to face with the experience. All my subsequent books are built around it. I tried to communicate a secret, a kind of an eclipse, and in the Kafka tradition even the eclipse is eclipsed. The secret itself is a secret.

Let me, therefore, not stick to the subject I have been given but rather tell you a few stories. One of them I heard was told not by a Jew but by Jean Cocteau, a French surrealist. It is only an anecdote, but it fits me and us very well. Jean Cocteau was asked, "Mr. Cocteau, if your house were on fire, what would you take away?" And he said, "The fire, naturally." I think what we took away from our tales and from our burning houses in European history was the fire.

A second story, not by Cocteau and not about him was about a *shammes*. A *shammes* means, in English, a beadle, someone who performs certain tasks in the synagogue. In American synagogues there is no beadle—they are all very high officials, very elegantly dressed. The *shammes* is one type that has completely disappeared from our American Jewish scene. Usually the *shammes*, the beadle, was a poor man, often hunchbacked, usually taciturn. I speak about one in my "Moishe–the–Beadle," and there is an authentic story about another: Somewhere in Russia, in a ghetto, a *shammes* called Moishe went mad; day after day he would come to the synagogue, ascend the *bima*, a kind of podium, bang his fist on the pulpit, and say to God, "*Ribbono shel Olam*, Master of the Universe, I want you to know that we are still here." Day after day. Then began the transports. The ghetto was decimated; it had fewer and fewer Jews. Still the beadle came, mad as he was, and with anger or was it laughter, he would pound his fist on the table, saying, "Master of the Universe, I want you to know, we are still *here*." Finally came the last transport, and he was the only Jew who remained in the ghetto. For some reason, the madmen were left behind, as they remained behind in my own town. He was alone in the ghetto. He came to the synagogue, again ascended the *bima*, opened the sanctuary, and banged his fist against the sanctuary, "Master of the Universe, I want you to know, *I* am still here." And then he stopped, only to murmur: "But *you*—where are *you*?"

I don't know what happened to Moishe–the–beadle. I don't even know what happened to Him, the One he addressed. I don't even know whether *I* am here. I say it because, when I think back twenty-five years—one generation, a quarter of a century—sometimes I wonder whether the person inside me who was a child during the war comes from the same root as I, has lived the same experiences, has seen what I have seen. I wonder whether there was a Holocaust at all.

The first three days of the war—in 1944—when the child entered the Kingdom of Night, I remember that the child did not believe—for three days he did not believe that there was a war; that there was such a thing as war. And for three days I didn't believe that the Jews were being killed. I still remember the dream I thought I had: I was with my father, and for three days and three nights the child I was kept saying to his father over and over, "It's not true; it cannot be. It is impossible that Jews could be killed in such a manner, and the world remain silent?" That was my question: Could the world remain silent? Later I found out that the world was silent and that the things which I *thought* happened did indeed occur.

But during the war all the Jews who were trapped inside had no idea that the outside world was aware of what was happening. I listened today to Dick Rubenstein. Of course I share his anger and his despair. Indeed you must know it was fortunate that Jews in the camps didn't realize what was happening in the world. Had the Jews in the camps known that Roosevelt and Churchill and De Gaulle and the Pope and everybody knew, and no one cared, I think they would have committed suicide. I think they would have chosen *not* to survive.

The only ones who *did* know were those who went to their death. I don't know whether you have ever had an occasion to see albums—albums of pictures taken as souvenirs by German officers, amateur photographers, to entertain their guests. It is unbelievable: they were taking pictures. I spent hours looking at those pictures, wondering how any man could have taken them, and how the life immobilized there is still there.

When you look at those pictures, what strikes you are the eyes. And then when you see the eyes, you understand what they were thinking. They went to their deaths without anger, without hate, without sadness, and without shame. I think that they went to their deaths with a terrible feeling of pity. They felt pity—pity for those in the outside world who could go on living with the knowledge of what was happening inside. And here I must disassociate myself from Dick. His was a very moving, eloquent, and disturbing address, in which he tried to explain his philosophy of how one survives or lives in a cruel, cold world of absurdity, what he termed the "God-is-dead world." I never spoke of God in that way, Dick. I never spoke of God at all. Maybe because I come from a little *shtetl* and because I was a *Yeshiva Bocher*—and still am, in a way. And maybe because, for years and years throughout my childhood, I learned that before I said "God is alive," I had to be prepared. I remember we had to go to the *Mikvah*—the ritual bath—in order to be worthy of affirming something as important as "God is blessed"; God is God.

Therefore, I never speak of God now. I rather speak of men who believed in God or men who denied God. How strange that the philosophy denying God came not from the survivors. Those who came out with the so-called God is dead theology, not one of them had been in Auschwitz. Those who had never said it. I have my problems with God, believe me. I have my anger and I have my quarrels and I have my nightmares. But my dispute, my bewilder-

271

ment, my astonishment is with men. I didn't understand how men could be so "barbarian," as you called it, Dick. I still don't understand it. Maybe because I come from a Yeshiva and that all I learned at the Sorbonne was nothing comparable to what I studied in the Yeshiva. I also don't understand how so many Jews remained human inside the camps. I will never understand it. You spoke of hate—that you don't want your children to hate. Let me reassure you, Dick, a Jew is incapable of hate. In the Bible, wherever hate is mentioned, it always refers to self-hate. The only hate that a Jew is capable of—unfortunately—is self-hate. But then he does it well. We cannot hate our neighbors; we cannot even hate our enemies. Look at Israel; Israelis do not hate the Arabs.

Let me tell you something else. Strange as it may sound, there was no hate involved in the relationship between Jew and German. We didn't hate the Germans, and the Germans didn't hate us. It was worse. You can hate only a human being. To them we were objects. Man doesn't hate objects. And we didn't hate them because we are incapable of hate, especially as they then represented the *Malach Hamavet*, the Angel of Death. How can you hate death? How can you hate something which is beyond you and which sometimes wears the mask of God? How can you? We didn't.

Furthermore, when I think of the Jews in the camps, what astonishes me is that so many of them remained human despite everything. I'll give you an example. As I told you, I came from a Yeshiva taken away straight from the Talmud. All of us—I wasn't the only one; when I say "I," I mean all of us—were taken away from the Yeshiva, from the Talmud, straight to Birkenau. And for three days I was in a daze, I couldn't believe what I saw. Then I awakened and I remember that immediately after, it must have been on the fourth or fifth day, I was sent to a commando. I have never told this story, because I consider it too personal. I was sent to a commando to carry stones. The man with whom I carried stones—I never saw his face, only his neck and I remember only his voice—the very first day he asked me, "Where do you come from?" I told him. "What do you do at home?" I said I was a *Yeshiva Bocher;* I studied. He said, "What tractate did you study?" I told him. He said, "What page?" I told him. He said, "Let's continue." I said, "Are you mad? *Here?* Without books, without anything and *why?*" He said, "We must continue. That is the only way." And believe it or not, we continued.

He was a famous *Rosh Yeshiva*, the famous head of a famous Yeshiva Talmudic school in Galicia. He used to recite a passage and I would repeat it, day after day. We studied Talmud to the very end. That a man like this not only studied but also taught Talmud in Auschwitz, that is a source of wonder to me. Also the fact that he was not the only one.

There was a man who smuggled in a pair of *tefillin*, phylacteries. It cost him I don't know how many rations, portions of bread. He smuggled them in and there were at least two hundred Jews who got up every day one hour before everybody to stand in line and to perform the Mitzvah. Absurd! Yes, it was absurd to put on the phylacteries. Do you know there were Jews there who fasted on Yom Kippur! There were Jews who said prayers! There were Jews who sanctified the name of Israel, of their people, simply by remaining human!

Within the system of the concentration camp, something very strange took place. The first to give in, the first to collaborate—to save their lives—were the intellectuals, the liberals, the humanists, the professors of sociology, and the like. Because suddenly their whole concept of the universe broke down. They had nothing to lean on. Very few Communists gave in. There were some, but very few. They had their own church-like organization—a secular church, but very well organized. They were the resisters. Even fewer to give in were the Catholic priests. There were very few priests who, when the chips were down, gave in and collaborated with the torturer. Yet there were exceptions. But you could not have found one single rabbi—*I dare you*—among all the *kapos* or among any of the others who held positions of power in the camps.

You say, Dick, that Hitler deprived the Jew of martyrdom. That is not true. Many Jews, especially the rabbis, could have saved their lives. In my town all the rabbis could have saved their lives, and do you know who wanted to save them? The priests. It's not the first time in history that they wanted alibis. The priests came to our rabbis—we had some thirty of them in our center—offering them refuge in the monastery, in the church. But, of course, what rabbi would choose it? I think there were two, out of at least fifty thousand rabbis in Eastern Europe, two who chose to escape individually. All the others preferred voluntarily, knowingly, to go with their Jews. How did these rabbis maintain their Jewishness and their humanity? *That* is the wonder! After all the system was so strong and the whole world was an accomplice!

What the Germans wanted to do was not only to exterminate the Jewish people physically; first of all, they wanted to exterminate them *spiritually*. Therefore, they invented this whole society—what we call in France *universe concentrationnaire*—with its princes and priests and high priests. The Germans wanted to deprave, to debase the Jew, to have him give up all values and dehumanize him. That was the first thing. Even the language in the camp—what kind of language was it? The most obscene language you could imagine, meant to create a climate, to impose an inhuman concept of man and of the universe upon the Jewish people.

There is a joke which is not funny. The joke is that, in one ghetto an SS officer tortured a Jew, and at one point clobbered him on the head while at the same time firing a blank shot. When the Jew came to, there was the SS man laughing, saying, "You are dead. But you don't know it. You think that you escaped us? We are your masters, even in the other world." It's a macabre joke, but it contains some truth. What the Germans wanted to do to the Jewish people was to substitute themselves for the Jewish God. All the terminology, all the vocabulary testifies to that. And in spite of all, here were these men who remained human and who remained Jewish and went on praying to God.

And here I will tell you, Dick, that you don't understand *them* when you say that it is more difficult to live today in a world without God. NO! If you want difficulties, choose to live *with* God. Can you compare today the tragedy of the believer to that of the nonbeliever?! The real tragedy, the real drama, is the drama of the believer.

\*     \*     \*

It took me ten years to write my first book. It was not a coincidence; it was deliberate. I took a vow of silence in 1945, to the effect that I would wait ten years to be sure that what I would say would be true. In the beginning people did not talk about what happened over there. Those who survived refused to reveal the darkness they had seen. Today you have novelists and sociologists, you have everybody writing about it. In the early days, those who were there did not touch on it: it was fire. Why didn't they? For many reasons.

First, because they were afraid that no one would believe them. Second, they were afraid that, in the very process of telling the tale, they would betray it. Certain tales must be transmitted orally or not at all, must be transmitted like secrets, as a whole, from mouth to ear, in whispers—like the real oral tradition which was never transmitted, never written down according to the Kotzker rabbi. I think it was Braque who said that literature is a wound turned fire; and we were afraid to invite that fire. You remember in the Bible what happened to the two children of Aaroni Hacohen, the high priest? One doesn't play with fire!

So we didn't speak about it because we were afraid of committing a sin. Even today all of my friends have the feeling that, when we write books and publish them, we have committed a sin. Don't ask me why. It's irrational. Something is wrong, something is impure. The real story, perhaps, will never be told. The real truth will never be communicated. The real vision can never be shared, so why speak about it?

I'll go even farther. Today, twenty-five years after the event, I wonder whether we shouldn't have chosen silence then. For some reason, I believe that had all the survivors gathered in a secret conclave, somewhere in a forest, and decided together—I know it's a poetic image, unfeasible, but I feel this sense of loss of this opportunity—if we had then all of us decided never to say a word about it, I think we could have changed man by the very weight of our silence. But then I also believe that mankind wouldn't have been able to bear it. It would have driven man and peoples to madness. That is why, I think, we spoke.

Then we also spoke for a different reason. Somehow the Jew in us is so strong that we believe in communication, we believe in transmission, we believe in sharing. I think the single factor in Jewish existence is this need to communicate. Therefore, we begin always with names; the Bible is full of names. Why do we have all these names—the father and the son, the father of the son—why? To give us this feeling of being linked, of having to continue. We must communicate. This is the central theme of Jewish existence and has been—always—throughout the four thousand years of our history. During World War II it was even more so. Hundreds of people in ghettos sacrificed themselves to enable one of them to get out of the ghetto and tell the tale.

When Shimon Dubnov, probably the greatest historian we have had, was led to the mass grave in Riga together with all the Jews, he shouted, "Jews, open your ears and open your eyes! Take in every cloud; take in every smile; take in every sound. Don't forget!" He was even then, even there, obsessed with the need to communicate, to tell *us* certain tales. In Auschwitz—worse, in Birkenau, in the Sonderkommando, the commando that worked in the crematoria— there were historians; men who wrote down, day after day, fact after morbid fact, dryly and soberly. They were conscious of the necessity to transmit. Why? Why did they do it? And what for? In whom could they believe? In man? That is what bewilders me and aston- ishes me: that they could still think of man and of God and of us, while they lived and died in an age in which both Jew and man were betrayed by man and God. This story of spiritual strength—I won't call it "resistance" because the word itself was devaluated—of the Jew has to be told. I think this is what makes us so humble. But here we touch, I believe, the very substance of what I call *Jewishness*— because I don't like the word *Judaism*. There are too many *isms* in this world. What do I call *Jewishness?*

There is a story in the Talmud, a very beautiful one. And it's relevant, because you spoke of martyrs, and we speak of martyrs. The story goes: When Rabbi Ishmael, one of the ten martyrs of the faith in Roman times, was led to his death, a heavenly voice was heard, saying, "Ishmael, Ishmael, should you shed one tear, I shall return the universe to its primary chaos." And the Midrash says that Rabbi Ishmael was a gentleman and did not cry. And I couldn't understand for quite a while: why didn't he cry? The hell with it! If this is the price to pay, who needs it? Who wants this kind of world? Who wants to live in it? Yet there are many reasons why he didn't cry.

One, he was a martyr. Two, he obeyed. Three, the last and most poetic ultimate reason why he didn't cry is because he wanted to teach us a lesson in Judaism. Rabbi Ishmael—contrary to his classical opponent, Rabbi Akiba—was a rationalist. Even while dying, he wanted to teach us a lesson: Yes, I could destroy the world, and the world deserves to be destroyed. But to be a Jew is to have all the reasons in the world to destroy and *not to destroy!* To be a Jew is to have all the reasons in the world to hate the Germans and *not to hate them!* To be a Jew is to have all the reasons in the world to mistrust the church and *not to hate it!* To be a Jew is to have all the reasons in the world not to have faith in language, in singing, in prayers, and in God, but *to go on telling the tale, to go on carrying on the dialogue,* and to have my own silent prayers and quarrels with God.

That is the lesson that Rabbi Ishmael, when he died, taught me; but then he was Rabbi Ishmael and I am only a teller of his tales. But then, perhaps, that is the meaning of Jewish existence, especially for a storyteller, to tell tales lived so many times by so many Jews, and I am only one of them.

# 16

# What Can America Learn from the German Church Struggle?

Theodore A. Gill

Coming at my enviable but impossible job of summarizing and applying the conference lectures, I discover a few things stick in my craw that I must mention or, otherwise, they will continue to irritate. So I will spit them out, but more as questions than as claims or charges. That is, after all, what I am capable of. The men and women whose essays appear in this volume are the experts. I have read them before, quoted them, taught from their books. I am not in their class on our present subject.

But I am in their field. And we are obviously not alone in that field. One of the most interesting revelations, creditable to this conference, is the startling sight of how widespread is the interest in the German Church Struggle. How arresting is the glimpse we get here of banked batteries of bright Ph.D. eyes, gimleting in on the church fight under the Nazis. And not just academicians either. Many of us are hooked on the subject. Among the standard enthusiasms, we have a new genre, the Church Struggle buff.

Nor is that a frivolous, throw-away observation, as it would be if it suggested turning recent bloody risks into seminar fun. Enthusiasms are essential to our human survival—I mean, to the *humanity* of whoever survives. And the Church Struggle is as currently suggestive an enthusiasm as one could have. That, I hope, is part of its appeal. But beyond that, there is the handiness of its packaging. It is an isolatable, discrete, manageable event. It is exceedingly knowable; it has a limited cast of characters, a limited number of events, a beginning, a middle, and an end. It is dramatic, too.

In addition, it is a kind of laboratory course in church history. Under as close a controlled situation as historical science can contrive, we now can observe a creed being born, an already classic confession being put together. So Barmen is not just a confession printed in the back of our prayer books for glazed-eye perusal when the sermon bores or announcements drag or the anthem dies. It is an instruction in the reading and understanding of all our older confessions; for here, written by men still alive, under pressure of events still reverberating among us, are the statements of faith required in our time. Here it is: a nourishing tuber ripped up out of its historical soil, with the clods of its political occasion clinging to it. We can know it all: from the street tumults and official threats to the housekeeping events of the breakaway synods themselves—how Barth sketched the Barmen confession while Asmussen and Breit napped after a heavy lunch; how Barth was overlooked in the invitations to Barmen until two days before, and then, what a scramble!; who preached on what text; who raised the money for printing; who thanked the ladies in the kitchen: church history in our terms. No wonder some of us fasten onto it.

There are probably darker reasons, too. This was internecine struggle. The impulses were fratricidal. Sibling things are down there in the mysterious murk—and the Oedipal business. Buffs cluster like flies to the lips of the wounds between brothers—the French Revolution, our own Civil War, now the Church Struggle. Again, the observation is not frivolous: Karl Barth was a Civil War buff.

But what has all this to do with *now?* The question has not waited until today to present itself to me. Two years ago, friends decided that one way to comment on developments in our own country right now would be to get a large feature film made about Dietrich Bonhoeffer, and soon. Easier said than done—and in this audience, only my wife and Dr. Bethge know what a bottomless swamp of legalese that teetering phrase crosses.

Yet, consider the possibilities: a child of plenty, personable, brilliant, many-talented, develops sweetly in his family privilege. He travels, he plays, he excels at the university, he enters the Christian traditional piety. He honors the government, preaches no politics, exalts the church, considers pacifism. He gets a great kick out of being around. Then his nation accepts a mad suitor; the atmosphere is suddenly electric with threat; Bonhoeffer goes into resistance. He does the best he can in a resisting church. At home he opposes, abroad he exposes the lie of his government and too many of its people. Sometimes in sight, sometimes out, he writes, preaches, teaches, exhorts, schemes. He refuses safety, enters the resistance, operates as a kind of double agent in his own country and abroad and a courier to the outside, joins a conspiracy against the life of the Head of State, is misunderstood by the church, betrayed by colleagues, imprisoned, hanged, burned to lost ashes in the Nazi ovens.

Years after the war, a friend collects and publishes letters and poems written by Bonhoeffer from prison. Realistic young students find in these fragments more suggestions for twentieth-century faith and life than in most of their other authorities, and the fascination and fame of Dietrich Bonhoeffer begin their enormous spread and usefulness.

The story, we submit, is worth filming on its own account. A complex hero is swept into historic events and the scenario quite honestly explodes into razzle-dazzle, hanky-panky, and derring-do with a real martyrdom for toppers. Such an account of personal development in the midst of earthshaking, earth shattering events, all true, will spark dramatic treatment over and over again.

But—and this is why I tell you about our project—as moviemakers we are interested in much more than the principal character and his tempestuous times. We are really interested in us and our own threatening period. But because Bonhoeffer's time was the upbeat for that whole discordant era in which we still flounder, we need take no liberties with his story to make it antiphonal to ours. If we tell his story straight, we think it may help us see around some of our own blind corners. It is not that we will be trying to learn from his history, so we will not have to repeat it; we *are* repeating it, it is all our history.

Would we be filming the 1930s or the 1970s when we showed a man who came to see the criminal potentiality in a conservatism that would clamp the lid on the status quo while a changing, churning history underneath the artificial order hastens the awful explosion such sealed conservatism ensures? Is it then or now when a desperate patriot decries the worked-out weariness of a once lively liberalism? Where are the intervening decades when a youth denounces the blood mysticism of the radicals, the maddening, senseless assumption of demagogues of every ilk that righteousness will come automatically when the right righteous are in, that the empowered "people" will naturally make things right? Would it be history we read or history we are caught up in when the script took up the earlier debate on law and order, Communism, racism, dissent, militarism? And what about our hero's struggle with issues of resistance, violence and nonviolence, assassination? How *déja vu* can you be?

Fortunately for you, the frantic ticket buyers, fighting your way into packed movie theaters, I will not script the film. But because to us the right parallels are so important, I have already made the (no doubt cinematically naive) suggestion that the German political development be shown in swift, separated scenes with overlapping action and dialogue, a twentieth-century people thus shown struggling with what are apparently the twentieth-century issues. Everything will depend upon playing these scenes straight, honestly, about Germany in the early 1930s. Everything will also depend upon playing them without one single verbal reference to Germany or Germans or Nazis or Hitler or Europe. Let there be not one ranter before a monstrous rally, not one goose-stepping soldier.

Instead, in one scene a troubled bourgeoise couple—serious, nervous, not at all "bad" or "wrong"—talking about law and order in terms of unnecessary violence and respect for the police and safety in the streets. That scene could bleed into another, dialogue switched in midsentence and finished in another voice where respectable men in a restaurant or beerhall discuss the same issue in terms of rowdies and aimless youths with their long hair, their folk songs, their wanderings. (I do not distort for my own purposes; see the newspapers and magazines of that day.) In neither discussion will causes be a matter of interest nor will justice be important enough to mention. Just control.

In a third scene, pleasant, responsible-looking businessmen in an office will be discussing with all dignity the problems raised by "the other race," especially the agitators among them, who are, of course, Communists. This dialogue can shift in midstream to tea-table women just as upset at what Communist agitators are doing to "those people" (though everybody has a good friend among them, some even a best friend). Even a wisp of "back where they came from" may be heard through the *Kuchen* and tea.

In a fifth scene, gentle old folk will be honestly agonized by inflationary threats to their security, hoping for almost any strong government moves that may save their small substance and so their painfully calculated future. On one of Berlin's raunchier streets at night, other old people, just as nice but not quite so gentle, will react

281

with the expected grim threats to the high school prostitutes and transvestites cruising the clubs where lipsticked, corseted Junkers pawed them fatly. (George Grosz will give you the picture.)

In still another scene a father may yell at his son that "not every forty-year-old is a criminal and an idiot for the simple reason that he is twenty years older than you are." (A quote certified by Peter Gay; as Richard Freedman remarked about it in the New York *Times*, "at least the cut-off date then was forty.") The son would not be guilty of a non sequitur, if his response brought up the fact that, in the recent past, right-wing extremists had got away with 354 murders, while twenty-two left-wing assassins had been severely punished.

Military men could be pictured assuring already assured military men that big military forces are essential to peace, that civilian governments know nothing of military matters, that peace depends on big preparation and overwhelming strength, that there are worse things than war. Farmers in the field will mouth the same line and add to it contempt for the "internationalists," for worrying about what other countries think. The same line can shift to a parish scene where ministers inveigh against "ecumenism" and the idea that other continents, other denominations have anything to add to their own superior tradition. And still another scene where church laymen agree vociferously that politics should be kept out of the pulpit, and that the economy is none of the church's business.

The goal, you see, is complete calendar ambiguity. Forty intervening years have to go curiously accordion pleated and translucent. We must wonder whether it is then or now on the screen. The earnest, nervous debates are on law and order, race, Communism, inflation, international monetary crises, internationalism, keeping the church out of politics, long-haired youth, respect for the flag, urban immorality, censorship. For those were the issues then. Fascism was then, as it is now, one response to those issues.

The generalized scenes become specifically German again when the nation turns to the politician who played most skillfully on its fears and retributions. Suddenly, perhaps, the screen is full of police clubbing young demonstrators on a summer twilight in a great city's streets, while, on the soundtrack, Adolf Hitler rasps his usual charges against Communist agitators and student rebels, and winds up with his standard law and order frenzy.

Surely the coincidences have registered themselves. If we are not in the same soup the Germans were, ours has many of the same noxious ingredients. The question is: how near are we? Now "nearness" is an unstable measure (as H. L. Mencken proved with his comment on first tasting "near beer": "Whoever named this is a very poor judge of distance"). When a United States senator supports a candidate for the Supreme Court because the candidate is mediocre and lots of folks are mediocre (and they need a mediocre voice to represent their mediocre attitudes on the highest tribunal) that is just a funny toe thrust in the ocean across which lies *Volk* justice and *Volk* courts. But it is in the same ocean. And when stop and frisk laws are discussed and no-knock entries are contemplated, that is not yet the suspension of all civil rights. But it does not enhance them. Armed Black Panther men dying by the tens in their pads are not six million naked men, women, and children in ovens and under the showerheads of death. But the smooth, official face has a family resemblance to other noncommittal fronts.

The nearness depends upon the analyst you consult. The varying evaluations are matter for splendid debate, with much questioning of each other as judges of distance. But what is more seriously disquieting than judgment of distance is sense of direction. Is there anything in American official life that moves massively *against* the drift? Anything that, no matter how near or far, is obviously going the other way?

Again, that may depend on your trusted observer. William Stringfellow sees only the exhaustion of the American revolutionary ethic. "We behold that wherever we turn: in the police aggressions against black citizens, in the attorney general's designs to neutralize the courts, in the usurpation of the federal budget and consequent corruption of the tax system by a virtually autonomous military-intelligence-scientific principality, by repetitious schemes to suppress dissent and intimidate the media, by an ironic policy of internal colonialism symbolized by the victimization of the welfare population."

But most disquieting to him (and to us looking back as well as looking around ourselves) is the tacit equating of the American Way of Life with religious idealism, and the hand-in-hand between chief priests and chiefs of state. That binding goes a long way back, of course, and takes us all in. For according to the gospels, for all practical purposes the ecclesiastical authorities acted as servants of the state in the confrontation with Jesus. In one version, the chief priests protest that Caesar is our king, we have no king but Caesar. In the dispute over jurisdiction between Pilate and Herod, they warn that if you release him, you will not be Caesar's friend. The ecclesiastics were, practically speaking, agents of the state. That is an all too familiar situation for chief priests to be found in. That was the situation in Nazi Germany. It was similar, Kierkegaard says, in Scandinavia a century ago. It is notoriously that way with the Dutch Reformed church in South Africa. It has been, in principle, the role of the white Anglo-Saxon denominations in most jurisdictions in this land both before and since the Civil War. On the issues of race and war, which is to say on virtually all issues, the white denominations and sects can be fairly viewed as the religious arm of the political establishment, or the same matter can be viewed the other way around: the incumbent political administration represents the terminal climax of the profoundly secular character of white Protestant denominationalism in America.

Dr. Stringfellow's astringent to ascerbic analysis would be fairly congenial to Professor Paul Lehmann, too. Recently, as he prepared to urge the trustees of Union Seminary to commit $400,000 of that school's endowment funds to make bail for the Black Panthers facing trial in New York City, he was asked by a reporter, "Do you think what you are talking about suggests a need for a Confessing Church, such as in Germany, just before Hitler came to power?"

Lehmann responded, "I think your question is natural enough in that one does bring to any type of human situation memories as well as hopes. Those of us who have lived through, even from a distance, an acute confrontation between church and state, such as that represented by the German Church Struggle in Nazi times, can scarcely avoid thinking about that a little bit. Realizing that historical parallels are never identical, it seems to me that the possibilities of a theological confrontation between a sensitive church, or a church endeavoring to be faithful to the gospel, and a developing over-extension of power in society, takes on a certain imminence particularly when the over-extension of power begins to distort the safeguards of the legal system. A further remark may be made in this connection. This is that one of the still open possibilities in American society is that church and state still have operational room vis-à-vis each other, and thus opportunities for sensitive explorations and sensitive judgments are still live not dead options. Indeed, explorations of avenues of reconciliation in terms of which law can really help make possible human freedom are at the top of any agenda about which church and state really face up to each other. So a good deal of my judgment depends upon whether the elasticity of the traditions of American society is sufficient to make room for an ongoing, serious exploration of the conscience of the body politic. So long as this is possible, there is a great sign of hope. This is why we must begin at the beginning and not wait until the dynamics of the situation have passed the point of no return."

Dr. Lehmann's answer is diplomatically hopeful. But to wind up our conference, the ill-informed question is enough. "Do we need a Confessing Church such as was in Germany just before Hitler came to power?"

Maybe. We need something. But now, thanks to this conference (or should I say, alas, because of this conference), I am quite clear that we do not need "a Confessing Church such as was in Germany." The Confessing Church has been thoroughly demythologized for me here. Or have I heard it wrong? Add up all the Sturm und Drang of the Church Struggle and though there are in it shining episodes of personal valor, and a lot of bad people were made very angry, and it messed up the *Gleichschaltung* record but good—was one development in that vicious regime ever thrown much off stride by the Confessing Church, even in its brief heyday?

One thing the Confessing Church did show us all. It showed us that in the adult world the church is not big enough anymore by itself to effect much. Dietrich Bonhoeffer found out at last what his father and brothers had been telling him since he was fifteen: the church was not important enough anymore in the things that matter most to justify giving his life to it. Theology was all right. Theology is a distinguished faculty in any European university. Some of father Bonhoeffer's best friends were theologians. But his brother Klaus said to Dietrich, "The church is just too peripheral an outfit, now." And at last Dietrich knew it too. That, at least, is how I interpret Bonhoeffer's turning to the *Abwehr* conspiracy. He had done his best to resist within the church by keeping its gospel pure. But at last he saw that even the Confessing Church was only a gnat nuisance to the state, and he wearied of keeping its hum in tune. He went to people who wanted action.

And the Confessing Church was too late, too often, to be much use as a model for us now. The questioner referred to "a Confessing Church such as was in Germany just before Hitler came to power." But there was no such Confessing Church then. It came later. It came late. Its principal prophet, Karl Barth, in the years just before Adolf Hitler came to power, while voting still meant something, rejected Paul Tillich's appeal to him to electioneer with him against the Nazis; he was busy with the purity of preaching and the exigencies of system. In 1931, when Bonhoeffer stopped in Bonn on his way home from Union Seminary, the young pastor pled with the theological titan for some specific and practical statements on the meaning of obedience in the developing situation; Barth demurred, finding Bonhoeffer impetuous. It was Adolf Hitler who saved Karl Barth's ethics by invading the sanctuary and demanding of the great teacher developments in his own teaching that he always knew were laggard.

And even after it got rolling, the Confessing Church was late in its perceptions. I simply cannot get gooseflesh over the systematic refinement in Barmen's discovery that the attacks on the Jews must be resisted because they were in reality attacks on Jesus Christ. That is not high theology. That is blasphemy, the unwitting blasphemy, I hope, of men playing a dandy hand of Doctrine. It was played out to the end, too. In the letter sent around preparing for the Stuttgart confession after the war, was there much about the guilt against the Jews? Was there anything?

We have little to learn from any church or any prophet who cannot recognize murder until it is murder in the cathedral. We have enough of those.

And then, the Confessing Church was just too limited. It influenced some. They did not all stick. And all together, did they do much? Yes, they put one fleeting, drowned fragrance in the otherwise universal stench. They were a winsome bunch; a winsome, crumbling bunch.

But, and here is the real question, how much of that good report has depended upon reading back into the Confessing Church record the valiance and sacrifice of one Confessing Church backslider, Dietrich Bonhoeffer, and prisons full of the men who took the ultimate risk: agnostics, atheists, Socialists, Communists; and among the crucial conspirators who were Christians? Was there a single one who was any longer much moved by Karl Barth-Barmen-Christomonist type considerations? Read their last letters: natural theology men, every one of them; in the pinch they were philosophic Christians (read Nikolaus von Halem's farewell letter to his mother: he bids her read Schopenhauer for consolation, "not the first book, but you know the great passage on World Will in the second volume," etc.), nineteenth-century Christians, Schleiermacher Christians, Enlightenment Christians every one. Have you looked recently at the surprising list of Bonhoeffer's prison reading? Did you think it was sheer cerebration and not physical experience that made Bonhoeffer turn on Barth at the end? It would be the first time for Bonhoeffer. He let his ideas go off the radical edge when he had lived awhile at the dead-end of the grand central tradition in Christian theology.

And now I have been brash and insensitive and holier-than-thou long enough. After all, we do learn from the Confessing Church.

As observed, we are reminded that the church by itself is not big enough to make the essential differences. So we look around for allies. And we waive blood tests when we marry consorts we need. And we learn the common language.

The Confessing Church shows us what happens when you are late, too. We need a much more sensitive and much farther out early warning system. We need a DEW line way, way out from the church. The Confessing Church, as a matter of fact, functions for us as a very distant censor, showing us a danger approaching. But most of the censors will be "human rights." Cross one of those, and the lights ought to go on in all Christian headquarters.

The DEW line we need cannot depend on esoteric coterie formulations. That does not mean I am *against* theology. Not at all. In a world with more time on its hands and some of the old guarantors of significance (like work) going, theology could shortly have a new life and vigor. But theology must now be a secret discipline. It is not a public operation. It is for those who get their fundamental orientation in the same place and in the same way, and want to think about that and celebrate that together. But the practical specifics of the life suggested by one's theology do not surface until you can talk about them in the *lingua franca* of man and men and freedom and justice and act on them in concert with people who never heard your secret talk, or heard it and walked out on it, but who are going your way.

Above all, and this has been my major dis-ease this week, we do not theologize before Jews. I have not touched on the Holocaust in my summary. It is fire, not to be touched by anyone. (But touching, tearing. Will you forget Richard Rubenstein, universalizing his desolation, yet never so Jewish as when he worries most about what identity he can give his sons. Or Elie Wiesel, a glowing spark thrown out of the Holocaust, so gratefully Jewish, yet never so universal as when he puts his faith in the faith of an old teacher and lives himself on the undramatic persistence of the people around him.) But since the Holocaust, what word can we hear but Bonhoeffer's who, on the little he could have known, said that thereafter the Germans could not speak evangelically again to the Jews. I enlarge it from Germans to Gentiles.

In a sermon at Stanford University, Dean Davie Napier confessed,

If I were a Jew . . . I would have to tell you that in view of what my people have suffered in 1900 years of Christian history in so-called Christian nations and implicitly if not explicitly in the name of Jesus Christ—as a Jew I would have to tell you that the name makes me sick. But as a Jew, I would know what you mean, perhaps better than you, by the Word of God and the Kingdom of God—and I would say, if you will not cudgel me with your name Jesus, I may even join you in the song "Oh Happy Day."

I find it a growing embarrassment that we should still have to so swaddle plainest humanity in Christological winding-sheets before we can show it; if that is the way it comes to us, then the least we can do is unwrap it in the church basement on Wednesday night—and not in the middle of a state university campus.

Humanize, humanize, that is the ticket: men, their freedom, their chances, their creativity, their relationships, fulfillments, hopes—that is what we keep our eye on, whatever or whoever it is that aims our vision. It is transgressions in these areas that give us our warnings.

DEW lines—way out in the human landscape, on every corner, in every ghetto, radar sensitivity—that is what we need!

And the screens of our receptivity must not be set so fine that they get clogged up with human peccadilloes, and never show the real threats. That means, for instance, that we go on with our good beginning at getting over the church's century-long lap fixation. Think what mischief our Christian prurience has done. Roehm was murdered and justice was strangled—but his sexually irregular life helped still the protest of good burghers who knew how much more important regular sex was to God than murder and the end of justice.

Add von Fritsch. And priests and nuns, casually destroyed, because "Christians" thought they knew what God was most interested in.

On the other hand, the moral grid must not be so wide-spaced that only great big Antichrists show on our ethical screens. Threats to men are human threats. Don't watch for waves of the future and cosmic surges and demonic clouds. They are all too airy, too gaseous to register. Watch for men giving trouble to men. The mesh on the moral screen must be man-sized.

And finally, we must keep our options open, keep our analyses fluid. That means no identification of the current enemy may become a fixation. The question was raised in this room, but not answered. Was Communism really the ultimate enemy in Germany? Was it so bad that nothing else was worse? Might it have been the revolution that should have come? It is a question now impossible to answer. But we must let it echo.

# Notes

## Chapter 1

1. Otto Diehn, *Bibliographie zur Geschichte des Kirchenkampfes, 1933-1945* (Göttingen: Vandenhoeck & Ruprecht, 1958); vol. 1 is a bibliography containing over 6000 items on the Church Struggle.

2. Six numbers were issued before it died out for lack of adequate financing: 10/1/59, 10/15/59, 11/15/59, 8/1/60, 9/15/60, 1/31/61; cf. "Research on Christianity and Totalitarianism," *Church History* (1960), 29:226-28.

3. Cf. John S. Conway, "Der deutsche Kirchenkampf," *Vierteljahrshefte für Zeitgeschichte* (1969), 17:423-49, and Beate Ruhm von Oppen, "Nazis and Christians," *World Politics* (1969), 21:392-424.

4. Cf. the report and discussion by Lucy S. Dawidowicz on the Yad Vashem Conference of April 1968, published in *Commentary* (1969), pp. 51-59.

5. Cf. my *Wild Tongues: A Handbook of Social Pathology* (New York: Macmillan Co., 1969), p. 93.

6. Karl Barth, *The Church and the Political Problem of Our Day* (New York: Charles Scribner's Sons, 1939), pp. 41, 43.

7. Hugh Martin et al., *Christian Counter-Attack* (New York: Charles Scribner's Sons, 1944), p. 135.

8. Dietrich Bonhoeffer, *Gesammelte Schriften*, ed. Eberhard Bethge (Munich: Chrs. Kaiser Verlag, 1958), 1:297-98.

9. Cf. Bernhard Pfister and Gerhard Hildmann, eds., *Widerstandsrecht und Grenzen der Staatsgewalt* (Berlin: Duncker & Humblot, 1956).

10. Cf. my "The Secular City and Christian Self-Restraint," *The Church and the Body Politic* (New York: Seabury Press, 1969), chap. 6.

11. Hans Buchheim, *Glaubenskrise im Dritten Reich* (Stuttgart: Deutsche Verlags-Anstalt, 1953), p. 17.

12. Koppel S. Pinson, *Pietism in the Rise of German Nationalism* (New York: Columbia University Press, 1936), passim.

13. Quoted in Horace M. Kallen, *Secularism Is the Will of God* (New York: Twayne Publications, 1954), p. 162n.

14. Eric Voegelin, *The New Science of Politics* (Chicago: University of Chicago Press, 1952), passim.

15. Jürgen Moltmann, *Theology of Hope*, trans. James W. Leitch (New York: Harper & Row, 1967), p. 43.

16. Quoted in Gabriel Vahanian, *The Death of God* (New York: George Braziller, 1961), p. 225.

17. Josef L. Hromadka, *Doom and Resurrection* (Richmond: Madrus House, 1945), p. 102; for more extensive discussion of this point with citations, see my "Protestant Churches and Totalitarianism (Germany 1933-1945)," in Carl J. Friedrich, ed., *Totalitarianism* (Cambridge: Harvard University Press, 1954), pp. 108-19.

18. Samuel Sandmel, "Bultmann on Judaism," in Charles W. Kegley, ed., *The Theology of Rudolf Bultmann* (New York: Harper and Row, 1966), p. 218. [This essay has been reprinted in Samuel Sandmel, *Two Living Traditions* (Detroit: Wayne State University Press, 1972). Ed.]

19. Arnold J. Toynbee, *A Study of History*, Somervell abridgment (New York: Oxford University Press, 1957), pp. 8, 22; see the brilliant critique by D. Eric Voegelin in *Order and History, I: Israel and Revelation* (Baton Rouge: Louisiana State University Press, 1956), p. 120.

20. Letter to seminary heads, dated 1/20/70.

21. Correspondence in my possession, dated 2/7/70.

22. *Trial of the Major War Criminals* (Nuremberg: International Military Tribunal, 1947), 9:268.

23. Cajus Fabricius, *Positive Christianity in the Third Reich* (Dresden: Püschel, 1937), pp. 23-24.

24. Cited in *Kirchliches Jahrbuch, 1933-1944*, ed. J. Beckmann (Gütersloh: C. Bertelsmann Verlag, 1948), p. 3.

25. Robert Welch, *The Blue Book* (Boston: Privately printed, 1959), pp. 68-69, 147.

26. Translated in full in *The German Phoenix* (New York: Doubleday & Co., 1960), appendix A.

27. "Die Bedeutung des Kirchenkampfes für die Ökumene," *Evangelische Theologie* (1960), 20:1-21.

28. Paul Gürtler, *Nationalsozialismus und evangelische Kirchen im Warthegau* (Göttingen: Vandenhoeck & Ruprecht, 1958), appendix doc. 8, pt. 4.

29. Hana Volavkova, ed., *I · Never Saw Another Butterfly. . .: Children's Drawings and Poems from Terezin Concentration Camp, 1942-1944* (New York: McGraw-Hill Book Co., 1962), p. 13.

30. Arthur C. Cochrane, *The Church's Confession under Hitler* (Philadelphia: Westminster Press, 1962), p. 19.

31. Elie Wiesel, *The Jews of Silence: A Personal Report on Soviet Jewry* (New York: Holt, Rinehart & Winston, 1966), p. 136.

## Chapter 2

1. Viktor Conzemius, "Eglises chrétiennes et totalitarisme national-socialiste," in *Revue d'histoire ecclesiastique* 63 (1968): 947.

2. Paul Gürtler, *Nationalsozialismus und Evangelischen Kirchen im Warthegau* (Göttingen: Vandenhoeck and Ruprecht, 1958).

3. Appended is a list of the principal official records of the Nazi party and state relating to the German Church Struggle:

Records of the Reichs Chancellery. Originals in Bundesarchiv, Koblenz, R 43 II 149-178a. Finding aid available. Selectively filmed, see G. Kent, *A Catalogue of Files and Microfilms of the German Foreign Ministry Archives 1920-45*, 3 vols., Stanford University Press.

Records of the German Foreign Ministry. Politisches Archiv, Bonn, especially *Staatsekretär, Vatikan;* Pol. III, *Vatikan;* and *Inland* II. Originals in Bonn. Selectively filmed. Finding aid, see Kent.

Records of the Reich Ministry of Justice. Originals in Bundesarchiv, Koblenz, R 22. Finding aid available.

Records of the Reich Ministry for Church Affairs.Originals in Potsdam. No information on finding aid.

Records of the Reich Ministry for the Occupied Eastern Territories. Originals in Bundesarchiv, Koblenz, R 6. Finding Aid, *Guide to Captured German Records*, No. 28. Microfilms available from U.S. National Archives (T-454)

Records of the NSDAP Part I–III. Originals in Bundesarchiv, Koblenz. Finding aid, *Guide to Captured German Records*, Nos. 3, 20, 35. Microfilms available from U.S. National Archives (T-81).

Records of the Reichsführer SS and Chief of the German Police, Part I–III. Originals in Bundesarchiv, Koblenz, except when of local provenance. Finding aid, *Guide to Captured German Records*, Nos. 32, 33 and 39. Microfilms available from U.S. National Archives (T-175).

Berlin Document Center, Biographical Materials. Originals in Berlin, only partially filmed, not generally released. Non-biographical materials. Originals in Bundesarchiv, Koblenz. Microfilms available from U.S. National Archives (T-580 and T-611). Finding aid, T-580, roll 999.

Rundschreiben, Anordnungen und Verfügungen des Stellvertreters des Führers. Originals in Bundesarchiv: Koblenz, Institute for Contemporary History: Munich, and Berlin Document Center. All incomplete: no finding aid or index.

Documents Prepared for the Nuremburg Trials 1946-48. Mimeographs and Photostats Available in National Archives, Washington, D.C.; Harvard University, The Library of the Law School.

Records of the Bavarian Political Police. Incomplete collection in Institute for Contemporary History, Munich.

Records of the Bavarian Ministries of the Interior and of Education. Originals in Munich Geheime Staatsarchiv.

Miscellaneous German Records, Part I–III. Originals in Bundesarchiv and elsewhere. Finding aid, *Guide to Captured German Records*, Nos. 5, 8, and 36. Microfilms available from the U.S. National Archives (T-84).

Kanzlei Rosenberg. Originals in Bundesarchiv, Koblenz, No. 8. *Einsatzstabs Rosenberg.* Originals in Bundesarchiv, Koblenz, NS 30. Records of the Beauftragte des Führers, etc. Originals in Bundesarchiv, Koblenz, NS 15. Finding aid, *Guide to Captured German Records*, No. 28. Microfilms available from the U.S. National Archives (T-454).

NSDAP Hauptarchiv, Group IX, Folders 487, 488, 489. Originals in Bundes-archiv, Koblenz. Finding aid, G. Heinz and A. Peterson, *NSDAP Hauptarchiv,* Stanford, 1964. Microfilms available from the Hoover Institution, Stanford.

## Chapter 4

1. A.J.P. Taylor, *The Origins of the Second World War* (London: Hamish Hamilton, 1961).

2. Gar Alperovitz, *Atomic Diplomacy: Hiroshima and Potsdam. The Use of the Atomic Bomb and the American Confrontation with Soviet Power* (New York: Simon and Schuster, 1965).

3. Arno J. Mayer, *Politics and Diplomacy of Peacemaking: Containment and Counterrevolution at Versailles, 1918-1919* (New York: Knopf, 1967).

4. Mayer, "Uses and Abuses of Historical Analogies" (Paper delivered at the Annual Meeting of the American Historical Association, 1967).

5. Peter Weiss, *Die Ermittlung. Oratorium in ll Gesängen* (Frankfurt: Suhr-kamp, 1965); and *The Investigation: a Play.* English version by Jon Swan and Ulu Graubard (New York: Atheneum, 1966).

6. Rolf Hochhuth, *Der Stellvertreter,* foreword by Erwin Piscator (Reinbek bei Hamburg: Rowohlt, 1963); *The Deputy,* trans. Richard and Clara Winston, with a preface by Albert Schweitzer (New York: Grove Press, 1964).

7. Guenter Lewy, *The Catholic Church and Nazi Germany* (New York: McGraw-Hill Book Co., 1964).

8. Saul Friedlaender, *Pius XII and the Third Reich: A Documentation,* trans. Charles Fullman (New York: Knopf, 1966).

9. For the invasion of the classroom by the Hochhuth industry, see Dolores Barracano Schmidt and Earl Robert Schmidt, eds., *The Deputy Reader: Studies in Moral Responsibility* (Chicago: Scott, Foresman & Co., 1965).

10. Lewy, pp. 309-21.

11. Eberhard Zeller, *Geist der Freiheit: der zwanzigste Juli* (Munich: Her-mann Rinn Verlag, 1954), p. 217.

12. Peter Hoffmann, *Widerstand, Staatsstreich, Attentat. Der Kampf der Opposition gegen Hitler* (Munich: Piper, 1969), pp. 465, 808.

13. She made a point of mentioning this to me when I saw her in 1953.

14. *Spiegelbild einer Verschwörung: Die Kaltenbrunner-Berichte an Bormann und Hitler über das Attentat vom 20. Juli 1944. Geheime Dokumente aus dem ehemaligen Reichssicherheitshauptamt* (Stuttgart: Seewald Verlag, 1961), pp. 262-63, 321-24, 435; and Christian Müller, "19. Juli 1944," in Hans-Adolf Jacobsen, ed., *20. Juli 1944: Die deutsche Opposition gegen Hitler im Urteil der ausländischen Geschichtsschreibung: Eine Anthologie* (Bonn: Presse— und Infor-mationsamt der Bundesregierung, 1969), p. 225.

15. Mother Mary Alice Gallin, *German Resistance to . . . Hitler: Ethical and Religious Factors* (Washington, D.C.: The Catholic University of America Press, 1961), p. 288.

16. *Volksgerichtshofs-Prozesse zum 20. Juli 1944.* Transcripts of tapes [of the court proceedings] from the audio-archives of the German Radio. Mimeo-graphed (n.p., April 1961), p. 136.

17. For further discussion, see my "Nazis and Christians," in *World Politics* (1969), 21:392-424.

18. Not even subtler presentations such as Gordon C. Zahn, *German Catholics and Hitler's Wars: A Study in Social Control* (New York: Sheed and Ward, 1962).

19. Zahn, pp. 143-72; Lewy, pp. 236-42 and 247.

20. For documentation refer to some of the earlier *Guides to German Records Microfilmed at Alexandria, Va.* (Washington, D.C.: The National Archives, 1960-   ). Later Field Commands records were filmed selectively, omitting the chaplaincy sections.

21. Edward N. Peterson, *The Limits of Hitler's Power* (Princeton, N.J.: Princeton University Press, 1969).

22. See below, chap. 10.

23. Magdalen Goffin, "A Contradictory Hero," in *The New York Review of Books*, August 21, 1969, p. 34.

24. See above, chap. 2.

25. See above, chap. 1.

26. George N. Shuster, *Like a Mighty Army: Hitler versus Established Religion* (New York: D. Appleton-Century Co., 1935).

27. John Brown Mason, *Hitler's First Foes: A Study of Religion and Politics* (Minneapolis, 1936).

28. Nathaniel Micklem, *National Socialism and the Roman Catholic Church, Being an Account of the Conflict between the National Socialist Government of Germany and the Roman Catholic Church 1933-1938* (London: Oxford University Press, 1939).

29. Lewy, p. 219.

30. Micklem, p. 229.

31. John S. Conway, *The Nazi Persecution of the Churches 1933-45* (London: Weidenfeld and Nicolson, 1968; New York: Basic Books, 1969), p. 409.

32. Ibid., pp. 449-50.

33. Anton Erb, *Bernhard Lichtenberg.* (Berlin: Morus Verlag, 1946).

34. It was not just that there was a popular outcry against the euthanasia program because the next of kin felt sympathy for the victims as relatives, as Lewy (pp. 266-67) and Conway (p. 283) argue, and no outcry against the extermination of the Jews because there had been Antisemitic propaganda; another important point of difference was the almost instant knowledge of the fate of the victims of the euthanasia program and the lack of it in the case of deported Jews.

35. Cf. Fred Mielke and Alexander Mitscherlich, *Doctors of Infamy: The Story of Nazi Medical Crimes . . .,* trans. Heinz Norden (New York: H. Schuman, 1949); Alexander Mitscherlich and Fred Mielke, eds., *Medizin ohne Menschlichkeit* (Frankfurt: Fischer-Bücherei, 1960).

36. Cf. Otto Ogiermann, S.J., *Bis zum letzten Atemzug: der Prozess gegen Bernhard Lichtenberg* (Leipzig: St. Benno-Verlag GMBH, 1968), pp. 120-25.

37. Ernst-Wolfgang Böckenförde, "Der deutsche Katholizismus im Jahre 1933; eine kritische Betrachtung," *Hochland* 53 (Feb. 1961): 215-39.

38. Hans Buchheim, "Der deutsche Katholizismus im Jahr 1933: Eine Ausein-

17. Ibid., pp. 474-75, 489.
18. Ibid., p. 482.
19. Ibid., p. 474.
20. Ibid., p. 482.
21. A good example is *The American Historical Association's Guide to Historical Literature* (New York: Macmillan, 1961), a prestigious work with "20,000 items selected and annotated by more than 230 experts . . . according to a plan devised by a committee of the American Historial Association." But nowhere, not even in the chapters on "Recent History" or "The World Wars," does this plan provide us with a section on the Holocaust. On it the entire bibliography has only one lonely item: the chapter on "International Relations" lists a book published in 1943. Moreover, in the chapter on German history Hajo Holborn, its compiler, does not list a single book or article on the SS, the concentration camps, or, except for one work covering the Second Empire, on Jews and Antisemitism.
22. I am not including here the guides to the vast holdings of Nazi documents captured by the Allies.
23. Jacob Robinson and Philip Friedman, *Guide to Jewish History under Nazi Impact*, Bibliographical Series no. 1 (New York: Yivo, 1960).
24. For an early survey, see Philip Friedman, "Research and Literature on the Recent Jewish Tragedy," *Jewish Social Studies* 12 (1950): 17-26.
25. *Fun Letstn Khurbn* [About the final catastrophe], nos. 1-10 (Munich, 1946-48).
26. *Bleter far Geshikhte* (Warsaw, 1948-    ).
27. *Yad Vashem Bulletin* (Jerusalem, 1957-    ), *Yad Vashem News* (Jerusalem, 1969-    ); *Yad Vashem Studies on the European Jewish Catastrophe and Resistance*. Vols. 1-5 (Jerusalem, 1957-63); vols. 6-7 (Jerusalem, 1967-68).
28. Ilse R. Wolff, ed., *Books on Persecution, Terror and Resistance in Nazi Germany*, Wiener Library Catalogue Series, no. 1, 2d rev. ed. (London, 1960). Also Catalogue Series, no. 2: *From Weimar to Hitler Germany, 1918-1933* (London, 1951), and Catalogue Series, no. 3: *German Jewry: Its History, Life and Culture* (London, 1958).
29. *Wiener Library Bulletin* (London, 1946-    ).
30. *Le Monde Juive* (Paris, 1946-    ). See also the Center's Catalogue no. 1: *La France: De l'Affaire Dreyfus à nos jours* (Paris, 1964); and Catalogue no. 2: *La France, Le Troisieme Reich, Israël* (Paris, 1968).
31. The Yivo journals: *Yivo Annual of Jewish Social Science* (New York, 1946-    )ʼ and *Yivo Bleter* (Vilna and New York, 1931-    ). The Yivo-Yad Vashem bibliographies, in addition to no. 1 (see above, note 23): Philip Friedman, ed., *Bibliography of Books in Hebrew on the Jewish Catastrophe and Heroism in Europe*, no. 2 (Jerusalem, 1960); P. Friedman and J. Gar, eds., *Bibliography of Yiddish Books on the Catastrophe and Heroism*, no. 3 (New York, 1962); Randolph L. Braham, ed., *The Hungarian Jewish Catastrophe: A Selected and Annotated Bibliography*, no. 4 (New York, 1962); nos. 5-8 cover the Hebrew press and nos. 9-11 the Yiddish press; no. 12, for books published in various European languages including English, is due to appear soon. For published works on the Holocaust we might use the excellent collection available

in the Judaica Room of the New York Public Library (42nd Street Research Branch).

32. *Bulletin für die Mitglieder der Gesellschaft der Freunde des Leo Baeck Institut* (Tel Aviv: Bitaon, 1957-   ); *Year Book of the Leo Baeck Society* (London: East and West Library, 1956-   ).

33. *Vierteljahrshefte für Zeitgeschichte* (Stuttgart, 1953-   ).

34. For the work of the Dutch institute, see its *Nederland in Oorlogstijd* (1946-50) and *Jaarverslag van het Rijksinstituut voor Oorlogsdocumentatie* (1945-   ). For the French institute, see its *Revue d'historie de la deuxième guerre mondiale* (Paris, 1950-   ).

35. Lucy S. Dawidowicz, "Toward a History of the Holocaust," *Commentary* 47 (1969): 51-56.

36. Ibid., p. 56.

37. Yaakov Shilhav, "A Turning Point in the Teaching of the Heroism and the Holocaust," *Yad Vashem Bulletin*, no. 12 (Dec. 1962): pp. 57 ff.

38. Jacob Gladstein et al., eds., *Anthology of Holocaust Literature* (Philadelphia: Jewish Publication Society of America, 1969).

39. Albert H. Friedlander, ed., *Out of the Whirlwind: A Reader of Holocaust Literature* (Garden City, N.Y.: Doubleday, 1968).

40. Leo W. Schwarz, ed., *The Root and the Bough: The Epic of an Enduring People* (New York: Rinehart, 1949).

41. Hana Volavkova, ed., *I Never Saw Another Butterfly . . . Children's Drawings and Poems from Terezin Concentration Camp 1942-1944* (New York: McGraw-Hill, 1962).

42. Charlotte Salomon, *Charlotte: A Diary in Pictures* (New York: Harcourt, Brace and World, 1963).

43. Salo Wittmayer Baron, *A Social and Religious History of the Jews: Ancient Times*, 2 vols, 2d rev. ed. (Philadelphia: Jewish Publication Society of America, 1952), 1: 3. It does not matter here whether we consider Judaism in religious or in cultural terms.

44. Malcolm Hay, *The Foot of Pride: The Pressure of Christendom on the People of Israel for 1900 Years* (Boston: Beacon Press, 1950); PB as *Europe and the Jews* (Boston: Beacon Press, 1960).

45. Leon Poliakov, *A History of Anti-Semitism*. Vol. 1: *From the Time of Christ to the Court Jews*, trans. Richard Howard (New York: Vanguard, 1964).

46. Hannah Arendt, *Origins of Totalitarianism*, chap. 4; Koppel Pinson, ed., *Essays on Anti-Semitism*, 2d rev. ed.; (New York: Conference on Jewish Relations, 1946).

47. See, for example, Peter Viereck, *Metapolitics: The Roots of the Nazi Mind* (New York: Putnam, 1961); Fritz Stern, *The Politics of Cultural Despair: A Study in the Rise of the Germanic Ideology* (Garden City, N.Y.: Doubleday, 1965); George L. Mosse, *The Crisis of German Ideology: Intellectual Origins of the Third Reich* (New York: Grosset and Dunlap, 1964).

48. Max Weinreich, *Hitler's Professors* (New York: Yivo, 1946).

49. Hans Peter Blauel and Ernst Klinnert, *Deutsche Studenten auf dem Weg ins Dritte Reich: Ideologien, Programme, Aktionen, 1918-1935* (Gütersloh: Sigbert Mohn, 1967). It is interesting but not unexpected that German students

outside the borders of the Reich tended to be the most radical. Thus, at Prague's German language university they even occupied buildings to force the ousting of a newly elected rector because he was Jewish.

50. Paul R. Massing, *Rehearsal for Destruction: A Study of Political Anti-Semitism in Imperial Germany* (New York: Harper, 1949).

51. Peter G. J. Pulzer, *The Rise of Political Anti-Semitism in Germany and Austria* (New York: John Wiley, 1964).

52. Eva Reichman, *Hostages of Civilization: The Social Sources of National Socialist Anti-Semitism* (Boston: Beacon Press, 1951).

53. Victor Klemperer, *LTI. Notizbuch eines Philologen* (Berlin: Aufbau Verlag, 1946). See also Dolf Sternberger/Gerhard Storz/W. E. Süskind, *Aus dem Wörterbuch des Unmenschen* (Munich: Deutscher Taschenbuch Verlag, 1962). A number of articles, more compilation than analysis, have studied this language as it applies to the Holocaust: Shaul Esch, "Words and Their Meanings: Twenty-five Examples on Nazi-Idiom," *Yad Vashem Studies* 5 (1963): 133-67; and two articles by Nacham Blumenthal: "On the Nazi Vocabulary," *Yad Vashem Studies 1* (1957): 49-66; "From the Nazi Vocabulary," *Yad Vashem Studies 6* (1967): 69-82.

54. Bill Kinser and Neil Kleinman, *The Dream That Was No More a Dream. A Search for Aesthetic Reality in Germany, 1890-1945* (New York: Harper & Row, 1969).

55. Norman Cohn, *Warrant for Genocide: The Myth of the Jewish World-Conspiracy and the Protocols of the Elders of Zion* (New York: Harper & Row, 1969).

56. André Schwarz-Bart, *The Last of the Just*, trans. Stephen Becker (New York: Atheneum, 1961).

57. Elie Wiesel, *A Beggar in Jerusalem*, trans. Lily Edelman (New York: Random House, 1970).

58. Elie Wiesel, *The Gates of the Forest*, trans. Frances Frenaye (New York: Avon Books, 1967).

59. Joseph Tenenbaum, *Race and Reich: The Story of an Epoch* (New York: Twayne, 1956).

60. Leon Poliakov, *Harvest of Hate: The Nazi Program for the Destruction of the Jews of Europe*, trans. from the French (Syracuse, N.Y.: Syracuse University Press, 1954).

61. Gerald Reitlinger, *The Final Solution: The Attempt to Exterminate the Jews of Europe, 1939-1945* (New York: A.S. Barnes, 1961); American hardcover edition (Beechhurst Press, 1953).

62. For example, Leon Poliakov and Josef Wulf, *Das Dritte Reich und die Juden: Dokumente und Aufsätze* (Berlin: Arani, 1955), or the collection *Dokumenty i materialy*, 3 vols. (Warsaw, Lodz, Cracow: The Central Jewish Historical Commission, 1946).

63. Raul Hilberg, *The Destruction of the European Jews* (Chicago: Quadrangle, 1961).

64. "Nazi Bureaucrats and Jewish Leaders," *Commentary* 23 (1962): 352.

65. See, for example, Jacob Presser, *The Destruction of the Dutch Jews*,

trans. Arnold Pomerantz (New York: Dutton, 1969). Few other studies are, unfortunately, available in English.

66. For an interesting early memoir about neutral and Red Cross efforts during the last days of the war, see Count Folke Bernadotte, *The Curtain Falls. Last Days of the Third Reich,* trans. Eric Lewenhaupt (New York: Knopf, 1945).

67. The most applicable monograph is still Guenter Lewy, *The Catholic Church and Nazi Germany* (New York: McGraw-Hill, 1964).

68. Henry L. Feingold, *The Politics of Rescue. The Roosevelt Administration and the Holocaust, 1938-1945* (New Brunswick, N.J.: Rutgers University Press, 1970). For an earlier popular account, see Arthur D. Morse, *While Six Million Died: A Chronicle of American Apathy* (New York: Random House, 1967); for a recent account, see Saul S. Friedman, *No Haven for the Oppressed* (Detroit: Wayne State University Press, 1973).

69. Apart from the details provided by Hilberg, the best history is Gerald Reitlinger's *The SS. Alibi of a Nation, 1922-1945* (New York: Viking, 1957); for two recent German studies, see Hans Buchheim/Martin Broszat/Hans-Adolf Jacobsen, *Anatomy of the SS State,* trans. R. Barry and others (London: Collins, 1968); and Herbert Jäger, *Verbrechen unter totalitärer Herrschaft. Studien zur nationalsozialistischen Gewaltkriminalität* (Olten: Walter-Verlag, 1967).

70. Rudolf Hoess, *Commandant of Auschwitz. The Autobiography of Rudolf Hoess,* trans. Constantine FitzGibbon (New York: Popular Library, 1961).

71. Cited in Leon Poliakov, "The Mind of the Mass Murderer," *Commentary* 12 (1951): 452.

72. For two such attempts, see Bruno Bettelheim, *The Informed Heart: Anatomy in a Mass Age* (Glencoe, Ill.: The Free Press, 1960); and Robert Jay Lifton, *History and Human Survival* (New York: Random House, 1970).

73. Hilberg, *The Destruction of the European Jews,* p. 669.

74. Oscar Handlin, "Jewish Resistance to the Nazis," *Commentary* 24 (Nov. 1962): 399. But Handlin's position becomes inconsistent when he also argues that "if there is a lesson to be salvaged from the Nazi period, it is that all of us are potential victims and all of us potential executioners."

75. The work of Yad Vashem reflects this emphasis; in fact, the Israeli Knesset wrote it into the constitution of the Memorial Authority. See Benzion Dinur, "Problems Confronting 'Yad Vashem' in Its Work of Research," *Yad Vashem Studies* 1 (1957): 7-30. For a serious attempt to analyze the problem of resistance, see Philip Friedman, "Jewish Resistance," ibid., 2: (1958): 113-31.

76. See Philip Friedman, "Problems of Research in Jewish 'Self-Government' (Judenrat) in the Nazi Period," *Yad Vashem Studies* 2 (1958): 95-113.

77. *Die Kontroverse: Hannah Arendt, Eichmann und die Juden* (Munich: Nymphenburger Verlagshandlung, 1964).

78. Hannah Arendt, *Eichmann in Jerusalem. A Report on the Banality of Evil,* rev. ed.; (New York: Viking, 1964). Thus her use of the term "Jewish Führer" as applied to Baeck. Rabbi Leo Baeck made impossible a judicious evaluation of his decision to conceal the facts of extermination from those

deported to the East. (Citation in original Arendt articles in *The New Yorker*, March 2, 1963, p. 42, but omitted in rev. ed. of the book, p. 119).

79. A good example is Jacob Robinson's book, which tries to refute Arendt page by page. His notes provide a good bibliography, but his interpretation, attempting even to exonerate Rumkowski of Lodz, does not contribute to our understanding. See *And the Crooked Shall Be Made Straight: The Eichmann Trial, the Jewish Catastrophe, and Hannah Arendt's Narrative* (New York: Macmillan, 1965). For the Eichmann trial itself, see Gideon Hausner, *Justice in Jerusalem* (New York: Schocken, 1968).

80. See H. G. Adler, "Ideas toward a Sociology of the Concentration Camp," *American Journal of Sociology* 63 (1958): 513-22; Hannah Arendt, "Social Science Techniques and the Study of Concentration Camps," *Jewish Social Studies* 12 (1950): 49-64; Samuel Gringanz, "Some Methodological Problems in the Study of the Ghetto," ibid. 12 (1950): 65-72.

81. See Anatol Kusnetsov, *Babi Yar*, trans. from the Russian (New York: Dial Press, 1967).

82. See Cecil Roth, "The Last Days of Jewish Salonica," *Commentary* 10 (1950): 49-55.

83. See Georges Wellers, *De Drancy à Auschwitz* (Paris: Editions du Centre, 1946).

84. Claud Lévy and Paul Tillard, *Betrayal at the Vel d'Hiv*, trans. Inea Bushnaq (New York: Hill and Wang, 1969).

85. Robert Katz, *Black Sabbath: A Journey through a Crime against Humanity* (New York: Macmillan, 1969).

86. However, we do possess a number of Yiddish works. See, for example, Mark Dworzecki, *Yerushelayim d'lite in kamf un umkum. Zikhroynes fun vilner geto* (Paris: Yidisher Folksverband, 1948); Joseph Gar, *Umkum fun der yidisher kovne* (Munich: Farband fun Litvishe Yidn, 1948).

87. H. G. Adler, *Theresienstadt 1941-1945: Das Anlitz einer Zwangsgemeinschaft* 2d ed. (Tübingen: J.C.B. Mohr, 1960). See also his *Die verheimlichte Wahrheit. Theresienstädter Dokumente* (Tübingen: J.C.B. Mohr, 1958).

88. The best memoir available in English translation is the Socialist Bund leader Bernard Goldstein's *The Stars Bear Witness*, trans. Leonard Shatzkin (New York: Viking, 1949); PB as *Five Years in the Warsaw Ghetto* (Dolphin Books, 1961); see also Philip Friedman, ed., *Martyrs and Fighters. The Epic of the Warsaw Ghetto* (New York: Lancer Books, 1954).

89. Emanuel Ringelblum, *Notes from the Warsaw Ghetto*, ed. and trans. Jacob Sloan (New York: McGraw-Hill, 1958); Chaim Aron Kaplan, *Scroll of Agony*, ed. and trans. A. I. Katsh (New York: Macmillan, 1965).

90. All authors and sources discuss the uprising (see above, notes 86 and 87). Also see the Yiddish works: Tovye Bozykowski, *Tsvishn falendike vent* (Warsaw: Hechalutz, 1949); Melekh Neustadt, *Khurben un oyfshtand fun di yidn in varshe*, 2 vols. (Tel Aviv: Histadrut, 1948); Jonas Turkow, *Azoy is es geven. Khurbn varshe*, 2 vols. (Buenos Aires: Zentral Farband fun Poylishe Yidn, 1948-50). For the German view, see the text and pictures of the macabre report presented to Hitler by the SS commander: The Stroop Report (PS-1061: "Es gibt keinen jüdischen Wohnbesitz in Warschau mehr!"), International Military Tribunal,

*Trial of the Major War Criminals,* 42 vols. (Nuremberg, 1947), 26: 628 ff.; English trans. in Office of United States Chief of Counsel for Prosecution of Axis Criminality, *Nazi Conspiracy and Aggression,* 8 vols. and 2 supp. vols. (Washington: G.P.O., 1946-48) 3: 718 ff.

91. We now have two monographs—one in German and one in Yiddish—on the ghetto in Lodz, officially known as "Ghetto Litzmannstadt." Josef Wulf, *Lodz. Das letzte Ghetto auf polnischem Boden,* Schriftenreihe der Bundeszentrale für Heimatdienst, vol. 59 (Bonn, 1962); Isaiah Trunk, *Lodzer geto* (New York: Yivo, 1962). See also Solomon F. Bloom, "Dictator of the Lodz Ghetto. The Strange History of Mordechai Chaim Rumkowski," *Commentary* 7 (1949): 111-22.

92. Eugen Kogon, *Der SS-Staat: Das System der deutschen Konzentrationslager* (Frankfurt: Verlag der Frankfurter Hefte, 1946). English PB as *The Theory and Practice of Hell* (New York: Berkley Publ. Corp., 1950). See also *Le Système concentrationaire allemande,* 1940-1944, in *Revue d'histoire de la deuxième guerre mondiale,* nos. 15-16 (July-Sept. 1954). For a monographic study of one camp, see Eberhard Kolb, *Bergen-Belsen* (Hanover: Verlag für Literatur und Zeitgeschehen, 1962).

93. Elie A. Cohn, *Human Behavior in the Concentration Camp,* trans. M. H. Braaksma (New York: Grosset and Dunlap [Universal Lib.], n.d.); David Rousset, *The Other Kingdom,* trans. Ramon Guthrie (New York: Reynal and Hitchcock, 1947).

94. Jean-Francois Steiner, *Treblinka,* trans. Helen Weaver (New York: Simon and Schuster, 1967; Signet PB, 1968). For one of the best memoirs about the killing centers, covering the Warsaw ghetto, Maydanek, Auschwitz, and other camps, see Alexander Donat, *The Holocaust Kingdom* (New York: Holt, Rinehart and Winston, 1963).

95. Elie Wiesel's report is, due to its stark and direct language, the most effective of these: *Night,* trans. Stella Rodway (New York: Avon Books, 1969). For two rather typical accounts that, unable to translate the horror into the language of normality, appear sensational, see Olga Lengyel, *I Survived Hitler's Ovens (Five Chimneys): The Story of Auschwitz* (Boston: Ballantine Books, 1954); Miklos Nyiszli, *Auschwitz: A Doctor's Eyewitness Account,* trans. S. Becker (New York: Avon Books, 1969).

96. Primo Levi, *If This Is a Man,* trans. Stuart Woolf (New York: Orion Press, 1959), PB as *Survival in Auschwitz: The Nazi Assault on Humanity* (Collier Books, 1961).

97. Tadeucz Borowski, *This Way for the Gas, Ladies and Gentlemen and Other Stories,* trans. Barbara Vedder (London: Jonathan Cape, 1967).

98. Primo Levi, *The Reawakening (La Tregua). A Liberated Prisoner's Long March Home Through East Europe,* trans. Stuart Woolf (Boston: Little, Brown, 1965); pub. in England as *The Truce.*

## Chapter 6

1. For the following two paragraphs, see such comprehensive studies as Eberhard Zeller, *Geist der Freiheit: Der zwanzigste Juli,* 5th ed. (Munich:

Gotthold Müller Verlag, 1965). 4th ed. translated by R. P. Heller and D. R. Masters as *The Flame of Freedom: The German Struggle against Hitler* (London: Oswald Wolff, 1967); Hans Rothfels, *Die deutsche Opposition gegen Hitler: Eine Würdigung,* new ed. (Frankfurt-Hamburg: Fischer Bücherei, 1969); Ger van Roon, *Neuordnung im Widerstand: Der Kreisauer Kreis innerhalb der deutschen Widerstandsbewegung* (Munich: R. Oldenbourg Verlag, 1967). For active attempts to overthrow and assassinate Hitler, see Hoffmann, *Widerstand, Staatsstreich, Attentat: Der Kampf der Opposition gegen Hitler.* 2d ed. (Munich: R. Piper & Co. Verlag, 1970).

2. Klaus-Jürgen Müller, *Das Heer und Hitler: Armee und nationalsozialistisches Regime 1933-1940* (Stuttgart: Deutsche Verlags-Anstalt, 1969), pp. 20-24.

3. See Hitler's speech before commanders of the army and navy in Berlin on February 3, 1933, in Thilo Vogelsang, "Neue Dokumente zur Geschichte der Reichswehr 1930-1933," *Vierteljahrshefte für Zeitgeschichte* 2 (1954): 434-35.

4. Hoffmann, pp. 43-46, 55-68.

5. Hoffmann, pp. 28-29.

6. Hoffmann, pp. 94-129.

7. Hoffmann, pp. 269-76, 306.

8. Hoffmann, pp. 328-41, 378-92, 440-86.

9. Hoffmann, pp. 602-36.

10. Willy Brandt, *My Road to Berlin,* as told to Leo Lania (Garden City, N.Y.: Doubleday, 1960), pp. 7, 144 ff.

11. Otto John, Papers, Stiftung "Hilfswerk 20. Juli 1944," Frankfurt.

12. *Constitution (Fundamental Law) of the Union of Soviet Socialist Republic as Amended by the First Session of the Seventh Supreme Soviet of the U.S.S.R.,* (Moscow: Progress Publishers, 1967), art. 126; cf. *Verfassung der Deutschen Demokratischen Republik* (Berlin: Staatsverlag der Deutschen Demokratischen Republik, 1969), art. 3, p. 10. See also Albert Norden, "Die Bedeutung des 20. Juli," *Die Weltbühne* 2 (1947): 553-60.

13. Henry Morgenthau, Jr., *Germany Is Our Problem,* (New York and London: Harper & Bros., 1945), facsimile of the "Morgenthau Plan" preceding p. ix; John Morton Blum, *From the Morgenthau Diaries: Years of War 1941-1945* (Boston: Houghton Mifflin Co., 1967), pp. 343-68.

14. Allen W. Dulles, *Germany's Underground* (New York: The Macmillan Company, 1947), passim.

15. Cf. the figures cited in Hoffmann, pp. 31-33.

16. Cf. Hoffmann, pp. 255-96.

17. Bruno Gebhardt, *Handbuch der deutschen Geschichte,* 8th ed. (Stuttgart: Union Verlag, 1963), 4: 177, 346-47, 352.

18. See William L. Shirer, *Berlin Diary: The Journal of a Foreign Correspondent 1934-1941* (New York: Alfred A. Knopf, 1941), pp. 142-43; Albert Speer, *Erinnerungen* (Frankfurt-Berlin: Propyläen Verlag, 1969), pp. 173, 181.

19. Speer, p. 184.

20. Author's recollection. See also Günther Weisenborn, *Der lautlose Aufstand: Bericht über die Widerstandsbewegung des deutschen Volkes 1933-1945* (Hamburg: Rowohlt Verlag, 1962), pp. 239-41.

21. *Trial of the Major War Criminals before the International Military Tribunal: Nuremberg 14 November 1945-1 October 1946*, vol. 31, (Nuremberg: International Military Tribunal, 1948), doc. 3033 PS, p. 498.

22. Hoffmann, pp. 429-30; Weisenborn, pp. 158-63; Annedore Leber, *Das Gewissen steht auf: 64 Lebensbilder aus dem deutschen Widerstand*, 9th ed. (Berlin-Frankfurt: Mosaik Verlag, 1960), pp. 62, 227.

23. Walther Hofer, *Der Nationalsozialismus: Dokumente 1933-1945*, (Frankfurt-Hamburg: Fischer Bücherei, 1957), p. 71.

24. Cf. the oath that Adolf Hitler was required to take upon being appointed chancellor, *Reichsgesetzblatt Teil I 1930* (Berlin: Reichsdruckerei, 1930), p. 96.

25. Hoffmann, pp. 571-601.

26. Hoffmann, pp. 266-96, 425, 432.

27. Rothfels, p. 189, n. 18.

28. Cf. David J. Dallin, *Soviet Espionage* (New Haven: Yale University Press, 1955), pp. 234-62; Paul Leverkuehn, *German Military Intelligence*, (London: Weidenfeld and Nicolson, 1954), pp. 175-83; W. F. Flicke, *Spionagegruppe Rote Kapelle* (Wels: Verlag Welsermühl, 1957), passim.

29. Gebhardt 4: 298-99.

30. Inge Scholl, *Students against Tyranny*, trans. Arthur R. Schultz (Middletown, Conn.: Wesleyan University Press, 1970), passim.

31. Ernst Niekisch, *Gewagtes Leben: Begegnungen und Begebnisse* (Cologne-Berlin: Kiepenheuer & Witsch, 1958), pp. 246-48.

32. Hoffmann, pp. 387-88; Bodo Scheurig, *Ewald von Kleist-Schmenzin: Ein Konservativer gegen Hitler* (Hamburg: Gerhard Stalling Verlag, 1968), p. 199.

33. Cf. Klemens von Klemperer, *Mandate for Resistance: The Case of the German Opposition to Hitler*, (Baltimore, Md.: Smith College [through] Barton-Gillet Company, 1969).

34. Speer, pp. 44-45, 420-64.

35. John W. Wheeler-Bennett, *The Nemesis of Power: The German Army in Politics 1918-1945*, 2d ed. (New York: The Viking Press, 1964), p. 459.

36. Kunrat von Hammerstein, *Spähtrupp* (Stuttgart: Henry Goverts Verlag, 1963), pp. 69-70; my translation.

37. Hoffmann, pp. 146-47.

38. Wilhelm von Schramm, *Conspiracy among Generals*, trans. and ed. R. T. Clark (New York: Scribner, 1956), pp. 44-65, 205-207.

39. Hoffmann, pp. 342-43.

40. "Generäle: Neue Mitteilungen zur Vorgeschichte des 20. Juli," *Die Wandlung* 1 (1945/46): 531; my translation.

41. Zeller, 5th German ed., p. 519, n. 19; Hermann Foertsch, *Schuld und Verhängnis: Die Fritsch-Krise im Frühjahr 1938 als Wendepunkt in der Geschichte der nationalsozialistischen Zeit* (Stuttgart: Deutsche Verlags-Anstalt, 1951), p. 22; Joachim Kramarz, *Claus Graf Stauffenberg 15. November 1907-20. Juli 1944: Das Leben eines Offiziers* (Frankfurt: Bernard & Graefe Verlag für Wehrwesen, 1965), pp. 41-46.

42. Cf. Hoffmann, pp. 371-78.

43. Eberhard Bethge, *Dietrich Bonhoeffer: Theologe, Christ, Zeitgenosse*, (Munich: Chr. Kaiser Verlag, 1967), pp. 734-37. English translation: *Dietrich*

*Bonhoeffer: Man of Vision, Man of Courage*, trans. Eric Mosbacher et al. (New York: Harper & Row, 1970). It is pointed out sometimes in discussions of the German opposition to Hitler that a few of the leading personalities were blood relatives or in-laws. For instance, Dietrich Bonhoeffer was a brother-in-law of Hans von Dohnanyi and Rüdiger Schleicher; an uncle of Stauffenberg, Count von Uexküll-Gyllenband, was also involved in the opposition. Therefore, it is said, it is clear that these people acted more as members of a class than as individuals who made individual ethical decisions. The argument is not based on any evidence beyond this speculation, and it is not cogent. Even a cursory examination of the dossiers of the Stiftung "Hilfswerk 20. Juli 1944" in Frankfurt will show that the vast majority of persons involved in the opposition to Hitler, even the leading ones, were in no way related to each other. On the other hand, how would one explain that persons such as Hitler's naval adjutant, Rear Admiral von Puttkamer, or certain members of the Stülpnagel family who were related to members of the opposition never sympathized with it but were actually on the "other side"?

44. Hoffmann, pp. 148-54; Christopher Sykes, *Troubled Loyalty: A Biography of Adam von Trott zu Solz* (London: Collins, 1968), pp. 271, 315.

45. Hoffmann, pp. 82-86; 140-41, 146-47.

46. Kramarz, p. 132.

47. Ibid.; this and the following quotations are my translations.

48. Hoffmann, p. 441.

49. Kramarz, p. 203.

50. Leber, *Das Gewissen steht auf*, p. 126.

51. Elfriede Nebgen, *Jakob Kaiser: Der Widerstandskämpfer* (Stuttgart-Berlin-Cologne-Mainz: W. Kohlhammer Verlag, 1967), p. 193.

52. Ibid.

53. Hoffmann, p. 611.

54. Hoffmann, pp. 611-12.

55. Hoffmann, p. 618; Annedore Leber, *Das Gewissen entscheidet: Bereiche des deutschen Widerstandes von 1933-1945*, in *Lebensbildern*, 4th ed. (Berlin-Frankfurt: Mosaik Verlag, 1960), p. 201.

56. Hoffmann, pp. 618-23.

57. Hoffmann, pp. 623-36.

58. Rothfels, p. 13.

59. *Trial of the Major War Criminals before the International Military Tribunal: Nuremberg 14 November 1945-1 October 1946*, vol. 33 (Nuremberg: International Military Tribunal, 1949), doc. 3881 PS, p. 424.

60. Film no. 3179-1, Bundesarchiv/Filmarchiv, Koblenz.

61. Hoffmann, pp. 628-29.

62. Friedrich von Schiller, *The Bride of Messina, William Tell, Demetrius*, trans. Charles E. Passage (New York: F. Ungar Pub. Co., 1962), p. 50.

63. Hoffmann, pp. 215-19.

64. Helmuth J. von Moltke, count, *Letzte Briefe aus dem Gefängnis Tegel*, 9th ed. (Berlin: Karl H. Henssel Verlag, 1963), pp. 17-22.

65. Bethge, p. 834.

## Chapter 7

1. Historians and other social scientists have disagreed as to why resistance within the Third Reich was not effective. Some have argued that the nature of the regime simply precluded any successful resistance. Others contend that self-limiting features of the resistance itself were more decisive than the external environment. The discussions within the working sessions of this conference found a synthesis by viewing Nazi Germany and its opponents as two parts of an interacting system. Out of this came an answer to the question: "Was resistance possible?"

In developing that synthesis I have not followed the exact order of the discussions of the working sessions, since they were too convoluted. Instead, I have written an independent essay which I hope captures the insights without distorting any of the contributions. The following draws, however, on all of the various papers, presentations, and discussions of the conference.

2. Romoser's arguments are developed at length, and without the crassness required by this brief summation, in "The Politics of Uncertainty: The German Resistance Movement," *Social Research* 31 (Spring 1964): 73-93.

## Chapter 8

1. Conway, (Toronto: Ryerson Press, 1968.)

2. "Nazis and Christians," *World Politics* 21 (1969): 392-424.

3. The classic statement of the sect-church difference, surely influenced by the German situation, was given by Ernst Troeltsch, *The Social Teaching of the Christian Churches* (New York: Harper, 1960).

4. Quoted by Koppel S. Pinson, *Modern Germany* (New York: Macmillan Co., 1966), p. 112.

5. Hanns Lilje, *Christus im deutschen Schicksal*, p. 18, quoted in Paul Banwell Means, *Things That Are Caesar's* (New York: Round Table Press, 1935), p. 17.

6. Ibid.

7. Ibid., p. 10.

8. Ibid., p. 87.

9. Ibid., p. 95.

10. Martin Niemöller, *From U-Boat to Pulpit* (New York: Willett, Clark & Co., 1937), p. 125.

11. Terence Prittie, *Germans against Hitler* (Boston: Little, Brown & Co., 1964), p. 95.

12. Niemöller, p. 154.

13. The classic study of elites, which first suggested several of these catagories, is Harold Lasswell, *Politics: Who Gets What, When, How? A Framework for Political Analysis* (New York: Meridian Books, 1958).

14. For Rosenberg's general philosophy, see the works cited, published in Munich, and his *Das Politische Tagenbuch 1934/5* and *1939/40*, ed. H.G. Seraphim (Munich, 1964).

15. Conway, *The Nazi Persecution of the Churches*, quotes one such speaker, p. 109.

16. Prittie, p. 97.
17. Means, pp. 169-70, and cf. Rosenberg as cited above.
18. Conway, p. 35.
19. Means, p. 70.
20. Prittie, p. 98.
21. Pinson, p. 496 f.
22. Means, p. 246.
23. Basel Miller, *Martin Niemöller* (Grand Rapids, Mich.: Zondervan Publishing House, 1942).
24. Prittie, p. 101.
25. Means, p. 247.
26. Conway, pp. 73-74.
27. Pinson, p. 512.
28. Miller, p. 80.
29. Ibid., p. 78.
30. Ibid.
31. Ibid.
32. Charles S. MacFarland, *The New Church and the New Germany* (New York: Macmillan Co., 1943). p. 113.
33. "Kundgebung des Deutschen Evangelischen Kirchenausschusses, 3 Marz, 1933," in Heinrich Hermelink, ed., *Kirche im Kampf* (Stuttgart: Rainer Wunderlich Verlag Hermann Leins, 1950), p. 29.
34. "Vertrauliches Hirtenschreiben des Generalsuperintendenten Dibelius in Berlin an seine Pfarrer, 8 Marz, 1933," ibid., p. 31.
35. Martin Niemöller, *First Commandment* (London: William Hodge & Co., 1937), p. 13.
36. Miller, p. 91.
37. Ibid.
38. Ibid., p. 92.
39. Means, p. 235.
40. Ibid., p. 255.
41. H. H. Kramm, *The Significance of the Barmen Declaration for the Oecumenical Church* (London: Society for Promoting Christian Knowledge, 1943).
42. Niemöller, *First Commandment*, p. 111.
43. See Conway, pp. 116 ff.
44. Wilhelm Niemöller, *Kampf und Zeugnis* (1948), quoted by Conway, p. 136.
45. Miller, p. 105.
46. Ibid., p. 112.
47. Ibid., p. 114.
48. Ibid., pp. 124-25.
49. Ibid.
50. Mary Alice Gallin, *Ethical and Religious Factors in the German Resistance to Hitler* (Washington, D.C.: Catholic University of America Press, 1955), p. 189.
51. Miller, p. 142.

52. Ibid., p. 137.

53. Ibid., pp. 149-50.

54. Ibid., p. 148.

55. Ibid., p. 153 f.

56. Gallin, p. 190.

57. Thus in November 1938, on the infamous "Crystal Night" when some one hundred and seventy synagogues were burned and twenty thousand Jews arrested, the Christian leadership was silent.

58. For an account of Nazi attacks on the churches in this period, see Conway, chap. 7.

59. Hans Rothfels, *The German Opposition to Hitler* (London: Oswald Wolff, 1961), p. 42.

60. Quoted by Conway, p. 220.

61. Gallin, p. 189.

62. Conway, p. 221, quotes the expression of Bormann in this regard.

63. Stewart W. Herman, *The Rebirth of the German Church* (New York: Harper & Bros., 1946), p. 60.

64. Rothfels, p. 43.

65. Thus the Nazis attributed the July 20, 1944 attempt on Hitler's life to "clerically dominated opposition groups" and used it as an excuse to imprison and execute even those who were not directly involved with the bombing.

66. Gallin, p. 189, quoting Dibelius.

67. Martin Niemöller, *God Is My Führer* (New York: Philosophical Library, 1941).

68. Gallin, pp. 140 ff.

69. Annedore Leber, *Conscience in Revolt* (London: Vallentine, Mitchell, 1957) p. 216. See also Eberhard Bethge, *Dietrich Bonhoeffer: Man of Vision* (New York: Harper & Row, 1970).

70. Roger Manvell and Heinrich Fraenkel, *The Men Who Tried to Kill Hitler* (New York: Coward-McCann, 1964), p. 47.

71. Ibid., p. 33.

72. Bethge, *Dietrich Bonhoeffer*, pp. 661 ff.

73. Manvell, pp. 35-37.

74. Ibid., pp. 75-76.

75. Ibid., p. 76.

76. Prittie, p. 121.

77. Ibid.

78. Ulrich von Hassell, *The Von Hassell Diaries* (Garden City, N.Y.: Doubleday & Co., 1947), pp. 282-83 and Gerhard Ritter, *The German Resistance* (New York: Frederick A. Praeger, 1958), p. 237.

79. Gerstenmaier thinks the Nazis were unaware of his involvement, while von Hassell believes the Gestapo held him hoping he would turn informer.

80. Plans of the *coup* had been given to the British Foreign Office. Hitler's success at Munich and Chamberlain's refusal to resist the Führer ended that early plot; see Gallin, pp. 7-14. On the general army attitude toward Hitler, see Alan Bullock, *Hitler, A Study in Tyranny.*

81. Manvell, p. 47.

82. See Lasswell, *Politics: Who Gets What, When, How?*, and Karl Deutsch, *Politics and Government* (Boston: Houghton Mifflin, 1970).

## Chapter 9

1. John L. Snell, *The Nazi Revolution: Germany's Guilt or Germany's Fate?* (Boston: D.C. Heath & Co., 1959). The following parenthetical text references are to this source.
2. Peter Viereck, *Meta-Politics: The Roots of the Nazi Mind* (1941; New York: Capricorn Books, 1965).
3. Ibid., p. 266.
4. J.S. Conway, *The Nazi Persecution of the Churches 1933-45* (New York: Basic Books, Inc., 1968), p. 3.
5. Adolf Hitler, *Mein Kampf* (Munich: Zentralverlag der N.S.D.A.P. Frz. Eher Nachf. GmbH., 1935). All citations from and references to *Mein Kampf* are indicated in text by page in parentheses; all translations are mine.
6. Walther Hofer, ed., *Der Nationalsozialismus Dokumente*, 1933-45 (Frankfurt: Fischer Bücherei, 1957), p. 16.
7. J. Ortega y Gasset, *The Revolt of the Masses* (New York: W.W. Norton & Co., 1957). First published 1932.
"It is not a question of the mass man being a fool. On the contrary, today he is more clever, has more capacity of understanding than his fellow of any previous period. But that capacity is of no use to him: in reality, the vague feeling that he possesses it seems only to shut him up more within himself and keeps him from using it. Once for all, he accepts the stock of commonplaces, prejudices, fag-ends of ideas or simply empty words which chance has piled up within his mind, and with a boldness only explicable by his ingeniousness, is prepared to impose them everywhere" (p. 70).
8. Alan Bullock, *Hitler: A Study in Tyranny* (New York: Bantam Books, 1961), p. 326.
9. Bullock, p. 354.
10. Hannah Arendt, *The Origins of Totalitarianism* (New York: Meridian, 1958), p. 356.
11. Leon Poliakov, "Anti-Semitism: Cause or Result of Nazism," in J.L. Snell, *The Nazi Revolution*, p. 31.
12. Gordon W. Allport, *The Nature of Prejudice* (Garden City, N.Y.: Doubleday, 1958), p. 391.
13. Adolf Hitler, "Racial and National Degeneration," in *Völkischer Beobachter*, Nov. 21, 1928, in Carl Cohen, ed., *Communism, Fascism, and Democracy* (New York: Random House, 1962), p. 412.
14. Richard Rubenstein, "Religion and the Origins of the Death Camps," *After Auschwitz* (New York: Bobbs-Merrill Co., Inc., 1966), esp. pp. 3-5.
15. I have not examined this possibility, but given the consistency of Hitler's application of his doctrine of one enemy to domestic politics, I cannot help but think that it had direct bearing on his effort to mobilize the German people and to bolster the general will for a war effort that proved to be fighting many different enemies on different fronts. In Hitler's world view, England, France,

the United States, and Russia were one enemy, and his having attacked them indeed made them so.

16. Will Herberg, *Protestant Catholic Jew* (Garden City, N.Y.: Doubleday, 1957), index under "American Way of Life."

17. Martin Kähler, *The So-Called Historical Jesus and the Historic Biblical Christ* (Philadelphia: Fortress Press, 1964), esp. Carl Braaten's introduction, p. 9.

## Chapter 10

1. *Evangelische Theologie* 28 (Oct. 1968): 555.

2. Friedrich Gogarten, *Einheit von Evangelium und Volkstum?* (Hamburg: Hanseatische Verlagsanstalt, 1933), p. 17.

3. "Karl Barth zum Kirchenkampf," in *Theologische Existenz heute* (1956), 49: 59.

4. Bethge, *Bonhoeffer* (Munich: Chr. Kaiser Verlag, 1970); English trans.: *Dietrich Bonhoeffer: Man of Vision* (New York, 1970).

5. K.D. Bracher, in *Stuttgarter Zeitung,* (Feb. 2, 1970), p. 14.

6. Ibid.

7. B.H. Forck, *Und folget ihrem glauben nach* (Stuttgart: Evang. Verlagswerk, 1949), p. 7.

8. Cf. "Entwurf eines Gutachtens zur Frage des Widerstandsrechtes nach evgl. Lehre," *Junge Kirche* (1952), 13: 192, 201.

9. Bracher, "Der 20. Juli-Vergangenheit-Gegenwart," in *Recht. Gerechtigkeit und Gewalt* (Stuttgart: Kreuz Verlag, 1969), p. 50.

10. (Munich: Chr. Kaiser Verlag, 1969), p. 31.

11. Hans Joachim Iwand, *Nachgelassene Werke* (Munich: Chr. Kaiser Verlag, 1965), 2: 253, 367.

## Chapter 11

1. Bethge (chap. 10) touched upon this aspect in his lecture. Conway (chap. 2) raised the serious question of why Barmen and the Confessing Church have apparently failed in post-war Germany.

2. Karl Barth, *Ad Limina Apostolorum* (Richmond, Va.: John Knox Press, 1968), p. 40.

3. It should have said justice, freedom, and peace, as Karl Barth later admitted.

4. It is, therefore, simply not true to say that those historians who subscribed to the Stuttgart Declaration "sought to show that the 'Bekennende Kirch' . . . has been uninterruptedly the opponents of Nazism, that they were now worthy of undertaking to govern the Church in the post-war world, and that the events of history had justified their previous political and theological stand."

5. Barth, *Eine Schweizer Stimme 1938-45* (Zollikon-Zurich: Evangelischer Verlag, 1945), p. 5.

6. Barth, "Lutherfeier 1933," in *Theologische Existenz heute,* no. 4, p. 5.

7. Barth, "Church Opposition 1933," ibid., no. 4, p. 20.

8. Cf. Barth, *Church Dogmatics II,* 1 (Edinburgh: T. & T. Clark, 1957): 127;

B.A. Gerrish, *The Faith of Christendom: A Source Book of Creeds and Confessions* (Cleveland and New York: World Publ. Co., 1963), pp. 129 f.

9. Cf. Barth, *Church Dogmatics I*, 2: 622 f.

10. Bonhoeffer, *Gesammelte Schriften* (Munich: Chr. Kaiser Verlag, 1958), 1: 240-61; English trans.: *No Rusty Swords* (New York: Harper & Row, 1965), pp. 326-44. Quotations are from the English text.

11. Ibid., p. 326.

12. Ibid., p. 343.

13. Ibid., p. 330.

14. Ibid.

15. Ibid., p. 334.

16. Ibid., p. 336.

17. Ibid., pp. 343 ff.

18. Cf. Ibid., p. 337.

19. Barmen remains a question to the Roman Catholic church to the extent that there is an ambiguity, even a contradiction in the "Dogmatic Constitution on Divine Revelation," especially between what is written in chapters I, III-VI *and* chapter II. But when one considers the overall greater stress that is laid upon "the one revelation" and upon "Holy Scripture," one is bound to say that Vatican II looks forward in the direction of Barmen and not backward to Vatican I and to the Council of Trent.

20. *"Church Opposition 1933,"* p. 20.

21. Barth, Foreword to *Theologische Existenz heute*, no. 4, p. 4.

22. Cf. Friedrich-Wilhelm Marquardt, *Die Entdeckung des Judentums für die christliche Theologie* (Munich: Chr. Kaiser Verlag, 1967).

## Chapter 12

1. Gordon C. Zahn, *German Catholics and Hitler's Wars* (New York: Sheed and Ward, 1962; PB, 1969); also my "The German Catholic Press and Hitler's Wars," in *Cross Currents* (Fall 1960).

2. Perhaps the most extensive of these adverse reviews, signed P.A.N., "Gordon Zahn vs. the Hierarchy," a 12-page Wanderer Forum pamphlet published by The Wanderer Press, St. Paul, Minn. (undated).

3. A wealth of published material is now available; a sampling of the more valuable titles in English is: J. S. Conway, *The Nazi Persecution of the Churches* (New York: Basic Books, 1968); Arthur C. Cochrane, *The Church's Confession under Hitler* (Philadelphia: Westminster Press, 1962); Guenter Lewy, *The Catholic Church and Nazi Germany* (New York: McGraw-Hill, 1964); Alfred Delp, *Prison Meditations* (New York: Herder and Herder, 1963); Helmut Gollwitzer et al., *Dying We Live* (New York: Pantheon, 1956). In German: Benedicta Maria Kempner, *Priester vor Hitlers Tribunalen* (Munich: Rütten & Loening Verlag, 1966); Johannes Maria Lenz, *Christus in Dachau* (Vienna: Buchversand 'Libri Catholici,' 1957); Johannes Neuhäusler, *Kreuz und Hakenkreuz* (Munich: Verlag Katholische Kirche Bayerns, 1946); Max Josef Metzger, *Gefangenschaftbriefe* (Meitingen: Kyrios Verlag, 1948); and Max Bierbaum, *Nicht Lob, Nicht Furcht: Das Leben des Kardinals von Galen* (Münster: Verlag Regensberg, 1957).

4. The Neuhäusler book is a case in point. See Zahn, *German Catholics and Hitler's Wars*, p. 87.

5. Carl Amery, *Die Kapitulation* (Hamburg: Rowohlt Verlag, 1963); in English: *Capitulation* (New York: Herder and Herder, 1967). Among other works in this vein are especially Hans Müller, *Katholische Kirche und National-sozialismus* (Munich: Nymphenburger Verlagshandlung, 1963), and two articles by E. W. Böckenförde, "Der deutsche Katholizismus in Jahre 1933: Stellung-nahme zu einer Diskussion" (*Hochland*, 1961-62) and "Der deutsche Kathol-izismus in Jahre 1933" (*Hochland*, 1960-61).

6. See especially the Lenz and Kempner volumes.

7. The only item from the war years is a carbon copy of a letter discussing arrangements to be made in case of a conflict between Mothers' Day observances and *unserer Feier* (unspecified). The item is dated May 4, 1942.

8. Despite the shortcomings already mentioned, Neuhäusler presents what is undoubtedly the most complete survey of the issues from the period covered by these documents.

9. Hirtenwort der Bayerischen Bischöfe zur Auflösung der katholischen Jung-männervereine und Jungfrauenkongregationen (to be read at all services Febru-ary 6, 1938).

10. Hirtenwort der deutschen Bischöfe (August 1936).

11. "Die ausgestreckte Hand des Papstes," Predigt des Herrn Kardinals am Papstsonntag, 13. Februar 1938, in St. Michael in Munich.

12. The most recent material is the collection published by Ludwig Volk, *Kirchliche Akten über die Reichskonkordatsverhandlungen 1933* (Mainz, 1969). Excerpts are published in the *Frankfurter Allgemeine*, November 25, 1969, under the heading "Eindämmungspolitik oder Dolchstoss?"

13. Faulhaber, Predigt in der Oberen Pfarr in Ingolstadt, May 24, 1936. A detailed notice of the measures taken against Catholic organizations had been sent out by the Munich chancery on July 30, 1935.

14. Ordinariat an die Hochwürdigen Pfarrämter u. Seelsorgsstellen der Erz-diözese, August 29, 1935.

15. Ordinariat an den Hochwürdigen Klerus der Erzdiözese München und Freising, January 26, 1938.

16. Predigt der H. H. Dompfarrers Johannes Kraus im Hohen Dom Zu Eichstätt, January 31, 1937.

17. Anweisung an die Pfarrämter und Kirchenvorstände der Erzdiözese, April 6, 1938. In this announcement Cardinal Faulhaber notes specially that this is the first opportunity for the bells of the other German churches to ring in unison with the "deutsch-oestereichischen" bells, a historical moment for religion and church as well as for the social and economic life of the nation.

18. Zahn, *German Catholics and Hitler's Wars*, p. 113.

19. Gemeinsamer Hirtenbrief der Oberhirten der Diözesen Deutschlands, June 7, 1934.

20. Lewy, pp. 152-53.

21. Faulhaber sermon, February 13, 1938; see n. 11.

22. Cochrane, p. 56.

23. Ibid.

24. Ibid., p. 110.

25. Aufklärung der katholischen Eltern über die "Deutsche Schulgemeinde," May 5, 1936.

26. Ordinariat an sämptliche Seelsorgestellen der Erzdiözese. Betreff: Neue Werbung für die deutsche Schulgemeinde, June 16, 1936.

27. Hirtenbrief des Hochwürdigsten Herrn Bischofs von Speyer—Ludwig Sebastian, April 11, 1937.

28. Predigt des Hochwürdigsten Herrn Bischofs Franz Rudolf am Hohen Osterfest, March 28, 1937, im Dom zu Trier.

29. Ordinariat an den Hochwürdigen Klerus der Erzdiözese. Betreff: Fall Al. Kober, Pasing, April 23, 1937.

30. Ordinariat an die Hochwürdigen Seelsorgestellen der Erzdiözese. Betreff: Jugendsonntag 1938, March 26, 1938.

31. Jugendstunde im Mai (Eucharistische Feierstunde) vom Weltfronleichnam des Eucharistischen Kongresses (undated).

32. Predigt Sr. Excellenz des Hochwürdigsten Herrn Bischofs Michael Rackl im Dom zu Eichstätt, April 12, 1937.

33. Predigt des Hochwürdigsten Herrn Bischofs von Eichstätt zu Ochsenfeld am Feste ChristiHimmelfahrt 1937 (carbon copy).

34. Faulhaber, "Flammenzeichen rauchen," Predigt des Herrn Kardinals vor der Marianischen Männerkongregation in München-St. Michael am 4 Juli 1937.

35. Ordinariat an Diözesanklerus zur persönlichen Information übergeben. P. Rupert Mayer S. J., München, Inhaftierung und Verurteilung im Juni/Juli 1937.

36. Ordinariat an die Hochwürdigen Stadtpfarreien und Pfarrkuratien Münchens. Betreff: P. Rupert Mayer, January 15, 1938.

37. Ordinariat an die Hochwürdigen titl. Seelsorgestellen der Erdiözese. Betreff: Kanzelverkündigung, January 20, 1938.

38. Kanzelerklärung der Bayerischen Bischöfe zu dem fortschreitenden Abbau der klösterlichen Lehrkrafte und klösterlichen Schulen. Am Sonntag, den 4. September 1938, zu vorlesen.

39. Kraus sermon; see n. 16.

40. Ordinariat. Betreff: Fall Schülle. Am Sonntag, den 24 Januar 1937 ist Nachfolgendes in sämtlichen Kirchen bei allen Gottesdiensten, mit Ausnahme etwaiger Kindergottesdienste, zu vorlesen.

41. Kraus, sermon.

42. Der Bischof von Berlin an den Herrn Reichminister fur Volksaufklärung und Propaganda, May 27, 1937.

43. Zahn, *German Catholics and Hitler's Wars.*

44. Cochrane, p. 223.

45. Beachtenswertes aus Staatlichen Gesetzen und Verordnungen, June 1, 1938.                    S

46. Oberhirtliche Erklärung zur "Abstimmung" über die Gemeinschaftschule, June 14, 1937.

47. Kraus sermon.

48. Verkundigung Verordnet vom Erzbischöflichen Ordinariat München und Freising mit Erlass Nr. 10900 vom 20. Juli, 1937.

49. Zahn, *German Catholics and Hitler's Wars.*

50. Ibid., passim.

51. Ibid., pp. 86-87.

52. Rackl sermon, April 12, 1937; see n. 32.

53. Ibid.

54. Kraus sermon.

55. Daniel Berrigan, *The Trial of the Catonsville Nine* (Boston: Beacon Press, 1970).

# Contributors

WILLIAM SHERIDAN ALLEN is professor of history at the State University of New York at Buffalo. He has previously taught at several universities including Wayne State University. He has studied at the Universities of Michigan, Connecticut, Göttingen, and the Free University of Berlin, receiving his Ph.D. from the University of Minnesota. His major work is *The Nazi Seizure of Power;* he is currently writing a history of the Socialist underground in Nazi Germany.

EBERHARD BETHGE studied theology at Berlin, Tübingen, and Halle. He joined Bonhoeffer's newly opened seminary of the Confessing Church in Finkenwalde in 1935 as a candidate for ordination, later becoming his assistant until March 1940 when the hidden seminary was closed for the second time by the Gestapo. He was arrested in 1944 in connection with the plot to kill Hitler and was freed by the Russians in April 1945. He has been assistant to Bishop Dibelius and a student chaplain in Berlin. In 1953 he was pastor of a German-speaking congregation in London; in 1961, leader of the Pastoralkolleg of the Englische Kirche im Rheinland. He has honorary degrees from the University of Glasgow and Berlin University and is honorary professor at Bonn. His publications include *Dietrich Bonhoeffer: Man of Vision;* several essays; and the editing of Bonhoeffer's collected works and *Letters and Papers from Prison.*

FREDERICK O. BONKOVSKY teaches at Vanderbilt University. He has been a Protestant pastor in Germany and in Massachusetts, assistant dean at Harvard College, and Fulbright fellow at the Free University and Kirchliche Hochschule in Berlin. His degrees are B.S. from Muskingum College, M.Div. from Yale University, and Ph.D. from Harvard University. He has contributed to scholarly panels and journals and is working on a book about ethics and international affairs.

**ARTHUR C. COCHRANE** is professor of systematic theology at Pittsburgh Theological Seminary. Born in Canada and educated there, he studied abroad and became one of the early interpreters of Karl Barth's work to the English-speaking world. During 1935-37 he was in Germany with the Confessing Church. His study, *The Church's Confession under Hitler*, was published in 1962. In 1963/64 he was visiting professor of theology at Yale University. His schools are University of Toronto, Knox Theological College, and Edinburgh University.

**JOHN S. CONWAY** was born in London and educated at St. John's College, Cambridge. After taking his doctorate in modern German history, he taught for two years at the University of Manitoba. For the past fifteen years, he has been a member of the history department of the University of British Columbia in Vancouver, and is at present professor of history there. He is the author of numerous articles and reviews dealing with twentieth-century affairs, and is a frequent contributor to newspapers and journals.

**FERDINAND FRIEDENSBURG**, 1886-1972, Dr. phil., Dr.jur.h.c., was professor at the Technical University of Berlin. He was trained as a mining engineer with a distinguished career in Civil Service and, among other high positions, was vice-president of the Berlin Police Department and Provincial Government President in Kassel; he was removed from office in 1933. As an outstanding Protestant layman, he served as Domherr of Brandenburg, and he was active in the Confessing Church. After the German defeat in 1945, he was recalled to a number of important political positions, also serving as a member of the Bundestag. He has written extensively on economics and politics, including a history of the Weimar Republic.

**HENRY FRIEDLANDER** was born in Germany in 1930. In 1941 he was deported to the Lodz ghetto and from there to Auschwitz, Neuengamme, and Ravensbrück. He emigrated to the United States in 1947. He received his Ph.D. from the University of Pennsylvania for a study of the German Revolution of 1918, served as staff member of the Committee for the Study of War Documents, and is presently teaching history at the City University of New York.

His most recent publication is "The Holocaust," in *The Study of Judaism: Bibliographical Essays* (1972).

**THEODORE A. GILL** has been a parish minister in New York City, dean of the chapel and professor of religious studies at Lindenwood College in Missouri, managing editor of *The Christian Century*, president of the San Francisco Theological Seminary, a senior secretary of the World Council of Churches, dean of the Detroit Center for Christian Studies, executive director of the Society for the Arts, Religion, and Contemporary Culture, and is now professor of philosophy and chairman of the Division of Arts and Languages at the John Jay College of Criminal Justice in the City University of New York. He was a student of Reinhold Niebuhr, Paul Tillich, Karl Barth, and Emil Brunner, and is the author of a cinematic biography of Dietrich Bonnhoeffer.

**PETER HOFFMANN** is professor of history at McGill University, to which he came in 1970. At the time of this conference he was associate professor at the University of Northern Iowa (1965-70). Born in Germany and receiving his early education there, he has done advanced study in both Germany and the United States (Ph.D., Munich). Among his writings in this field are *Widerstand, Staatsstreich, Attentat: Der Kampf der Opposition gegen Hitler* (1969), and several studies, in professional periodicals, of the July 20, 1944, attempt on Hitler's life.

**FRANKLIN HAMLIN LITTELL,** professor of religion and director of graduate religious studies at Temple University, has been chairman of the project since its inception. After the war he served for nearly ten years in various United States agencies in Germany. Among his articles and books in the field of the Church Struggle and the Holocaust have been "The Protestant Churches and Totalitarianism (Germany, 1933-45)," in C. J. Friedrich: *Totalitarianism* (1954); "Die Bedeutung des Kirchenkampfes für die Ökumene," in *Evangelische Theologie* (1960); *The German Phoenix* (1960). He is an alumnus of Cornell College, Iowa, Union Theological Seminary (where he studied with Reinhold Niebuhr), and Yale University (Ph.D.); he holds the honorary doctorate from Marburg.

**HUBERT G. LOCKE,** assistant to the chancellor and associate professor of sociology and social welfare at the University of Nebraska at Omaha, served as a member of the Planning Committee for the First International Scholars' Conference on the German

Church Struggle and as vice president of the Walker and Gertrude Cisler Library Board, Wayne State University, which launched the first efforts in an American university to establish an archival collection of documents related to the Church Struggle. He is a graduate of Wayne State University, the Chicago Theological Seminary, and the University of Michigan. He holds honorary degrees from the University of Akron, the Chicago Theological Seminary, and Payne Theological Seminary at Wilberforce University. He is author of *The Detroit Riot of 1967* (Wayne State University Press, 1969), *The Care and Feeding of White Liberals* (1970), and numerous articles.

**WILHELM NIEMÖLLER** studied Protestant theology at Bethel, Münster, Erlangen, and Greifswald. From 1925 to 1930 he was pastor at Schlüsselburg and from 1930 to 1963 at Bielefeld. In the German Church Struggle he was one of the founders of the Councils of Brethren, was a member of the Westphalia assembly of the Confessing Church, and participator in the Confessing Church synod. Since 1945 he has been in charge of the archives of the Confessing Church in Bielefeld and spends his full time editing the history of the Church Struggle. In 1959 he received an honorary doctor's degree from the University of Göttingen.

**BEATE RUHM VON OPPEN** was born in Switzerland and educated in Germany, Holland, and England. She did research on Germany for the British Foreign Office during and after the war, and later at the Royal Institute for International Affairs and at Nuffield College, Oxford, broadening out into international and comparative politics. She has also worked on captured German documents at Alexandria, Virginia, in 1959/60. She was tutor at St. John's College, Annapolis, 1960-1963, and again since 1971. In the intervening years she was a member of the history departments at Smith College and the University of Massachusetts, and of the Institute for Advanced Study and the Center of International Studies at Princeton. Her publications include *Documents on Germany under Occupation 1945-54* (Oxford University Press, 1955) and *Religion and Resistance to Nazism* (Princeton, 1971).

**RICHARD L. RUBENSTEIN** is professor of religion at the Florida State University. He has degrees from the Jewish Theological Seminary and Harvard University and has written several books, including *After Auschwitz: Radical Theology and Contemporary Judaism* (1966), and various articles.

MICHAEL D. RYAN is associate professor of theology at Drew University, Madison, New Jersey. A graduate of Augustana College, Sioux Falls, South Dakota, he began his studies in theology at the University of Tübingen in 1957 as a Fulbright fellow. He received his B.D. and Ph.D. degrees from Drew University. The title of his doctoral dissertation was "The Role of the Discipline of History in the Theological Interpretation of Albrecht Ritschl." He has taught in the religion department at Concordia College, Moorhead, Minnesota, and is a member of the National Society for Religion in Higher Education.

ELIE WIESEL, author, born in Romania, deported from Hungary to Auschwitz in Poland and Buchenwald in Germany, now resides in the United States. His books range from his autobiographical *Night* to his evocation and celebration of Hasidism in *Souls on Fire*. His obsessions are the Holocaust and its mystery, Israel and its mission, man and his solitary confrontation with God. He was recently appointed Distinguished Professor of Jewish Studies at New York City College.

GORDON C. ZAHN is professor of sociology at the University of Massachusetts-Boston. He received his Ph.D. from the Catholic University of America and has written several books on subjects relating to war and peace, with special focus on the Nazi experience, notably, *German Catholics and Hitler's Wars*, based on a year as a Fulbright research fellow at Würzburg, and *In Solitary Witness: The Life and Death of Franz Jaegerstaetter*. His most recent works are *The Military Chaplaincy: Role Tension in the R.A.F.* (University of Toronto Press, 1969), and *Thomas Merton on Peace* (McCalls Books, 1971).

# Index

The manuscript was prepared for publication by Marguerite C. Wallace. The book was designed by Joanne Kinney. The typeface for the text is Linotype Century cut by Linn Boyd Benton in collaboration with T.L. De Vinne; and the display face is Albertus designed by Berthold Wolpe.

The text is printed on Nicolet Natural Text paper and the book is bound in Columbia Mills Llamique cloth over binders boards. Manufactured in the United States of America.

## DATE DUE

| | | | |
|---|---|---|---|
| | | | |
| | | | |
| | | | |
| | | | |
| | | | |
| | | | |
| | | | |
| | | | |
| | | | |
| | | | |
| | | | |
| | | | |
| | | | |
| | | | |
| | | | |
| | | | |
| | | | |
| | | | |
| | | | |

30-505  JOSTEN'S

51034